BLOOD LIBEL

THE INSIDE STORY OF GENERAL ARIEL SHARON'S HISTORY-MAKING SUIT AGAINST **TIME** MAGAZINE

BY

URI DAN

SIMON AND SCHUSTER
NEW YORK

Copyright © 1987 by C.B.U. Publishing Corporation
All rights reserved
including the right of reproduction
in whole or in part in any form
Published by Simon and Schuster
A Division of Simon & Schuster, Inc.
Simon & Schuster Building
Rockefeller Center
1230 Avenue of the Americas
New York, New York 10020
SIMON AND SCHUSTER and colophon are registered trademarks of
Simon & Schuster, Inc.
Designed by Irving Perkins Associates
Manufactured in the United States of America

10   9   8   7   6   5   4   3   2   1

Library of Congress Cataloging in Publication Data

Dan, Uri.
  Blood libel.

  1. Sharon, Ariel—Trials, litigation, etc.
2. Time, Inc.—Trials, litigation, etc.   3. Trials
(Libel)—New York (N.Y.)   I. Title.
KF228.S48D36   1987   345.73′0256   86-26197
ISBN 0-671-60554-2   347.305256

CONTENTS

FOREWORD   11

YES, I WAS AT BIKFAYA   19

PART I
HOW IT ALL BEGAN   27

PART II
PREPARING FOR TRIAL   65

PART III
THE TRIAL BEGINS   127

PART IV
THE TURNING POINT   171

PART V
THE VERDICTS   209

APPENDIX   253

INDEX   261

It is not the critic who counts,
not the one who points out how the strong person
  stumbled,
or how the doer of deeds might have done them
  better.
The credit belongs to the man who is actually
  in the arena,
whose face is marred with sweat and dust and
  blood;
who strives valiantly;
who errs and comes up short again and again;
who knows the great enthusiasms, the great
  devotions,
and spends himself in a worthy cause;
who, if he wins, knows the triumph of high
  achievement;
and who, if he fails, at least fails while
  daring greatly,
so that his place shall never be with those
  cold and timid souls who know neither victory
  nor defeat.

                              —*Theodore Roosevelt*
                              1920

FOREWORD

IN ISRAEL IT IS FAR EASIER TO MAKE HISTORY than to write it. Sometimes it requires only one brief order to achieve a memorable historic act—or to commit a colossal historic blunder. But to describe it afterward is much more difficult, especially in the Jewish state, where every citizen has his own version of what took place, particularly if he or she wasn't there on the spot.

I was there. As an adviser to the Israeli minister of defense, Ariel Sharon, I accompanied him into Lebanon at noon on June 6, 1982, when the Israeli tanks moved forward to carry out the most massive antiterror campaign in modern and probably ancient history.

Sharon's statement that day became his battle cry throughout the war: "Israel has decided to destroy the kingdom of the PLO local, regional, and international terror—in Lebanon, with its capital in West Beirut."

I was also there in Washington ten days earlier, accompanying Defense Minister Sharon to his meetings with Defense Secretary Caspar Weinberger at the Pentagon and with Secretary of State Alexander Haig at the State Department.

During their confidential discussions Sharon, among other pressing topics, vehemently highlighted the dangers of local and international terrorism, quoting from a heavy file marked "National Security Issues, May 1982," prepared by the Ministry of Defense.

On this sunny day in Washington, Sharon presented Weinberger and Haig with facts and figures concerning the alarming situation created in the northern part of Israel by the PLO. Sharon emphasized that Palestinian terror organizations, under PLO leadership, had set up a "state within a state" in Lebanon. Sharon added that since the so-called ceasefire between Israel and the terrorists went into effect in July 1981, the PLO had substantially increased its build-up in Lebanon, procuring and absorbing hundreds of artillery pieces, rocket launchers and mortars.

Sharon told them that not only were Syria, Libya and Iraq all giving aid to Palestinian terror organizations, but the Soviet Union and her East-European satellites also went on providing the PLO with important military and political support.

11

Using charts and maps, Sharon stated that the PLO had been and was perpetrating atrocities against civilian targets both in Israel and abroad. PLO attacks were never directed against military targets, but rather against defenseless civilians, including women and children.

Still pointing to the maps, Sharon explained how the Syrian army, protected by an umbrella of SAM anti-aircraft missile batteries, was occupying the major portion of Lebanese soil and actually serving as a defense for the PLO bases.

Sharon summed up, his voice rising in line with the intensity of his feelings: "The PLO is closely involved in international terrorism. It provides training facilities and arms to terrorist groups such as the Red Brigades in Italy, the Baader-Meinhof gang and Neo-Nazi groups in West Germany, the Japanese Red Army, and subversive organizations in Latin America. In return these groups have aided the PLO in its operations abroad.

"The terrorist organizations' presence in Lebanon has served as a base for anti-Israel and international terror. It has constituted an obstacle on the road to a comprehensive Middle East peace and a stimulus for Soviet expansion and subversion in the region and the world."

When the war erupted several days later, Washington was therefore the least surprised capital in the world. The United States had, however, never given a green light for the campaign, nor had Sharon requested one. The Israeli prime minister, Menachem Begin, called the antiterror campaign the Peace for Galilee operation, since that part of Israel had been under the constant threat of the PLO guns and hit squads.

But it was also a war against the terrorist organization that, between 1965 and 1982, according to the *Israel Defense Force Journal,* killed 1392 people and wounded 6432 others—Jews and non-Jews alike, both in Israel and abroad.

On June 9, in a unique air strike, the Israeli air force destroyed the Syrian surface-to-air Russian-made missile complex in Lebanon. Between June 12 and June 14 the Israeli army accomplished the takeover of the southern and eastern suburbs of Beirut and achieved a linkup with the Lebanese forces. The siege of West Beirut then got under way. Yasser Arafat and other terrorist leaders, with twelve thousand of their men, were trapped.

The Lebanese forces, known generally as the Christian Phalanges, had been trained and secretly supported by Israel since 1976. Previously, under the Israeli Labor party government, headed by Yitzhak Rabin and Shimon Peres, the Israelis had decided to help the Christian minority in Lebanon, who were engaged in a cruel civil war waged against them by the PLO. For more than a decade the Christian Phalanges had been led by the Gemayel family—father Pierre and his two sons, Bashir and Amin. When Begin and Sharon replaced the Labor party government leaders in 1977, they continued with the Labor party's policy of helping the Lebanese Christian community.

Once the siege of West Beirut had got under way, the Israeli government, as well as a large part of the Labor party opposition, urged the Christian Phalanges to "take part in the liberation of their capital." But except for minor operations under the command of Bashir Gemayel—who directed the Lebanese forces politically and militarily—the Israeli army alone bore the heavy burden of the siege. Hundreds of Israelis were killed and wounded tightening the noose around the terrorists in West Beirut.

Throughout the remainder of June, July, and part of August, with the Israelis unleashing bombing raids and heavy artillery shelling against West Beirut, President Ronald Reagan's special Middle East envoy, Philip Habib, was busy negotiating for the lifting of the siege. During the night between August 12 and August 13 Yasser Arafat finally capitulated, passing his message through Philip Habib to General Sharon that he was ready to leave town with the rest of the terrorists on the terms laid down by the Israelis. Earlier during the day of August 12 the Israeli air force had engaged in a massive strike on West Beirut.

The expulsion of ten thousand PLO terrorists from West Beirut started on August 21, under the supervision of the multinational force, led by the U.S. Sixth Fleet, with the participation of France and Italy. The terrorists boarded ships in Beirut port, sailing to seven different destinations. Two days later Bashir Gemayel was elected the new president of Lebanon, scheduled to take office within one month.

Returning from another quick trip to Washington, Sharon arrived home on the first of September and proceeded directly to Aley, near Beirut. With Philip Habib he participated in a farewell luncheon given to the commanders of the multinational force on the occasion of their having completed the mission of supervising the expulsion of the terrorists.

Israeli intelligence warned that about two thousand terrorists had remained behind in West Beirut, which, according to the agreement, was out of bounds to the Israelis. The intelligence reports also emphasized that these terrorists still held a gigantic arsenal of armaments, left behind by their expelled friends, who were permitted to take with them only light personal weapons. Sharon had previously warned Habib about this.

On September 12 the multinational fleet sailed away from Beirut. On the same night Sharon secretly met with Bashir Gemayel at his home in Bikfaya. They agreed that political negotiations would start between the president elect and an Israeli mission, headed by Foreign Minister Yitzhak Shamir, with the aim of signing a peace treaty with Israel. The first meeting was scheduled for Wednesday, September 15, in Lebanon.

But the day before the proposed meeting, around 4:00 P.M. on Tuesday afternoon, a remote-controlled bomb killed Bashir Gemayel in his office in the suburb of Ashrafiya, East Beirut.

On the same night Prime Minister Begin, Defense Minister Sharon, and Chief of Staff Rafael Eitan ordered the Israeli army divisions to move into West Beirut. Thousands of Israeli soldiers advanced in tanks to take control of key points and road junctions. A heavy battle started in the early hours of September 15. Israeli intelligence insisted that two thousand terrorists had infiltrated back into their hideouts in West Beirut. Begin and Sharon were apprehensive that the terrorists would again take control of the Lebanese capital and that all the agonizing effort of the war, including the heavy Israeli casualties, would be submerged in the new chaos.

With the Israeli forces again suffering casualties, the Lebanese forces were finally integrated into the new battle. On the eve of September 16, with the approval of Sharon and by order of General Eitan, Phalangist units entered two of the Palestinian neighborhoods that had long been known as terrorist bases and training centers for international terrorists such as Baader-Meinhof (West Germany) and the Red Brigades (Italy). These were the suburbs of Sabra and Shatilla.

On the same evening the Israeli government met in Jerusalem and received a specific report on the integration of the Phalangists into the battle of West Beirut.

On Friday night, September 17, Sharon learned that "something had gone wrong" with the Phalangists in Sabra and Shatilla. He ordered the chief of staff to get them out of those places immediately.

But only late on Saturday afternoon, September 18, were Begin and Sharon informed that the Phalangists had in fact committed a terrible massacre in Sabra and Shatilla. News agency reports began to arrive in Israel with horrifying accounts of women and children killed by the Phalangists. No Israeli commanders or soldiers had accompanied the Phalangists into Sabra and Shatilla. Because of this the intelligence data had been uncharacteristically poor.

Israeli intelligence is generally regarded as one of the best in the world, but regretfully in this instance it went dramatically wrong. No early intelligence report even hinting at a massacre had been shown to Sharon or Begin.

The massacre aroused an enormous and spontaneous uproar in Israel and across the world. In addition to the deep and genuine shock, the tragic event was promptly exploited by Begin's and Sharon's political rivals inside Israel and abroad, particularly in the USA and Western Europe. The Labor party opposition jumped on the bandwagon, with the object of immediately toppling Begin's government.

The report of the investigation by Assad Germanos, a Lebanese military attorney, published in November 1982, stated that in Sabra and Shatilla 460 people were killed, of whom 15 were women and 20 were children, all the rest being men. The breakdown according to ethnic origins was as follows: about 300 Palestinians, and 100 Lebanese, and the remainder Syrians, Algerians, Pakistanis and Iranians.

Sensitive to the civilian casualties, Begin's government, with the approval of Minister Sharon, decided ten days after the massacre to establish a commission of inquiry. In parallel, the U.S. prompted the return to Beirut of the multinational force, displacing the Israelis from the positions they had taken up at the Beirut airport.

Foreword

The inquiry commission, headed by Yitzhak Kahan, president of the Supreme Court, started its investigation immediately, holding sessions in Jerusalem. The commission thus became known as the Kahan Commission.

The mandate of the commission was defined as follows: "The matter which will be subjected to inquiry is: all the facts and factors connected with the atrocity carried out by a unit of the Lebanese Forces against the civilian population in the Shatilla and Sabra camps."

The commission held 60 sessions, hearing 58 witnesses. In response to the commission's requests, the cabinet secretary, the Office of the Minister of Defense, the general staff of the Israel Defense Forces, the Ministry for Foreign Affairs, and other public and governmental institutions provided the commission with many documents, some of which were, in the course of the deliberations, submitted to the commission as exhibits.

On February 8, 1983, in Jerusalem, the Kahan Commission published its conclusions, exonerating the Israeli political and military echelons from any direct involvement in the tragic events. It stated: ". . . We have no doubt that no conspiracy or plot was entered into between anyone from the Israeli political echelon or from the military echelon in the IDF. and the Phalangists, with the aim of perpetrating atrocities in the camps. The decision to have the Phalangists enter the camps was taken with the aim of preventing further losses in the war in Lebanon; to accede to the pressure of public opinion in Israel, which was angry that the Phalangists, who were reaping the fruits of the war, were taking no part in it; and to take advantage of the Phalangists' professional service and their skills in identifying terrorists and in discovering arms caches. No intention existed on the part of any Israeli element to harm the noncombatant population in the camps . . .

". . . We assert that in having the Phalangists enter the camps, no intention existed on the part of anyone who acted on behalf of Israel to harm the noncombatant population, and that the events that followed did not have the concurrence or assent of anyone from the political or civilian echelon who was active regarding the Phalangists' entry into the camps . . ."

16

". . . We assert that the atrocities in the refugee camps were perpetrated by members of the Phalangists, and that absolutely no direct responsibility devolves upon Israel or upon those who acted in its behalf."

At the same time, however, the commission found that Sharon and other high-ranking Israelis bore "*indirect* [author's emphasis] responsibility for what occurred in the refugee camps." According to the commission's findings, Sharon and several Israeli generals *should have foreseen* the dangers in allowing the Phalangists to enter Sabra and Shatilla. The commission therefore recommended that Sharon be removed from his post as minister of defense.

The recommendation was adopted the same week by the Israeli government. Sharon decided to accept Begin's suggestion that he remain in the government as minister without portfolio and as a member of the cabinet for security affairs.

On Monday, February 14, 1983, while Sharon was busy moving out of the Defense Ministry, the Israeli media published a press release by *Time* magazine. It said that the issue dated February 21, carrying Sharon's picture on the cover, stated that the magazine had learned that on September 15, 1982, at Bikfaya, Sharon had discussed with the Gemayel family the need to avenge the murdered president elect, Bashir Gemayel, and that this had been followed by the massacre at Sabra and Shatilla. Prime Minister Begin in a special statement in the Israeli Parliament denied *Time*'s story and called on the magazine to apologize to Sharon. *Time* did not respond.

Sharon thereupon decided to sue *Time* magazine for libel, since, as far as he was concerned, *Time* was accusing him of direct responsibility for the massacre, of having planned it cold-bloodedly with the Gemayel family—a premeditated mass murder.

Prime Minister Begin, after losing his right-hand man, Sharon, as defense minister, decided in August 1983 to resign from the government. "I cannot bear it anymore," the seventy-year-old ailing premier explained.

Sharon was reelected in the Israeli general elections, which took place in July 1984. In September of the same year he was appointed minister for trade and industry in the Israeli National Unity government, under the premiership of Shimon Peres

Foreword

(Labor), his longtime political opponent, whose opposition persisted during the period of the Sabra and Shatilla upheavals.

Two months later, in November 1984, Ariel Sharon arrived in New York to carry out his legal campaign against Time, Inc.

I was there again, on the spot, accompanying him during the long and arduous libel trial.

Yes, in Israel it is harder to write history than to make it.

But in New York, through their verdicts, a jury of six Americans both made and wrote history. Here is that history as I lived it.

YES, I WAS AT BIKFAYA

PIERRE GEMAYEL GAVE HARDLY ANY INDICATION that he'd lost his son only eighteen hours earlier. Bashir Gemayel, Lebanese president elect and the hope of the Christian community, lay dead, his coffin on a bier. A remote-control bomb had killed him outright; the funeral was due to take place four hours later, there in Bikfaya.

The bereaved father's face was impassive. His eyes were dry. He sat ramrod-straight on a highbacked chair to the right of Israeli Defense Minister Ariel Sharon. On a velvet-covered sofa at Sharon's left sat Amin, Pierre Gemayel's remaining son. Between them was a representative of the Israeli intelligence body, the Mossad.

Sharon's voice was appropriately low. "Sheikh Pierre, I have come to convey the condolences of Menachem Begin, Israel's prime minister, of the entire Israeli government, and of the people of Israel on the death of your son, President elect Bashir Gemayel." The Mossad represenive translated his words into French.

From my seat slightly to the right of and behind Sharon I listened intently. This was habitual with me at all the many open— and secret—meetings the Israeli defense minister invited me to attend. As his media adviser I followed every word. The worldwide media campaign waged against Israel during the Lebanese war had made this even more essential. Sometimes I acted as French-Hebrew translator during Sharon's contacts with the Christian leaders of Lebanon, but this time I wasn't needed. The senior representative of the Mossad interpreted for the bereaved father and Sharon.

I couldn't know then, of course, that this conversation in Bikfaya, the picturesque home village of the Gemayel family, would become pivotal in a libel suit brought by Sharon against *Time* magazine in New York. And not only couldn't I know, I couldn't even imagine that *Time* magazine would claim in a New York courtroom that I hadn't been there, there at the meeting in Bikfaya. In the corridors of the federal courthouse in Manhattan's

Blood Libel

Foley Square, David Halevy, *Time*'s reporter in Israel, grinned wolfishly and said, "But you weren't even at Bikfaya."

David Halevy himself certainly wasn't at the meeting. Even he didn't deny that. Nevertheless he was able to tell *Time*'s readers what was said there, what had been decided there. An American jury solved the extraordinary anomaly: it found he was a liar.

Yes, I was there at Bikfaya observing as always every detail. I followed the conversation at that meeting in Bikfaya. I listened very closely.

Most of the hundreds, probably nearer thousands, of Sharon's meetings I have attended for more than thirty years were interesting, illuminating, and often dramatic. The meeting at Bikfaya was dull; somber, to be sure, but infinitely dull. The conversation between Sharon and Pierre Gemayel said nothing. It was boring, perhaps the most boring conversation I had ever attended with Sharon, although the circumstances were dramatic enough: the Gemayel family was in mourning for its murdered son, the president elect of Lebanon.

And it was this most boring conversation of Sharon's that became probably his most famous throughout the world. And all because *Time* magazine published a lie, because it published "information" regarding something it knew nothing about: it published details of a conversation it had never heard, it reported something that had never happened.

It stated that there in Bikfaya, on a day of mourning and condolence, Sharon had encouraged the Gemayel family to take revenge on the Palestinians. *Time* claimed to know of a discussion that had taken place there, paving the way for the massacre at Sabra and Shatilla.

The American jury solved that anomaly too. These six ordinary, honest, perceptive Americans found that *Time* magazine, in the persons of certain employees, had been negligent and careless. The jury members specifically singled out David Halevy.

As a young military reporter in the fifties I had heard Sharon, the commander, speaking to Israeli paratroopers before antiterror raids into Jordan, Egypt, and Syria. I had heard Sharon speak to his soldiers in the Sinai desert during the Suez campaign of 1956. I had heard the astonishing calm with which Sharon talked to his officers during the bitter days and nights of the Suez Canal crossing in the Yom Kippur War of 1973. Even amidst the thunderous crash of shells and shrill whistle of rockets his voice remained controlled.

I had heard many of Sharon's fateful talks before and during the Lebanon war. I heard him in late May 1982 at the Pentagon and at the State Department warning Caspar Weinberger and Alexander Haig that Israel would not tolerate terror from Lebanon any more than it would tolerate terror anywhere in the world. I heard his voice begin to rasp after numerous talks with envoy Philip Habib in Beirut, Tel Aviv, and Jerusalem in June, July, and August 1982. Sharon warned Habib, President Ronald Reagan's special Mideast envoy, that if Israel were not allowed to complete its task in Lebanon, "terror would continue to strike; not only against Israel but also against the United States."

This was eight months before the Syrian-Palestinian-Shi'ite terrorists blew up the American Embassy in Beirut, killing several Americans; nearly sixteen months before a Shi'ite kamikaze team murdered two hundred and fourteen marines in Beirut; three years before a TWA aircraft was hijacked by Syrian-backed Shi'ites to Lebanon in June 1985; and over three years before an American Jew was murdered by Palestinian terrorists, who threatened to kill Americans first when they hijacked an Italian liner, the *Achille Lauro,* in October 1985.

During these conversations I had felt, despite their fascination, that Sharon was sometimes talking to the wall. All Philip Habib and his friends in the State Department wanted was to keep the PLO in Beirut as a political organization; to stop Israel's military advance in Lebanon—to prevent Sharon from carrying out his essential task.

Sharon had had to fight both Israeli politicians and the American envoy to attain at least one major goal: the expulsion from Beirut of the PLO with its light weapons at the end of August 1982.

That same month I had been present at a fascinating conversation in Bashir Gemayel's Beirut office in the HQ of the Christian forces at Karantina. It was just before Bashir's election as president of Lebanon.

At noon Sharon had stood on a top floor of the Beirut Electricity Company Building. It was late summer, hot and clear. As he gazed toward the shimmering horizon where the blue of the sky and the Mediterranean met, the Israeli victory seemed complete. Members of the PLO expelled from Beirut by the Israel Defense Forces packed the decks of the first ship leaving the harbor under the watchful eyes of Israeli soldiers. These were members of the very same organization that most Israeli and international experts—and so many journalists—had said in ignorant self-assurance would never be expelled from Beirut.

This achievement gave Sharon's meeting in the Karantina a special flavor. The common enemy of the Jews and the Christians—both minorities in the Middle East—had been beaten back. The PLO was broken. The PLO that had taken so many victims in Israel and was sworn to the annihilation of the state. The PLO that had waged bloody war for so many years against the Christians of Lebanon. This PLO had been expelled from its capital of terror in West Beirut.

Pierre Gemayel was still head of the clan. In his father's presence Bashir Gemayel resembled nothing so much as a schoolboy called before the headmaster. Sharon sat opposite them in the paneled room, air-conditioned against the August heat. Pictures of the Gemayel family covered the walls. Bashir's officers settled themselves on the couch as a young secretary served coffee in tiny cups.

Pierre Gemayel, as always immaculately dressed in suit and tie, congratulated the Israeli security forces. "You have achieved a great thing," he told Sharon. Bashir nodded in agreement. In less formal garb of short-sleeved shirt and brown slacks, he looked younger than his thirty-five years. It was hard to believe that this fresh-faced young man had already had so much deep experience of life—that within a few days he would be president of Lebanon.

Sharon responded in his usual straightforward manner. "Sheikh Pierre, now is the time for you to decide. We started this war to destroy the PLO in Lebanon. We have paid a heavy price. But when you make peace with us, together we can ensure the safety and security of both our countries. That will be another, positive, by-product of the war."

I remembered this optimistic conversation when Sharon and I arrived in Bikfaya at midmorning on that fateful Wednesday,

September 15, 1982. The stone cottages were all hung with black-draped photographs of Bashir Gemayel. Thousands of people were gathered on the road leading to Pierre Gemayel's home. When Sharon arrived, driven in a Lebanese-registered car, they made way for him, their faces expressing grief and shock. Sharon's security guards gripped their weapons firmly, but there was no need for the gesture. Several of the local people approached Sharon and shook his hand, almost as though trying to draw courage from him. Perhaps they even felt he needed their encouragement and their thanks.

In Pierre Gemayel's spacious living room people gathered in hushed groups. Sharon was shown to a more isolated area, where he was received by Amin Gemayel, Bashir's brother and now heir to the presidency.

This was the first time they'd met. Amin, elegantly attired in a dark-blue suit, rose, saying to Sharon: "I am aware of the talk you had with Bashir." Sharon knew he was referring to the Bikfaya meeting at Bashir's home some three days earlier, when it had been arranged that on Wednesday, September 15, Israeli Foreign Minister Yitzhak Shamir and Sharon were to arrive in Lebanon and meet with Bashir, the president elect, to discuss the principles of a peace plan. Now, on that same Wednesday, one of the two parties to the peace plan lay in a coffin.

Sharon was gratified that Bashir's successor knew about the meeting, but Amin was still an unknown quantity. They had no chance to talk as just then Pierre Gemayel came through a low doorway and approached their corner. Tall and spare, still immaculate in a black suit with snowy handkerchief protruding from his breast pocket, Pierre had a smile of greeting for his guest. He was calm and controlled. The only visible sign of personal grief was the grayish pallor of his face.

Everyone rose—Defense Minister Sharon; the mustached and graying General Yehoshua Saguy, head of Israeli military intelligence; the head of the Israeli security service; two Mossad representatives; and aides from the Israeli entourage.

I sat slightly to the left of Pierre Gemayel, next to Sharon, who sat on the sofa, and I listened to the conversation.

Sharon spoke with urgent sincerity. "Sheikh Pierre, we feel

your pain and Lebanon's pain. Please accept the condolences of the people of Israel and their government." A Mossad representative translated into French. A second Mossad man sat to the right of Pierre taking notes.

Pierre Gemayel answered in a mild tone, almost as if there had been no tragedy. "We thank the government of Israel, the people of Israel, and you yourself, General Sharon, for sharing in our grief. You are the only country in the world that helped us in our hardest hour. The Christians of Lebanon will never forget."

Amin Gemayel sat unmoving, his arms folded across his chest.

Later Sharon would comment on the bereaved father's self-control. "I have thought about it. I too have suffered personal tragedies. I know how a man feels when something like that happens. But his calm made me feel this was a man who had the situation under control. He was in charge."

Sharon told Pierre that the Israeli government would maintain its relations with the Lebanese Christians and continue with the support it had provided over the years. Sharon also said that "the Israeli army is entering West Beirut." The conversation stopped intermittently for translation. Sheikh Pierre said the Christians in Lebanon needed Israel's continued help. He said he knew of the talks Sharon had had with his murdered son Bashir, especially emphasizing the last one, on September 12. These talks, said Pierre, were very important.

Sharon assured Pierre that he was aware of the importance of that last talk with Bashir—concerning a peace plan between Israel and Lebanon. "We will continue the political process we started," said Sharon.

All the Israeli representatives—all of them senior officials—heard Sharon's words, as I did. We heard every syllable of his conversation in this closed group with Pierre Gemayel. And none of us, other than the translator, said a word.

Revenge or anything remotely resembling it was never mentioned. There were no ambiguous movements of body or hand—from Sharon, from Pierre, or from Amin Gemayel.

In total only 15–20 minutes elapsed from the time the meeting started until Sharon took his leave. This was, after all, a condolence visit. He didn't want to intrude on the family's personal grief. Pierre Gemayel warmly shook Sharon's hand and personally accompanied him to the door. Grieving villagers clustered outside. Pierre Gemayel raised his hand in dignified greeting. The mourners made way for Sharon, shaking his hand as he passed.

The paragraph in *Time* magazine bore not the slightest resemblance to the actual conversation at the meeting in Bikfaya.

Time's cover showed Begin's and Sharon's pictures under the headline "Verdict on the Massacre." The cover story inside included a head, "The Verdict Is Guilty." And in the body of the story on the conclusions of the Israeli commission of inquiry investigating the events at Sabra and Shatilla was the paragraph that turned a polite, deferential conversation in Bikfaya into a meeting of Murder Inc.

HOW IT ALL BEGAN

AT 5:00 A.M. ON FEBRUARY 14, 1983, MY PHONE RANG.

Ariel Sharon, the Israeli minister of defense, was on the line.

"Did you hear about the disgusting lie that *Time* magazine published about me?" he asked in a voice simultaneously grieved and angry. He didn't wait for my reply. "I heard them quoting the lie on the radio, claiming that I had encouraged the Phalangists to take revenge on the Palestinians. That's what they wrote, that the massacre in Sabra and Shatilla occurred because I encouraged the Gemayel family during my visit to their house in Bikfaya to take revenge on the Palestinians for their murder of Bashir."

"Yes, I heard the Israel radio broadcast after midnight," I answered.

"How could *Time* publish this terrible invention without checking it?" he continued. "It's not just an Israeli newspaper bent on publishing any fabrication. Issue an immediate denial."

"I remember the meeting in Bikfaya very well," I said to Sharon. "You didn't say a word that could be interpreted as a call for revenge. Neither did Pierre Gemayel nor Amin Gemayel mention the subject." Pierre was the father and Amin the brother of the assassinated president elect of Lebanon, Bashir Gemayel.

"Publish a denial immediately," Sharon repeated. "But I don't think that will be enough this time. I'll take them to court for libel."

So, on February 14, 1983, Ariel Sharon's libel action against *Time* magazine began.

At the time I was working as the defense minister's media adviser. I knew that the two evening papers in Israel close their operations very early and that they might quote *Time* magazine's lie. In order to get the denial published that day I had to call *Yediot Ahronot* and *Ma'ariv* and dictate the denial over the phone. Then I called the Voice of Israel and the army radio in an attempt to prevent the lie's being spread.

This was, of course, put out as an announcement by a "Ministry of Defense spokesman." The moment that the minister of defense instructed me to publish the denial, it became an official, departmental announcement. Many months later, during the legal process in New York, *Time* magazine tried to claim that we had not published an official denial. But, as it turned out, this was just one of their many excuses. After phoning the newspapers I called Ministry of Defense spokesman Danny Weinreich. I dictated the wording of the denial to him and told him to bring it to the attention of the rest of the media.

The defense minister's schedule was very crowded that day, for Sharon was to bid farewell to the chiefs of the army and the Defense Ministry departments, eighteen months after taking office on August 6, 1981.

The Lebanon war as not yet over, but Israel still held all the aces. The Israeli forces were deployed from south of Beirut to the northern frontier of Israel, securing the Galilee region, for which purpose Israel had gone to war. But the man who had run the war day and night since June 6, 1982, was on his way out. The Israeli politicians, not the enemy, had brought him down. That was why the war continued until June 1985. That was why Israel forfeited many of her achievements in Lebanon.

For the situation in Lebanon there was no substitute for Arik Sharon as minister of defense. Moshe Arens, who had been Israel's ambassador in Washington, and Yitzhak Rabin, more experienced than Arens in military affairs, both ran away from Lebanon, chased by the Shi'ite enemy.

No one except those very close to Sharon could have realized how disturbed he felt that day, believing, as he did, that a terrible personal wrong had been done to him and that a terrible blow had been struck against the security of Israel.

Ordinarily one might expect a political leader forced out of office to say a few conventional parting words with an appropriately sad expression. But Sharon, wearing a dark-blue suit that emphasized the paleness of his face, bore himself as if it were a perfectly normal day at the Defense Ministry. He knew that the eyes of both friend and foe were fixed on him. Television cameras from all over the world were focused on him. The media, some happily, announced that Sharon's downfall had finally arrived.

At the beginning of the day he went into his office for a few minutes. His secretary, Sarah, gave him a sheaf of cables that had been received from people all over—from the U.S., from France, from Scandinavia. He glanced at a few of them. They were messages of support. Without saying anything, Sharon handed me several.

"It is an embarrassment to the State of Israel that you have been forced to leave your position as minister of defense" one of them read. "It's a disaster for Israel that a man like you has been forced to resign from his position as minister of defense. I'm sure we'll hear more of you." "Israel's enemies from the USSR to the Arab countries are celebrating their victory today" read a third cable.

Sharon got up, leaving the pile of telegrams on his desk. He turned toward the other wing of the ministry and walked down the corridor to the conference room of the chief of staff. Around the U-shaped table, top army officers and the chief of staff were waiting for him. He knew everyone well. Some of them, such as Chief of Staff Rafael Eitan and his deputy, Moshe Levy, had been his junior officers when he commanded the paratroopers in the fifties. He had fought with many of the others in Israel's wars.

When the photographers had left and the doors were closed, Sharon pulled out a little note pad that he always carried with him. He didn't say a word about Sabra and Shatilla, about the Kahan Commission of Inquiry, which had investigated the tragedy and found him indirectly responsible. He talked only about the future. The defense minister's message to one of the best armies in the world was conveyed just as if it were a regular meeting, one of the hundreds of meetings he had run as minister of defense. He spoke of the lessons the Israel Defense Forces should derive from the war: how and when to use the air force; the need to "improve immediately" night-combat fighting techniques; the need to be even better prepared to deal with the enemy's antiaircraft missiles, even though, in an astonishing operation, the IDF had succeeded in destroying all the Soviet-made Syrian missile batteries in the Beka'a Valley in Lebanon in June 1982.

Sharon said just a few words, but they were to the point. I felt that some of the generals found it hard to understand what was going on. They had been expecting to see a beaten man, a man complaining that he'd been thrown to the wolves. All of them related to Arik differently—with opposition, hate, fear, ad-

31

miration—but all, without exception, were united in their appreciation of him as an extraordinary military leader.

When he went back to his office there were newsclips on his desk. *Ha'aretz,* the only respectable Israeli daily, had a long article commanding the front page under the banner headline "Secret Excerpts from the Kahan Inquiry Published in *Time* Magazine. On the Eve of the Massacre, Sharon Spoke with the Gemayel Family About the Need for Revenge." *Davar,* the Labor opposition mouthpiece, carried an almost identical headline. The leftist paper *Al Hamishmar* ran a headline so large it looked like 24 point: "Sharon Met with the Gemayel Family After Bashir's Murder and Talked About the Need for Revenge."

Sharon was visibly angry as he turned the pages. *Ma'ariv* printed lengthy quotes from the *Time* story. My denial was there all right—all of the one and a half lines they'd given it. Only *Yediot Ahronot,* the most popular Israeli daily, had published the complete text of the denial under *Time*'s story, which was bannered "*Time:* On the Eve of the Massacre Sharon Told the Gemayel Family to Avenge Bashir's Death. Ministry of Defense: It's a Lie." Right at the end was the denial of the Defense Ministry spokesman: "This is an evil and completely groundless article, like other stories without any vestige of truth published about Minister Sharon on previous occasions. These stories are a premeditated and deliberate part of the continuous defamatory campaign by various elements against Minister Sharon."

"See how the lie takes wing," Sharon observed to me. "Look how blatantly they lie. Do you think," he continued, "that I could sue *Time* magazine for libel? In Tel Aviv? In New York? I'm going to look into it today," he said firmly. "I've already arranged a meeting with Dubi Weissglas this afternoon." Weissglas was the leader of the team of lawyers that had advised Sharon during the Kahan Commission's inquiry into the tragic events of Sabra and Shatilla.

Sharon now hurried to the large conference room on the ministry's fifth floor, where the heads of the defense establishment, joined by executives from the military industries and weapons-systems experts, were waiting for him. Everyone fell silent when he came into the room, accompanied by his wife, Lily, who would remain at his side.

Sharon made his speech brief. He addressed them not as a minister whom the government has decided to transfer from his post but more like someone who had just taken up the Defense Ministry burdens. Everything must be done to ensure that Israel did not lose its deterrent capacity, he said. This risk does exist. It's in our hands to keep Israel strong enough to prevent war. "One of the ways of doing this," he said, "is to minimize dependence on outside sources—to manufacture our own arms, including the Lavi jet fighter-bomber. It's the plane of the nineties."

Hundreds of ministry employees were waiting for him on the second floor when he'd finished. Clerks from his office were waiting for him there. They all wanted a parting photograph with "the minister," as they called him when they didn't use his nickname, Arik. Many faces were tear-stained.

"There's a boy, a soldier, standing and crying," said one of the clerks. "It's Oron."

I found myself shaking. I hadn't known my son was also coming to the office to be with Arik on this painful day. Arik called to him to come in. Oron's eyes were red and brimming with tears.

"Hey there, there's nothing to cry about, my boy," Arik said, comforting him. "Nothing's happened." Oron's tears didn't stop. Arik put an arm around the boy's shoulders and called for a photograph. Oron couldn't say a word. There was only a painfully forced smile.

Thereafter it was like an assembly line, ending with the Christian Lebanese poet May Moor, who had arrived from Beirut to say farewell. A courageous woman who had come out openly in favor of peace between Israel and Lebanon, she had staunchly stood by her belief despite threats to her life.

"To us you are a modern Hannibal," she told Sharon at the beginning of her moving speech before the flashing cameras and forest of microphones. "You not only saved Israel from the PLO, you saved us too, the Christians."

Sharon sat across the table from her, under photographs of David Ben-Gurion and Menachem Begin, listening silently. The Israeli press would in due course make cynical use of May Moor's words.

Finally, two farewell meetings had been arranged for Sharon with the chief of staff and the head of the security service. I asked him to give me five minutes between meetings. "You must read this letter. Peter Malkin brought it this morning," I said to him. Peter was the man who had caught Adolf Eichmann. One of the finest fighters who ever served in the Mossad, the Israeli Central Intelligence Agency, Peter Malkin had caught Eichmann on Garibaldi Street in Buenos Aires in 1960. A very cool man, with common sense and deep sensitivity, Peter had sent Sharon a letter in his round script.

> I saw the ministers saying goodbye to you on TV during the Cabinet meeting. They were like sardines in a can. One eye closed and one eye covered in oil. They were jealous of you even then. They knew that everywhere you go you'd be watched. The press and the cameras will follow you everywhere. Some people are born with a talent for painting. You were born with a talent for leadership. And for that, they can't forgive you. . . . Next time, don't be in such a hurry. Don't leave your friends running after you, breathlessly trying to match your pace. Next time, give us smaller victories at greater intervals. If you do that, I haven't any doubt that one of these days you'll be prime minister of Israel.

It was a wonderful letter for one of the saddest days in Sharon's long and stormy career.

Peter, with his highly original style, had put his finger on sensitive issues: the victories in Lebanon, the expulsion of the Palestine Liberation Organization from Beirut, the fracturing of the PLO, the destruction of the Syrian missiles. They were indeed big victories in a very short time. And it was hard for Sharon's enemies to digest them.

"What's the date today?" Sharon asked me.

"The fourteenth of February."

Sharon wrote the date at the top of the letter. He always dates anything he considers of documentary value.

At three o'clock that afternoon Sharon left the Ministry of Defense without looking back. The chief of staff in his red beret was waiting for him at the exit. They walked together past an honor guard made up of all the different services of the IDF. A cool breeze lifted Sharon's silvery forelock. His face was set. As he later told me, Sharon was thinking at the moment that it was the Jews who had handed him over to his enemies.

Sharon's face showed all the pain, all the emotion when we met in his apartment an hour later. The lawyer Dov (Dubi) Weissglas was standing in the living room holding the morning and evening papers. He explained to Sharon some of the difficulties of a libel suit. The huge costs involved. The further defamation that would inevitably be published both before and during the trial. He described how *Time*'s legal counsel would cross-examine Sharon during the trial, how they would interrogate him on everything he'd done and especially what he had not done throughout his life.

"You were with me all the time during the Kahan Inquiry," Sharon answered firmly. "You know all the evidence. I'm not going to put up with the media's lies any longer." He squared his shoulders. "I've decided to fight. Today *Time* magazine printed one of the worst lies ever published about me. It's the biggest weekly newsmagazine in the world. I want to take them to court."

Prime Minister Menachem Begin found *Time*'s accusation so outrageous that he attacked it that same evening, calling it "a libel."

The ailing seventy-year-old Begin was under continual attack from leftists and the Labor party, headed by Shimon Peres, who tried to unseat him, using the Sabra and Shatilla massacre as their latest weapon. Undeterred, he made a firm declaration in the Knesset, the Israeli parliament.

Mr. Speaker, members of the Knesset:

I read Appendix Number Two to the Final Report of the Commission of Inquiry, which decided it will be privileged and top secret, and, of course, I will not reveal its contents. But I am able to say, on the basis of this knowledge, that what is written in *Time* magazine, as if the Minister of Defense, after the assassination of Bashir Gemayel, went to Beirut and talked to the family of the assassinated [victim] about revenge upon Palestinians or on those suspect[ed] in the murder, this whole story is entirely a lie and false and has no substance. Since the Commission does not exist anymore and cannot itself deny it, I announce this denial from the Knesset podium and I call on the Editorial Board of the famous magazine distributed around the whole world, *Time,* to apologize immediately to the Minister of Defense and to the State of Israel for the distribution of this libel.

Blood Libel

It is very rare for an Israeli prime minister to use the Knesset podium to deny a press story categorically. Begin, who had gone to the Knesset to make a statement on the adoption of the Kahan Commission Report, found it appropriate to do so and to draw a clear distinction between the report and the *Time* story.

More than a year later, when Sharon's attorneys were digging into *Time*'s files in New York, they found this Telex sent the following day by Harry Kelly, *Time*'s Jerusalem bureau chief.

> That must have been one heck of a news release on the Inquiry cover [the *Time* story], specifically on that fairly innocuously worded "*Time* has learned" [para]graph about Sharon's meeting with the Gemayel family. It was on page one in the papers Monday. Somebody at the Defense Ministry was commenting it was all lies. Then the Press Office put out a statement that the Defense Ministry response was not an official denial. Then later in the Knesset Monday Begin called it "bald lies and slander" and called on *Time*'s editors to apologize to Sharon and the State of Israel for "disseminating this libel." And I don't think anybody's had a chance to read the story yet: at least our copy hasn't arrived. We must have struck a nerve. Cheers.

The Telex had been sent to *Time*'s chief of correspondents, Richard L. Duncan, in New York. Neither he nor Kelly, who received the magazine with the story the next day, Wednesday, February 16, nor anybody else at *Time* made any effort to discover why Prime Minister Begin called the story a "libel" or what nerve was struck. For *Time*'s people the news release remained "that fairly innocuously worded '*Time* has learned' graph about Sharon's meeting." So—"Cheers."

Two weeks later attorney Weissglas brought suit in an Israeli court against Time, Incorporated and *Time*'s international edition for libeling Sharon. On March 1, 1983, *The New York Times* published *Time*'s reaction: "Richard L. Duncan, chief of correspondents for Time-Life News Service said a *Time* correspondent in Jerusalem had told him of Israel radio reports of the suit, but, he said, 'We have not heard anything from Sharon or his office. We haven't heard from a lawyer.' Asked if Time-Life stood behind the story, Mr. Duncan replied that the company did."

Sharon asked me over and over during the ensuing weeks how it was that an organization as impressive as *Time* hadn't bothered either to investigate the basis of Begin's official denial or to apologize for its mistake.

"Of course they think you're through," I replied. "*Time* magazine, like several Israeli journalists and politicians, think you're washed up politically. They believe all the lies that have been written about you, so they didn't dream that you would dare to sue them. Or they thought that if you did sue, they'd be able to prove you are a cold-blooded murderer!"

Sharon was often asked why he chose to sue *Time* on this one specific paragraph when apparently even more serious things had been written about him over the years. He explained to me where the difference lay. "I have nothing against opinions that are opposed to my views or against those who attack me on that basis. But to lie—that's another story. In contrast to the many other lies that have been written, *Time*'s lie was not only the worst, because it accused me of killing innocent people; it was written as if it were all fact. *Time* has written incorrect things about me in the past. However, in this most serious instance, the things were not written broadly and generally but directly, as if they were facts. They were written in a way that allowed for a libel suit. The paragraph in *Time* was written so that it was possible to refute it factually." Sharon thought for a moment and then added, "There is no such thing as a perfect crime. Inevitably each criminal eventually makes his own mistake. *Time* made theirs too, and it will cost them dearly."

This was *Time*'s mistake:

> One section of the [commission's] report, known as Appendix B, was not published at all, mainly for security reasons. That section contains the names of several intelligence agents referred to elsewhere in the report. *Time* has learned that it also contains further details about Sharon's visit to the Gemayel family on the day after Bashir Gemayel's assassination. Sharon reportedly told the Gemayels that the Israeli army would be moving into West Beirut and that he expected the Christian forces to go into the Palestinian refugee camps. Sharon also reportedly discussed with the Gemayels the need for the Phalangists to take revenge for the as-

sassination of Bashir, but the details of the conversation are not known.

Sharon had analyzed the *Time* paragraph, line by line and word by word, scores of times, both to himself and with his friends and lawyers. The *Time* story said that on a certain day, at a certain place, in a very well-defined conversation between him and the Gemayel family, Sharon had discussed with the Phalangists "the need for revenge" on the Palestinians for the assassination of Bashir Gemayel.

According to *Time,* all this was included in the unpublished Kahan Commission Secret Appendix, which meant that it was not even possible to check this awful story, because, for security reasons, the appendix had not been cleared for publication. Nevertheless "*Time* has learned"—it was *Time*'s scoop, which other papers didn't have.

Sharon regarded the paragraph very seriously because it had been published *after* the findings of the Kahan Commission. As far as Sharon was concerned, the *Time* story created the impression that the Kahan Commission of Inquiry was hiding something from the Israeli people and the world at large. How could the commission have found him guilty only of indirect responsibility if the Secret Appendix—according to the *Time* story—concerned details of his talks with the Gemayels about the need to take revenge on the Palestinians? It was as if Israeli law and top government officials had conspired to keep the truth a secret: the "truth" being that Israel's minister of defense and the Phalangists had plotted cold-blooded murder.

Sharon went over and over Secret Appendix B at the government secretariat offices, as he was entitled to do, not only as a party against whom findings had been made by the commission but also as a minister of the government. He found not one iota of the information *Time* had published.

And so the *Time* paragraph became a new "act of accusation," Sharon said, because the Kahan Commission Report had already been published, and *Time* had based its story on it. "The Israeli government should have taken care of *Time,*" he added. But because he knew that the government and its diligent attorney general would do nothing of the kind—because, unfortunately, a lack of response is typical Jerusalem behavior whenever Israel is in any way humiliated—he decided to proceed on his own.

Time, which had published the lie, nevertheless could not have known—since they weren't interested enough to investigate—why Sharon had decided to remain in the government without portfolio after the findings of the Kahan Commission were published. Had *Time* taken the trouble to find out about this rather than being satisfied with the false story written by their reporter, David Halevy, they would perhaps have published the several denials of the story that were issued in Israel.

Sharon's reason for staying in the Begin government was precisely that he had decided to fight. On February 8, 1983, a Tuesday morning, when the Kahan Commission published its findings, Sharon was at home on his farm. His assistants and lawyers, who analyzed the report in a room at the Jerusalem Hilton, described the findings to him, including the commission's recommendation to the government to remove him from his position as minister of defense.

Sharon's immediate reaction that morning had been to resign not only from his position but also from the government. "I won't remain in the government as a minister without portfolio," he had said emphatically. "Absolutely not. They can all go to hell. I'm going back to work on the farm." Sharon sincerely believed that he had been treated unjustly. After serving his country devotedly and unceasingly for thirty-eight stormy years, he thought perhaps now was the time to retire, to say thank you and goodbye. But when he had cooled down, after a conversation with Prime Minister Begin, he reconsidered.

He was sorry that Begin had not accepted his suggestion to reject the conclusions of the commission of inquiry. Sharon had explained to Begin that the conclusions were very serious indeed and that they did not reflect what actually had happened at Sabra and Shatilla. "Menachem, you know the truth. We were not involved in it," Sharon said. The findings unjustifiably sullied the names of IDF generals, the chief of staff, the prime minister, and Foreign Minister Shamir, quite apart from Sharon himself, the defense minister maintained.

In a situation like this, Sharon had said to Begin, a motion should be introduced in the Knesset calling for rejection of the commission's findings. It was entirely within the government's authority to introduce a motion of this sort. No government could continue with such a report hanging over it. If the government falls because of this, Sharon had suggested, "we'll call for elections. We'll once again ask for the confidence of the people against this backdrop—rejection of the findings of the commission. I believe that a majority of the nation will support us."

But Begin had accepted the advice of the Likud ministers who were Sharon's rivals and counseled him that if Sharon were to leave the Ministry of Defense, public opinion would calm down and the government, unaffected, could continue to funtion.

On the evening of that same dark day Sharon went ahead with his original schedule and held a large reception at the Tel Aviv Hilton for Admiral Lompunda, Zaire's minister of defense, and a delegation sent to Israel by the government of President Mobutu. There were hundreds of people at the reception, and they followed Sharon's every move and gesture. Television cameras took close-ups of him. But his behavior and expression remained unchanged. Sharon knew how to keep the tremendous turmoil he was feeling buried deep.

In a way Sharon felt that if he resigned and worked his farm, it would simply be a relief. His wife and sons wanted him at home, calm and relaxed, in the fields, tending the sheep, going horseback riding. On the other hand, he sensed that even if he did quit politics, his enemies would continue to hound him. They would refuse to accept that he had given up all activity at the national level and would always be fearful that he was there, albeit on the farm, threatening their political careers.

At the same time Sharon knew that his supporters would not leave him alone either. Even if he wanted to isolate himself from politics, they would still come to him. Army people, settlers from Judea and Samaria—they would all come knocking at his door, asking how he could remain uninvolved in his country's affairs when things were so turbulent. Israel, after all, was a country fighting for its very existence.

Moreover, Sharon knew himself better than anyone else did.

He knew that after he had been at the farm for a while he would become restless, frustrated because he was not involved in national affairs when such fateful events were occurring—militarily, economically, and in the settlements. Sharon knew that he could not cut himself off from all this, especially as he believed he had something to contribute, at least as much as any other minister in the government.

At the age of fifty-five he was too young to cut himself off from his tempestuous way of life in the service of Israel. He could not escape the fact that he was a controversial leader, one who dealt with matters that either were controversial or else became that way after he took them up, a man capable of arousing heated debate and strong commitments.

Whether it proved to be a curse or a blessing, Sharon decided to continue playing an active role in the nation's leadership. Lily and their boys saw it as a curse.

Sharon came to the conclusion that the quickest way to regain influence over what was going on (and shorten his term of political exile) would be from a position in the government, not from the farm. He decided that he wouldn't allow his being out of the Ministry of Defense to lead to his retirement from the government. If he were to resign as minister of defense, this would constitute resignation from the government. And to be reinstated as a member of the government, even as a minister without portfolio, would require approval by a special vote of the Knesset. This is customary when any minister joins a government. Sharon foresaw the danger implicit in this step. His opponents, both in the opposition and among his own party fellows, would try to ensure that approval of his return did not pass a Knesset vote. So, with Begin's cooperation, Sharon directed and caused the government to vote instead on shifting him from the Defense Ministry to minister without portfolio—all perfectly permissible within the law.

The New York suit could now begin.

ARIEL SHARON AND MILTON GOULD MET FOR THE
first time in a spacious, wood-paneled fifteenth-floor conference
room in the Manhattan offices of Shea and Gould. Only the small
group of people there knew the purpose of the meeting. Sharon's
security guards, discreet as always, sat outside in the corridor.

Gould and Sharon were formal. It was "Mr. Gould" and "General Sharon." Watching them, I saw two commanders: seventy-
four-year-old Milton Gould, his deep-set eyes penetrating under
bushy white brows, and across from him the silver-haired, fifty-
five-year-old general.

Only the two commanders spoke at the outset of this first strategy session for the forthcoming battle. Everyone else watched and
listened: Arnold Forster, a warm-hearted Jew and longtime
fighter for the Israeli cause in the ranks of the Anti-Defamation
League, who had only recently joined Gould's firm; Richard
Goldstein, one of Gould's partners, a Jewish lawyer of the younger
generation in a three-piece suit and sporting a well-trimmed mus-
tache; and several aides on both sides.

Gould raised a lot of questions at the meeting. He was as eager
and alert as someone half his age. He was one of the last of a great
school of professionals. He hadn't followed the fashionable trend
of specialization. His list of clients included some of the most
prominent American names of the past fifty years, and the types
of cases he had handled also showed that half-century spread. His
attitude toward Sharon was interesting. He showed infinite respect, of course, but also curiosity.

Yes, Gould had read the paragraph in *Time.* It was awful.

"It's nothing but a lie," Sharon told Gould firmly. "I've decided to fight it."

Sharon had investigated a number of firms before he'd selected
Shea and Gould at 330 Madison Avenue, off Forty-second Street.
All of his friends had urged him to go to this particular firm, as
one of the most seasoned and respected in Manhattan. He'd also
been advised that Shea and Gould would take the case without
fee—for expenses only. Perhaps the reason for this was what
clinched the decision for Sharon. Gould and Forster, he'd been
told, believed that what *Time* had published was a lie.

Now Gould's questions were coming steadily. Sharon described his Bikfaya meeting. "It was only a condolence call."

"Are there authorized minutes of the meeting?" Gould wanted to know.

Mindful of the confidentiality of classified documents, Sharon was careful. "Such minutes do exist."

"Can they be produced in court?"

It wasn't so simple, Sharon explained. "I'll have to go to the government and ask for them. I think I'll get them, because there was nothing secret at that meeting. Anyway, it's all been published. But there's no absolute assurance."

"Were there other people at this meeting aside from Pierre and Amin Gemayel and yourself?" Gould continued.

"There certainly were. It was reported in the Kahan Report. The head of the Israeli military intelligence, the head of the Shin Bet—that's the secret service—Mossad representatives, and Uri Dan."

Gould turned to me. "You'll be able to testify in court about what was said in that conversation?"

I nodded.

The meeting continued for about two hours. Gould repeatedly went over all the material; Sharon patiently recapped the background several times.

Finally Gould gave a brisk and satisfied nod. "If I have the minutes of the conversation and Uri Dan's testimony—well, we'll prove the lie," he said confidently. "And we'll sue *Time* for fifty million dollars in damages."

Sharon was amazed. "How did you arrive at that figure?" he asked jovially. "Not that I mind—but what's the basis for your claim?"

Gould smiled, a smile born of long experience. "Simple. Make it less and no one will take your suit seriously." Then he added, "You'll have to freeze the legal proceedings in Tel Aviv until after the trial in New York."

The first meetings at Shea and Gould's offices took place in May and June 1983, shortly after Sharon had become minister without portfolio. Before the June meeting Sharon visited Montreal, where he'd been invited by Jewish community leaders to a banquet to raise funds for Jerusalem's Shaare Zedek hospital. There a storm broke loose that reverberated across the continent.

Arab and Canadian supporters of the PLO had joined with leftist Jewish youngsters, including a sprinkling of Peace Now followers, to protest Sharon's visit. They ran ads in the newspapers and scattered posters throughout the city. They distributed handbills. Sharon was shown wearing an SS uniform. The poster legends were all the same. "IDF brutality." "The criminal government of Israel." The specter of Sabra and Shatilla was produced again and again.

Sharon would never get used to it. "What hatred! What lies!" he protested.

The Canadian Mounted Police provided heavy security around his hotel. Outside, a raucous pro-PLO demonstration shouted denunciations, while inside, in the banqueting hall, Sharon accepted a boisterously warm welcome. Several of the guests came over and hoisted him onto their shoulders. Sharon evoked peals of laughter with the opening sentence of his acknowledgment. "If you could manage to pick *me* up, then you'll manage any mission at all for Israel," said the very heavily built minister with a wide smile.

The noise from the outside even penetrated the hall. Young Jews had gathered in a counterdemonstration, and the two groups stood opposite each other yelling vituperative slogans. To the horror of the security guards, Sharon left the banquet and went outside. He stood at the entrance to the hotel for about fifteen minutes, simply looking at the two groups, whose violence was increasing. The Zionist camp was slowly getting the better of things. Sharon waved hello, and some of the youngsters broke away to come over and shake his hand. The Montreal demonstration fueled Sharon's determination to punish *Time*.

Back in New York again for the second session with the lawyers, Sharon did a painstaking recap of the Bikfaya meeting. Every detail, every word had to be clear. There could be no blurring. On the desk was the *Time* story with its glaring headline: "The Verdict Is Guilty." The paragraph accusing Sharon of encouraging murder was outlined in red.

Gould emphasized the need for absolute precision. He wanted

every scrap of information. Where were the minutes of the meeting? Did Secret Appendix B contain what *Time* had published?

"No. Absolutely not." Sharon was emphatic. "How could the documentation include something that was never said? I never encouraged them to take revenge." It was essential, he knew, that the lawyers have at their command not only the facts but also the reasoning.

"Not even by a hint?" Gould was determined there should be no loopholes.

The events of Bikfaya, Sharon said, were precisely as described in the Kahan Report. The minutes of the conversation had been transcribed according to standard Mossad procedure. Each of these meetings with the Lebanese had been organized by the Mossad, the Israeli equivalent of the CIA. The Mossad was in charge of Israel's relationship with the leaders of the Christians of Lebanon. The minutes weren't in stenographic form. They were written in tight, concise summaries. Sharon couldn't recall the precise wording, "but it couldn't have been different from what I said to Pierre Gemayel."

Gould emphasized the cardinal importance of the contents of both these minutes and Secret Appendix B. That would be the hub of their entire case.

"All those documents," Sharon assured him, "were given to the commission of inquiry—the minutes of all the conversations and meetings with the Lebanese. My office transferred thousands of documents to the commission. So did other government agencies." He reiterated the reasoning behind the facts. "If the minutes of the Bikfaya talks had said what *Time* accused me of, I wouldn't have been made indirectly responsible; I would have been directly responsible."

Gould wanted to be sure that back in Jerusalem Sharon would make a legal request to see the documents, as he was entitled to do. "You must understand," the attorney said, "that suing *Time* magazine for fifty million dollars is serious. It's essential that we know the document of the Bikfaya talks contains nothing even resembling what *Time* said it did. And if it doesn't, as an official document of the State of Israel it will support Sharon's description of the conversation."

Sharon had his personal reasoning too. "In my opinion, it's important to prove that what was published about me is a lie. I'll have a hard time explaining why we are suing for fifty million dollars. My opponents will make the most of that. They'll make it look as though my whole purpose is to make money."

Like Sharon and Forster, Gould was certain the Israeli government would let Sharon have the documents. "There's nothing secret in them," Sharon had explained. "No military operations were discussed. It was a condolence call at the Gemayel home, a conversation between myself and Lebanese Christian Arabs. We knew perfectly well that the whole thing would be transmitted to Damascus, to the Syrians, in very short order."

Sharon's Israeli lawyer, Dubi Weissglas, also attended this meeting with the New York lawyers. He was completely familiar with everything connected with Sabra and Shatilla after all the months in which he had represented Sharon before the Kahan Commission. While Sharon and Gould talked, Weissglas started the follow-through. He called the Ministry of Defense in Tel Aviv and asked for an outline of the conversation at Bikfaya. Shortly thereafter he was back in the conference room with a summary of the minutes. Translating as he went along, he read them to Gould.

Gould was astonished. "That's all there was?"

"That's all," said Sharon grimly. "I told you it was a brief condolence visit. There was no discussion at all—certainly not of the Palestinian camps."

Gould took the notes Weissglas had made while talking to Tel Aviv.

Even with his awareness of all the conflict and disagreement in Israel, both at government level and in the country as a whole, Sharon couldn't imagine that the State of Israel would refuse to allow him access to the key documents at issue. It was so obvious that they were essential to support his words—and proof that *Time* had lied.

Sharon was convinced he wouldn't have any difficulty with the Israeli government; or rather, he wanted to be convinced. Proof that there was nothing secret about the events at Bikfaya was essential to clear not only his own name but also that of Israel—

there could be no distinction between the two. If *Time*'s statement were true, it would make not only Sharon but also the State of Israel an accomplice to murder, because as minister of defense he represented Israel at that moment.

Even with a lifetime of bitter experience, Sharon retains a directness of thought that some people might describe as naïveté. I see it as innocence. That innocence is one of the secrets of Sharon's strength. He succeeds precisely because he doesn't get entangled in maneuvering and manipulation, he can go straight to his target and reach it. What his opponents deride as naïveté, as a lack of political finesse, enables him to move forward and not get sidetracked. While his adversaries are wallowing in the shallows of internecine argument, Sharon simply sweeps forward with the main current. When he set out in the summer of 1973 to create the Likud bloc in Israel, to unite the opposition, because that was the only way to unseat the Labor party, his efforts were dismissed as infantile. But they succeeded, and the derision gave way to astonishment. It was exactly the same later in 1973, when he firmly believed it was possible to cross the Suez Canal and take the battle to the enemy. He did it while the other generals and the government were still dithering in doubt and fear.

And at Gould's office in New York this same innocence, this certainty, made him persevere. He was convinced the Israeli government would give him the minimal weapon he required in order to disprove the lie: a document or documents that were innocuous, that had no military or political significance.

Gould and Goldstein too were convinced. They were heartened by Sharon's confidence, and, in addition, they were wrapped in the wholly democratic fabric of American society, which is much less convoluted than Israel's. Secrecy laws in the United States aren't so complex. Above all, the lawyers couldn't imagine that the State of Israel would not grasp that its own name was in jeopardy here.

On June 22, 1983, Ariel Sharon's suit for libel against *Time* magazine was filed in the City of New York.

DAVID HALEVY, *TIME*'S ISRAELI-BORN JERUSALEM reporter, in interviews with the Israeli press and in stories he spread about himself, projected the image of a fighting IDF combat officer. But he readily disclosed Israel's most zealously guarded security information and defense secrets while exploiting the contacts he had developed as an army reserve officer. The principal rationale he advanced for publishing his scoops, regardless of their accuracy, was his anxiety for Israel—for its immediate future, for its ultimate destiny. There could be no greater patriot.

"Dudu" Halevy, who in 1983 looked older than his forty-two years, was born in Jerusalem to a family with left-wing leanings, members of the Mapam party. Even in Israel their position had been on the extreme left of that party. For some time Dudu was a member of the Hashomer Hatzair movement. Both party and movement have always openly declared their virulent dislike of Begin and later of Sharon. At Tel-Aviv University, Halevy joined the more moderate Mapai party, later known as the Israel Labor party. He was active in the party's young guard in the halcyon years when Labor reigned supreme and its leaders never even dreamed of Begin and Sharon taking over from them.

Politics proved grist for Halevy's mill. At Tel-Aviv University he combined his studies of the Middle East with editing first the student journal, *Dorban,* and later the Labor party's youth organ, *Ramzor.* It is worth noting that Halevy never actually worked on a big Israeli newspaper. He limited his activities to small papers, where his ferreting could cause party scandals. Many years before Halevy cozied up to Labor leader Shimon Peres, he was spokesman for another Labor luminary, Yigal Allon.

From the outset we knew it would be difficult to make clear to the jury in New York that Halevy had been politically motivated as long as he could remember. But we could demonstrate to the federal court that Israel's highly politicized system, especially that of the Labor party and its more extreme offshoots, taught hatred of the so-called right.

At the end of the sixties Halevy became a stringer for *Time* in Jerusalem. That activated the other aspect of his personality, the hard-hitting reporter. The ideologue cum reporter volunteered in

1970 to serve as an IDF reserve officer during the war of attrition on the Suez Canal. It was a long-drawn-out and arduous war, with heavy casualties. Halevy served for three months. Many, many other Israelis also volunteered and served longer, but Halevy cashed in on his three months. Apparently discarding his patriotism along with his uniform, the hard-hitting reporter immediately publicized his heroism at the Suez Canal.

Reserve officer Halevy was mobilized for the Yom Kippur War in 1973. So were hundreds of thousands of ordinary Israelis. He suffered a neck wound during a war that left nearly three thousand dead and more than five thousand wounded. After the war the patriot volunteered his services for about a year, acting as a battalion commander. Many of his peers volunteered too, but much less ostentatiously.

Halevy was especially talented in ensuring that his voluntary service, his heroism, and his old injury remained in high relief. I believe it was much to the detriment of Israel that he and a few other like-minded souls strenuously cultivated this macho image, promoting their bravado into the headlines. Then, when Halevy returned to his job at *Time,* the various personalities alternated. One or another would jockey to the fore, depending on the demands of the current script.

Time's Jerusalem bureau chiefs were nearly always foreigners, Americans who understood little or no Hebrew. They obviously didn't have Halevy's qualifications or his access to the antechambers of the Israeli government. Somehow or other the bureau chiefs became dependent on Halevy. In an internal, confidential memo obtained from *Time's* files by Sharon's legal team, a *Time* correspondent described Halevy's absorption into the magazine's bloodstream:

> ... What I do know is a bit of how Murray [Gart] and first Marsh [Clark], then Don Neff eased into a closer and closer arrangement with Halevy, culminating in a correspondent's job [for Halevy]. I talked it over several times with Murray, who seemed totally motivated by the quality of several of the exclusives that Dudu filed as a stringer....
>
> ... Halevy ... having been instead a Mossad partisan in the

bitter dispute over the 1973 war, when [Moshe] Dayan allegedly ignored warnings that the Egyptians were about to attack. . . .

. . . If pushed to the wall on this one, while not defending Dudu as a figure free of intrigue himself, I would say this is typical Middle East bullshit throughout, reinforced by the fact that the writer somehow turns out to be the injured party.

My inclination is not to pursue this any further, pending some of my ongoing talks with Halevy, because we just won't get to the bottom of it. I am feeling more concerned about other, more recent and less glamorous aspects of Dudu's behavior. . . .

In the spring of 1977 Halevy positioned himself at the side of Shimon Peres, then running for premier as head of the Labor party. It was a tough electoral campaign for Israel. Labor had ruled the young state since its birth in 1948. In 1977 the then prime minister, Yitzhak Rabin, had had to resign after disclosure of his wife's infringement of local monetary regulations by holding twenty thousand dollars in a Washington, D.C. bank account. Shimon Peres, Rabin's longtime rival in the Labor party hierarchy, came to the fore as a candidate in the race against Menachem Begin.

Most of the Israeli media backed Labor. Political pundits declared Shimon a sure winner. So in joining the intimate special staff of Peres' electoral train, Halevy was apparently on the winning side. Even CIA reports to President Jimmy Carter predicted that Peres would grab the brass ring. The result, however, was quite different. May 17, 1977, was a day of political upheaval for Israel. For the first time in the country's history the Labor party was exiled to the political wilderness. Menachem Begin won: he became prime minister, and Ariel Sharon became one of the most prominent members of his cabinet.

Israel doesn't yet have the traditions of fair play so intrinsically a part of the political principles of older democracies such as the United States, where the immediate antagonisms of electoral campaigns aren't sustained indefinitely.

The generations-old hatred that Labor leaders and their supporters had for Begin, his Likud party, and the "Begin people" was exacerbated by Begin's victory. From the moment he came to power they concentrated on unseating him, actively assisted by vicious attacks from most of the Israeli media. *Time*'s postelection story, outdoing even them, included the infamous "Begin rhymes with Fagin," probably its ugliest editorial thrust until the canard about Sharon. Halevy continued reporting for *Time,* while his disappointment at the failure of his idol Peres, archenemy of Begin and Sharon, simmered toward the boil.

On August 22, 1977, *Time* published a story about Israeli military assistance to the Christian minority in Lebanon. The information was known to a lot of Israeli journalists, but they respected military censorship regulations, which precluded publication of stories endangering defense and foreign relations. *Time,* however, published the scoop, this time genuine, and headlined its story "Israel's Secret War." A special box contained a particularly interesting paragraph:

> In the meantime, reports *Time*'s Jerusalem correspondent David Halevy, the secret Israeli operation began in May 1976 when three Israeli missile boats sailed from Haifa to Jounieh Bay, near the Christian "capital" north of Beirut. Aboard one boat was Yitzhak Rabin, then Israeli premier, and his defense minister, Shimon Peres. Soon the Israelis were joined by two boats from the mainland, one carrying Camille Chamoun, then a Lebanese cabinet minister, the other carrying Lebanese Christian Phalangist Party leader Pierre Gemayel—both boats guided and guarded by Israeli frogmen. Though the two Lebanese Christians, leaders of competing factions, refused to meet with each other, they both appealed to Rabin for direct Israeli intervention in the civil war then raging in Lebanon.

The story was substantially correct, with a single exception. Shimon Peres, the defense minister, was not on the missile boat. Only Premier Rabin sailed to the secret meeting.

Since Halevy had free access to Peres, he could have checked his information before filing his story. But the explanation for the error more likely lies in Halevy's political bias. As I was told several months later by Brigadier General (Res.) Ephraim Poran, who at the time was Rabin's military aide, "We believed that Halevy put Shimon Peres on that missile boat only because he wanted to do a favor for his friend, to show that Peres also went on important secret missions. Rabin could not deny it even if he wanted to, since our relations with the Christians in Lebanon at that time were secret, including his visit. So how could Rabin deny a detail in the story since he couldn't confirm that it ever took place?''

Again Halevy's fingerprints were noticeable. The evidence showed that Halevy had included something secret in stories that no one could check, and, if there was a denial, Halevy could easily explain it to *Time*. "Well, of course, it is so secret that they have to deny it."

With the inexorability of a Greek tragedy, Halevy similarly led *Time* to Sharon's libel trap in New York. Halevy fed *Time* interesting "secret" stories. Then he stirred into the mixture an error such as the one about the missile boat. It worked; the road was open to a story without any foundation. All secret of course.

Meanwhile one aftermath of the war was an increasing moral deterioration among some of the senior officer echelons of the IDF. Certain officers systematically began using Israeli newsmen to harm their adversaries in the army or in the political establishment. Others did likewise to further their professional advancement. In the course of doing so they occasionally revealed critical military secrets to reporters. Careerism and political involvement not only hurt them but also damaged journalistic ethics and the level of professionalism in the Israeli press. Many Israeli reporters routinely published lies or incorrect statements about people whose politics they disliked.

At *Time*, Halevy's reporter personality didn't change. He overlooked or never absorbed the fact that he was supposed to observe American journalistic standards and acted precisely like the Israeli reporter he was. After all, he had grown up among Israeli journalists. The sole difference was that they published their falsities in Hebrew in Israel, while Halevy published his in English for *Time*.

Reserve General Avigdor (Yanosh) Ben-Gal, who was OC Northern Command and commander of hundreds of tanks in the Lebanon war, described the collaboration between himself and his close friend Halevy (*Monitin*, March 1984):

> ... Dudu has many friends in the upper and intermediate echelons of the army command, and we all love and appreciate him

and like to chat with him. It may be assumed that all of us acted as Army Spokesmen for him. But we all did so bona fide and to some extent also to affect conditions and to hit out at people we felt could damage the system. One of our larks, when we met him and were short of cash, was to have meals at the expense of American Express. We certainly had some great food. Through him we found out where the nouveau[x] riche[s] were eating.

What was it we talked about? We discussed ways of increasing efficiency, correcting things, and how to prevent the recurrence of disasters like the Yom Kippur War. How to create motivation among the tired and satiated citizens of the country. We felt extremely close to him, because he was just one of us. I had many man-to-man talks with him when I opened up and spoke of my problems and got his advice. Dudu was always much less open; he is a very introverted person. The main points of contact were when he helped me with his connections. During the "Peace for the Galilee" war the relations between us became very much closer. He was sent to establish a base for *Time* in Beirut and we spent long nights talking from sunset to sunrise. The effect was mutual. It was more an interchange of ideas. We weren't trying to persuade each other because we held the same ideas on a large scale. I supplied him with thoughts and ideas and didn't search for them in his articles, because the conversations with him weren't official, like talking to a newspaperman. I was just talking to him as I always talk to Dudu. . . .

Time's clashes with the government of Israel go back a long way, although their frequency and violence increased after Begin's accession to power, culminating in Sharon's suit for libel. When Ezer Weizman served as minister of defense in 1978, for instance, *Time* published a story about a clash on the West Bank. From Jerusalem, Dudu Halevy sent New York a Telex in which he quoted Weizman's reaction to the story: "Yesterday Weizman called me at home and told me the following: 'Lousy story [his profile]—but what a terrible, lying, libelous story on Beit Jala. I do not want to see you again, you and your magazine stink.' "

Time could have saved itself all the trouble, damage, shaken credibility, and gigantic expense occasioned by Sharon's libel suit if it had only learned the lesson given to it by the Israeli prime minister himself, Menachem Begin. On September 24, 1979, the newsmagazine published a sensational story:

> ... Begin took a day off from his governmental duties. He was driven to a secluded laboratory, where three non-Israeli neurological experts examined him. One of the specialists was Dr. Jack Fein, a prominent brain surgeon at the Albert Einstein College of Medicine in New York City. After the examination, the doctors recommended that Begin restrict himself to a three-hour workday and try to rest as much as possible. They apparently feared that the medication that Begin takes for his heart condition has affected his body's ability to recover from the stroke. "I am concerned about Mr. Begin's health," said Dr. Fein, "but I admire his courage. . . ."

This new "*Time* learned" David Halevy scoop was published in the magazine in a special box titled "Fears for Begin's Health." It concluded: "Even one of Begin's protective aides admits deep concern: 'It seems that his physical condition is deteriorating quickly. I do not know when, but he will have to quit the premiership. It might happen tomorrow, next week—or next year.' "

The historical facts are that Begin, whose fragile health was not a secret, still controlled his government nearly four years after that story appeared in *Time*. So his political death was announced prematurely by wishful-thinkers Halevy and *Time*. Moreover, Begin—who seemed "less and less in control" according to *Time* in September 1979—masterminded the bombing of the nuclear reactor in Baghdad in June 1981, defeated Shimon Peres again in the elections in the same month, and went to war in Lebanon in June 1982.

But all of this is beside the point. Mr. Begin could not persuade *Time* on that occasion that he was still going to direct the affairs of Israel notwithstanding *Time*'s "informed speculation," which turned out to be pure guesswork. But what Begin could have denied, and did very firmly, was the story about the three mysterious physicians who checked him in "a secluded laboratory." Begin himself and all of his aides made it known to *Time*'s bureau in Jerusalem that it never took place, it was sheer fantasy. The false "Begin health story," as it would be known in the New York federal court five years after its publication, bore Halevy's unmistakable imprint. There were several "secrets" that only Halevy knew about, such as "a secluded laboratory" and "three non-Israeli neurological experts."

The protests from Premier Begin's bureau arrived very quickly on the desk of Dick Duncan, chief of *Time*'s correspondents in New York. Duncan wrote a "personal and confidential" report about it to editor in chief Henry Grunwald and managing editor Ray Cave. All three of them, as well as Halevy, would be put in the witness box of the federal court later. The confidential letters found their way to Sharon himself when, through the discovery process in New York, his lawyers obtained *Time*'s personnel and secret files.

Duncan's letter concerning the "Begin health story" affords an illuminating inside look into the workings of the upper echelons of *Time* when its editors are confronted with a false story:

> Here is a review of where we stand as of Wednesday, October 26th on the Begin health story. Dean Fischer [*Time*'s Jerusalem bureau chief at that time] has given me a lengthy memo by packet recounting his experiences in rechecking the story. I have talked with David Halevy, and he will be filing what he promises to be dramatic confirmation of the story late Thursday or early Friday. It will be distributed to you. We will need to evaluate this account in light of David's personal and professional position. On the other hand, we must recognize the difficulty of getting anyone on the record in Israel on a story which is so obviously to the detriment of this government. David will also be coming back here to talk to me. He will be arriving this weekend.
>
> At this moment, on the basis of the information given to me by Fischer and of my talks with Halevy, I believe our story is wrong. Inescapably, that conclusion then requires a further decision as to whether Halevy was either (a) inexcusably shoddy in his reporting or (b) intentionally misled us, or (c) was the victim of an incredibly well orchestrated disinformation plot.

Halevy never fulfilled his promise to file a "dramatic confirmation" of the story. He just led Duncan, Grunwald, and Cave by their noses.

One of the explanations chief of correspondents Duncan offers for the false story is that Halevy was "the victim of an incredibly well orchestrated disinformation plot." This finally is what Halevy would have liked Duncan and company to believe—that he was "a victim"—while in fact he was victimizing his editors, and all of them later would be victimizing Sharon, as they had done before to Begin.

Continuing his confidential letter dealing with the "sources" of Halevy's falsity, Duncan said:

> Dudu has told Fischer that his original source for the story was "A." He also said he had discussed it with "B." He also says he had confirmed the story with "C." In confirming the story, he says he talked to Dr. Jack Fein in New York and "D." Both Halevy and Fischer agreed that Fischer supervised Halevy as to his sources and what they said. Stunned by Begin's early morning phone call denying the story and by reports that Dr. Fein (who was quoted in the story) also denied that the meeting had taken place, Fischer began to make some phone calls. He called "C," who said the story was "fantastic." He called Begin's two doctors, who denied any knowledge of the meeting and denied knowing Dr. Fein. He called "D," who denied any knowledge of the meeting and said that his wife, not he, answered the phone when Dudu called. He called Dr. Fein, who said "he never asked me specifically if I was in attendance." Fein denied having any knowledge of the examination. He telephoned "A," who denied any knowledge that the meeting had taken place and that he was Dudu's source. He did not call "B," who figures only as a tipster and a close friend of Halevy's. Denials from "C" and "A" are, I think, routine, given the fact of Begin's vehement denial. Begin's personal protest is not routine, and I consider that it essentially discredits the story. "D" 's denial is very disturbing because he does not appear to be someone who would come under quick pressure from the government. Somewhat the same evaluation applies to Fein.
>
> "I have asked Strobe [Talbott] for his sources' evaluation of our report. The best intelligence neither confirms nor discredits it at this point."

Halevy would repeat the same mind-boggling tales in his long days of testimony in New York in an attempt to explain how he allegedly knew about what Secret Appendix B had to say about

Sharon, relying on such "secret sources" as "Israeli General No. 1" or "Source C," and the like.

But with "Begin's health story" Duncan still tried to behave reasonably correctly. He stated in his letter:

> In my judgment, the balance of the evidence is that our story is wrong. I have sent Ray [Cave] a suggested admission to this effect which would follow "C"'s letter in the magazine. I also think that Dean Fischer has reacted well in this situation. He methodically went back to the sources and spotted the problem. In his dealings with "C" he overspoke when he suggested we might make an "apology," but I'm afraid that is the kind of communication error which can happen under pressure. Halevy's case rests on establishing that there is indeed, as he says, a huge "cover-up." It is possible, but I'm afraid that he must prove that case, and prove it with much better evidence than he has for the original story."

Still, *Time*'s arrogance does not permit its editors to apologize. As Duncan says, Dean Fischer, the Jerusalem bureau chief, "overspoke" when he suggested a printed apology to C—who was Dan Pattir, press counselor to Prime Minister Begin. Duncan makes a special effort to rationalize Fischer's overspeaking, probably in order to protect him from the rage of the gods, Grunwald and Cave. During Sharon's libel suit, editor in chief Grunwald will elaborate in the federal court on the distinction between "regret" and "apology" according to *Time*'s special code.

One month later *Time* had no choice but to print in its letters section the following letter by Dan Pattir:

> Your report "Fears for Begin's Health" (Sept. 24) is regrettable for the serious misinformation it contains. On the basis of the most authoritative examination of the real facts, I am able to inform your readers that contrary to your correspondent's assertions, the Prime Minister did not take a day off from his governmental duties shortly before the Haifa summit with President Sadat, he was not driven to a "secluded laboratory" or to any other location for a physical checkup, and he had never met with a team of "three non-Israeli neurological experts." He could therefore never have been examined by them. In particular, the Prime Minister never met with a Dr. Jack Fein. Hence, no such team could have given

any medical advice to the Prime Minister. Following the Prime Minister's release from the Hadassah Medical Center, and after a brief rest period at his home, he resumed his regular daily duties, with the full approval of the two physicians who treated him, Professor Mervyn Gotsman and Professor Sylvan Lavie. The story in your report, that the Prime Minister has to put in a shorter working day, or is working less hours, is incorrect. Given the totally unfounded nature of your report, it is proper that your readers be informed of the above facts.

In smaller print *Time* added its personal comment:

Time has rechecked all aspects of its story which was based on what it believed was firsthand knowledge of a meeting between Prime Minister Begin and three consulting neurologists. *Time* was apparently misled as to the meeting and regrets the error. *Time* stands by its report that for a period of weeks following his stroke on July 19 the Prime Minister's work load was significantly reduced.

"*Time* was apparently misled" means that *Time* put the blame on somebody else, not that something was rotten in its fact-checking kingdom.

"*Time* . . . regrets . . ." This was the maximum *Time* was ready to concede to Mr. Begin.

After all, it was only an "error."

But still one might have supposed that *Time*, the world's leading newsmagazine, would have learned something about Halevy and about its own faulty news-reporting and editing processes. *Time* actually was sicker than Begin.

The upshot was that Duncan put Halevy on probation. Duncan had never before done this to any of his more than eighty correspondents. On February 13, 1980, still suffering from the fallout from "Begin's health story," *Time*'s chief of correspondents sent the following letter to Halevy:

Dear David,

This is the letter I promised you confirming our conversation in Athens. I must tell you that I did not come away from our conversation feeling satisfied that I really knew the full story on a number of the points we discussed. But I did feel that there was sufficient reason to say just that to you, and then drop the subject completely, because we are going ahead on a different footing now. I want to make this work, and I feel you do too.

The gist of our agreement, as I understand it, was that I felt your work recently to be unsatisfactory and, that without necessarily agreeing with me on all points, you accepted conditions, necessary to correct that situation.

The conditions for the period of one year, in which you will be on this probationary status, are as follows:

1. The fullest possible sourcing on all reports, which includes the name if possible, but if not, then the closest kind of characterization of the nationality and affiliation of the source. When it is not possible to put this kind of information on the wire, it must at least be available to the bureau chief or to me in some manner.

2. Multiple sourcing when at all possible.

3. A consistent effort on your part to report, and also to suggest, the "meat and potatoes" everyday (or every week) stories from the bureau, not just specials and exclusives.

4. A more obvious effort on your part to insure that what you report to *Time* (and to the *Washington Star*) is printable, reliable information, reflecting not just informed speculation, but the *most likely true situation*. As part of this, I would like to see on your part more effort to evaluate the reliability of various sources, and the likelihood that they in fact *know* what they are saying.

On our part, I realize that we must continue to understand the special nature of some of your source relationships and the information you get from them. You spoke to Dean [Fischer] and me about needing better guidance on the use of attribution and sourcing on your files, and you have a right to expect that Dean will give it to you. And so will I.

Dudu, I want very badly to get you and the magazine back on the highly productive relationship we have enjoyed in the past. For various reasons, that relationship seems to be suffering. The points I have made in this letter are designed to help things work again. I realize they may cramp your style some, and where they are unreasonable you can certainly ask for relief. But what I want to do is get you, and your best reporting, back into print, in sizable and important stories. I hope you agree with me that it will work this way. I believe it will.

In retrospect the "Begin health story" affair was the writing on the wall. But *Time*'s editors chose not to read it.

ON AUGUST 4, 1983, SHARON MET PIERRE GEMAYEL
again. It was the first visit since his condolence call at Bikfaya. In
contrast to the brief conversation then, the August meeting was
lengthy, and the political exchanges were particularly important
for Lebanon.

"Unless people in Lebanon are going to stand up and speak up
for strengthening ties with Israel," Sharon warned Gemayel, "Israel will withdraw from Lebanon, and in all likelihood your country will revert to the state it was in during the years preceding the
expulsion of the PLO from Beirut."

The wisdom of hindsight shows that this was a kind of final
warning from Sharon, acting as a friend, to Gemayel, and
through him to the Christian community Gemayel represented.
"You have only a few weeks, perhaps only days, to act. The onus
is on you to prove to Israel publicly in word and deed that you
regard it as your friend," Sharon admonished him.

Again unlike the Bikfaya visit of September 15, 1982, which
Sharon had made as minister of defense, this was a private call.
Sharon made this clear with his very first words: "Although I
spoke to the prime minister this morning just before I left for
Beirut, I have not come as a representative of the government but
as someone who was very active in defense matters concerning Israel and Lebanon." Sharon thought for a moment and then
added jestingly, "The Lebanese affair turned me into a shepherd.
I get up every morning at half past four and tend to my flock."

Sharon was in Beirut at the invitation of commanders of the
Christian Lebanese forces. From the time he had left the defense
ministry they had repeatedly invited him to a farewell party in
Beirut. But the invitation strangely had got stuck at secret high-
level bureaucratic echelons in Jerusalem.

Sharon had been following the situation in Lebanon with grave
concern. In the absence of a clear Israeli initiative and policy, it
was deteriorating rapidly. He had little faith in the practical
value of the May 17, 1983, agreement between Israel and Lebanon, the terms of which had been dictated by the United States
and which was lauded as a high point of American diplomacy in
Lebanon. Sharon thought Washington was making a grave mistake both in relying on Syria to assure a balance of forces in Leba-

non and in simultaneously encouraging Lebanese President Amin Gemayel not to strengthen ties with Israel beyond the May agreement.

The visit to Beirut gave Sharon a chance to speak from the heart to the Lebanese representatives and also to inspect the situation in the field. Often, when talking to Lebanese and American diplomats, he had commented, "The situation in Beirut will become normal only when the terror in West Beirut has been eliminated and it becomes an open and safe city: when I can spend a holiday with my family at the Commodore Hotel."

This was far from the case in the Lebanese capital in August 1983. Arik landed in an Israeli helicopter at Damour, the Christian town where hundreds of citizens had been massacred by the Palestinians during the seventies and which had started returning to life only after the Israeli forces entered Lebanon.

Sharon's small convoy wended its way through the streets of West Beirut, so familiar to Sharon. Occasionally, when it got caught up in a traffic jam, some Lebanese would recognize him and wave in astonishment. They were doubtless amazed to see the Israeli best known in Lebanon, whom so many terrorists would have wanted to eliminate, traveling like this through the city of terror, even though he was accompanied by Israeli and Lebanese security men.

Pierre Gemayel received Sharon in the spacious offices of his party, not far from the port. He appeared as erect and calm as ever. And, as always, he was immaculately dressed, wearing a gleaming white shirt and formal tie. The room was air-conditioned against the shimmering August heat. An ornate chandelier hung from the high ceiling. The walls were covered with pictures of Pierre's two sons, the dead Bashir and the Lebanese president, Amin.

Sharon and Gemayel sat down at a round table. Fadi Frem, commander of the Lebanese forces, translated Gemayel's French into English:

"The Lebanese need the Americans just as much as the Israelis do. But Lebanon is very important from your point of view with regard to the future relationship with the Arab world. One day you will have to hold out your hands to the Arabs, and Lebanon can be your best bridge toward achieving this."

Sharon listened attentively to Pierre's thirty-minute monologue. He noted the points made by Gemayel.

Sharon then addressed him. "Sheikh Pierre, we expelled the PLO from Lebanon and smashed them. This was the purpose of our war. As a by-product, we gave Lebanon a chance to change and again become a part of the Western world under the leadership by the United States. But I want to emphasize that in spite of our deep friendship with the U.S., we have never once relied on anybody, not even them. We have never once believed that somebody else would fight our battles for us. Assistance, cooperation, coordination, yes! But nobody can defend us except ourselves. And this is the same for you, for the Lebanese."

Sharon paused to reflect. "Don't expect the United States to solve your problems. It will solve only its own. I told you this before, Sheikh Pierre, at our first secret meeting in January 1982 at Bashir's house. Camille Chamoun was there too. It was only about six months before the outbreak of the war. I warned you that the United States would try to solve other problems in the Middle East—its relationship with Syria and the rest of the Arab world—and the Lebanese nation would pay the price.

"And that is exactly what happened," Sharon continued, speaking completely frankly. "Months passed and Lebanon didn't take a single step on its own. Everything was dictated by the United States. And this is what has brought Lebanon back to the tragic situation it finds itself in today."

Gemayel responded firmly. "For over eight years the Palestinian terror destroyed us, and nobody came to help us—not the United States, not Europe, nor the Arab states. You came and rescued us, and also the West. But Lebanon is so weak now that it needs America more than anything else."

Sharon agreed that good relations with the United States were important. "But you have to speak up loud and clear if you want a close partnership with Israel," he added. "We had so many casualties in the war that nobody in Israel will accept that the Christian leaders in Lebanon are not prepared to come forward openly in favor of full cooperation with Israel, or at least to demonstrate a change in Lebanese politics concerning Israel.

"We embarked on the war in Lebanon," he said emphatically, "depending only on ourselves to destroy the PLO. As a result of

63

this, Lebanon was offered a historic opportunity, a golden chance. A situation like this may occur perhaps once in fifty years—the possibility of being free and independent of foreign forces. But to achieve this there has to be a change in your policies toward us."

Sharon's voice deepened as he tried to convey the tension, the anxiety. His face was grim as he summed the matter up. "I am afraid Lebanon is losing its last chance for independence, that you are going to lose this opportunity. You have perhaps only a few days left. This is the Lebanese tragedy. Nobody will be able to stop the downward momentum if you don't act quickly—not Habib, not Draper [Morris Draper, U.S. Special Envoy to the Middle East], not Robert McFarlane [National Security Adviser], and not George Shultz. This is my last message to you, Sheikh Pierre."

Pierre Gemayel sat lost in thought. Sharon got up. Gemayel rose to accompany him. "I understand you, General," he said. "The Jews left Israel and have returned after two thousand years, thanks to people like you, but try to understand our position. . . ."

Sharon and Gemayel parted on good terms. Sharon knew the father would inform his son, the president, of what they had talked about. However, he also felt that this aged representative of the Christian community would not take any initiative to change the situation and that Christian Lebanon was doomed. It was with infinite sorrow that Sharon recognized the inevitable.

In the afternoon Lebanese officers accompanied Sharon to the place in Beirut where Bashir had been assassinated. A monument, erected by the Christians, marked the spot. Sharon stood in front of it for a few minutes. He was very conscious that at this spot, where the explosion had killed Bashir, the chance that an independent Lebanon would enter into a peace agreement with Israel had also died. Of all the members of the Gemayel family, Bashir had been the only one who not only understood independence but who also knew how to go about achieving it. From the point of view of Syrian intelligence the right man had been killed with that suitcase full of explosives.

PART
II

PREPARING FOR TRIAL

THE FALL OF 1983 WAS THE FIRST TIME SHARON SAW

the federal courthouse in New York, where his suit against *Time* would be tried. He arrived filled with curiosity, closely observing lawyers, judge, and surroundings like a general reconnoitering the field of battle. He was impressed by the neatness and order of the judge's chambers, by the dignity of the legal process, even if, at this juncture, things didn't seem particularly favorable for him.

At the pretrial proceeding Sharon witnessed the first clash of the two legal teams. Maintaining that Sharon had no case in libel, *Time*'s lawyers demanded that the suit be summarily dismissed. This was the first of their several attempts to prevent Sharon's case from getting to open court.

Time's first contention was that Sharon already had such a bad name that nothing could make it worse; therefore, even if their story were held to be libelous, he had no cause of action. *Time*'s lawyers got their teeth into this theory and wouldn't let it go. Doggedly they kept reiterating that Sharon had come out so badly from the Kahan Commission Inquiry that the *Time* story couldn't have blemished his reputation any further, even if the story were inaccurate. In other words, *Time* said, Sharon was libel-proof.

Sharon found it all fascinating. He had had little previous experience of the legal process. Occasionally he'd been on the sidelines of a military trial when called as a character witness. But even his own stormy military career had never brought him to center stage. Now, however, he was in the thick of it—not at home in Israel but in a foreign country and in a suit initiated by himself. Despite his personal involvement, all his natural curiosity was aroused.

During a recess at the first pretrial session he joshed Richard Goldstein, who was assisting Milton Gould in arguing the plaintiff's case. "Listen, this is very interesting. Do you think I could be a law clerk in New York? Maybe carry that big black briefcase of yours?" Between wars in the fifties, he told Goldstein, he'd finished law school. But he'd never gone into practice.

Sharon's lawyers didn't take lightly *Time*'s argument that Sharon was libel-proof. Perhaps Judge Abraham Sofaer really would dismiss the case. So it was an occasion for relief when, in

December, the judge rejected *Time*'s contention that Sharon's reputation was indefensible. Sharon indeed had a cause of action for libel. The judge spelled it out in a most interesting interim decision.

> . . . No finding or statement in the [Kahan] Report or in the [*Time*] article [Sofaer stated] is comparable in its seriousness and potential reputational impact to the statement upon which this suit is based. Though the Commission seemed dubious of Sharon's claim that the danger of atrocities did not concern him, at no point did it find Sharon had lied. Furthermore, while the *Time* article states that Sharon resigned as Defense Minister because of the Cabinet vote, Sharon nevertheless chose to resign, and was simultaneously offered another Cabinet position with the potential for continuing influence. Sharon remains a Minister today; and the article recites that he is still respected by many people, presumably for a lifetime of public service and achievements, particularly in military combat.
>
> Finally, *Time* cannot reasonably rely on Sharon's public complaint that the Commission's condemnation placed upon him "the mark of Cain" in attempting to show he was already regarded as a liar and abettor of murder before the alleged libel was published. Sharon's exaggerated protest no doubt stemmed from his having been deemed accountable even indirectly for so heinous an event in human history. His interpretation of *Time*'s alleged libel, which *Time* has taken great pains to show can also be exaggerated, is that it was intended to convey the impression that he had approved or solicited the massacre, not merely blundered in failing to anticipate and prevent it. . . .

The criteria for indirect responsibility, as defined by the Kahan Commission, the judge said, were so rigorous that even if someone couldn't meet them, that didn't automatically give him a bad name. In other words, Judge Sofaer himself pronounced judgment on the criteria of the Kahan Commission:

". . . The Commission explicitly imposed a standard more stringent even than negligence in evaluating the conduct of Israeli officials. . . . The Commission imposed what it termed "personal" responsibility upon Sharon, but only on the basis of the uniquely stringent standards it applied. . . ."

The commission's conclusion that Sharon should have foreseen the Christian massacre of Palestinians, and consequently was indirectly responsible for it, led Judge Sofaer to rule that the criteria of the Kahan Commission were far more rigorous than those generally applied when establishing negligence and responsibility.

The judge's ruling recalled a similar opinion when, three days after the commission's report was published, Amnon Goldenberg, chairman of the Israel Bar Council, said publicly, albeit very low-key, that the measure of responsibility applied by the commission was too strict. Sharon had been present at the council's lunch meeting when Goldenberg made his mild comment. However, mild or not, it was immediately denounced by political hacks and the media, who so thoroughly squashed the observation that it never went any further.

For the same reason, Sofaer's interim judgment made little impact in Israel. The pack baying for Sharon's blood wasn't going to publicize anything that made him less responsible for Sabra and Shatilla, indirectly or otherwise. In fact, it wanted the public to forget the indirect aspect, initially imposed by the super-rigid criteria of the Kahan Commission.

Sharon didn't know anything about the judge except that he was Jewish, but he was impressed by the dignity with which Sofaer conducted the proceedings. It pervaded the entire room.

Judge Sofaer had been assigned to the case purely by chance. His speaking some Hebrew and Arabic and spending part of every summer on vacation in Jerusalem weren't factors when his name was drawn from "the wheel." It was this random system used in New York's federal court that had put Sofaer on the bench for the libel suit against *Time*.

It was only much later that Sharon found out that "his" judge was capable of understanding the Middle East scene as well as being a master of the American legal labyrinth. Born in 1938, Abraham David Sofaer was a graduate of Yeshiva University and was widely known for his energy and intellect, both faculties much needed and used during the tough months of the *Time* libel suit. Although he already had a deservedly illustrious reputation, the *Sharon* v. *Time* case made him the focus of world attention, while his every move was minutely checked by the media and the jurists. Sofaer never let either of the giant litigants sway his judgment.

The dark-haired, rather pale judge made this clear to the reporters from the outset: "I don't know Sharon. I am aware of *Time,* but I don't know the people there. When you get into a case, it's the issues and evidence that count. You can't say that because you're Jewish, you can't sit on a case involving Israel. I don't see any problem."

Sharon was fascinated when he heard that the judge had been born in Bombay when India was still under the British raj, that he came from a family observing Jewish traditions, and had grown up speaking some Hebrew and some Arabic. Sharon had special respect for the strong family ties characteristic of the Sephardic Jews. Sofaer's family had come to the United States when he was a fourteen-year-old boy.

Sofaer's preoccupation with history and international affairs had led him to send a letter to *The New York Times* after President Anwar Sadat's historic peace mission to Israel in November 1977. In his letter he called on the Palestinians to support peace efforts in the Middle East, describing himself as a "Jew who is unambivalently proud of his Arab heritage." A note under the letter stated that Sofaer's grandparents had been born in Egypt and Iraq.

SHARON HAD LESS CONFIDENCE IN HIS AMERICAN
lawyers at Shea and Gould. Did they believe that the paragraph
published by *Time* was a lie? Were they convinced that Sharon's
allegations were well founded?

For quite some time I had reason to believe that a number of
them had doubts. Not that they thought Sharon wasn't being absolutely truthful in his answers to them. But somehow, they felt,
the real truth fell somewhere between the version *Time* put
forward and Sharon's contentions. Arnold Forster, who knew
Sharon well and who was well versed in the problems of Israel
and the Middle East, was perhaps the only one who believed in
Sharon completely from the start.

The attorneys, like many Americans, had come to regard *Time*
as a linchpin of American culture and a standard for entertain-
ment, even for reporting. They simply could not comprehend the
supreme arrogance shown by *Time*'s editors, nor could they con-
ceive of the extent to which those editors had been duped by
Dudu Halevy. Also, it must be borne in mind, some of Gould's
assistants, young Jewish lawyers from New York, were far removed from the Israeli scene. However, in the course of their
meetings with Sharon—to whom Gould and his associates related
with a good deal of respect right from the start—they came to ap-
preciate his forthrightness and learned how easy it was to talk to
the big man, even on the most sensitive topics. "I'm here to answer all you want to know—but you don't dare to ask!" Sharon
quipped. They also came to recognize Sharon's firmness and his
ability to stand his ground—as distinct from aggressiveness—and
on occasion his tendency toward impatience.

Still, it was difficult for them to believe that, without any investigation as to source, *Time* had published a sheer fabrication
in a cover story. "At every meeting Richard Goldstein cross-
examined me about this," Weissglas related. " 'Are you sure it
didn't happen?' he would say. 'Have you read all the documents?
Are you sure that there is nothing in there that *Time* can surprise
us with at the trial? After all, there's never smoke without
fire. . . .' "

"I've thought it over time and again, but, believe it or not,
there simply is nothing," was Weissglas' reply.

Gould and his assistants pressured both Sharon and Weissglas to try to work out where the contents of such a paragraph could have come from. It didn't seem possible to them that *Time* had just invented this.

At another time a combination of guesswork on the part of the American lawyers and of Weissglas and Sharon led to the conjecture that a report filed by two Dutch journalists might have been the source. These two journalists had volunteered a very dubious story to the Kahan Commission. According to their account, while visiting Beirut after the events of Sabra and Shatilla, they had apparently heard from a Phalangist officer that Sharon had spoken about avenging the murder of Bashir. There was no mention of their testimony in the commission's report, but their story was published in the Israeli press. It left no more of an impression among informed persons than a run-of-the-mill sensational, cheap story in the *National Enquirer*.

The attorneys asked Sharon to obtain a copy of the transcript of the Dutch journalists' evidence before the commission as well as copies of what they had written in the Dutch newspapers. Sharon's lawyers still naïvely believed that in publishing its cover story *Time* must have relied on some source—possibly on the evidence of the two Dutch journalists. However, it did seem bizarre that a publication of *Time*'s stature should need information from two second-rank journalists for a story as important as "Sharon's revenge discussion."

Sharon, by then back in Israel, read their evidence. It was identical to what had been published in the Israeli press. Sharon made brief notes of what he read to give to his lawyers. He had no idea then of the unnecessary trouble he was heading for—through no fault of his own.

Time's lawyers, a team headed by Thomas Barr from the firm of Cravath, Swaine and Moore in New York, were in direct contact with Milton Gould. On one of their visits to Gould's offices, in an off-the-record chat, Gould mentioned that his side had a transcript of the main points of the minutes of the conversation at Bikfaya—that is, the same piece of paper on which Weissglas had made notes in the course of his telephone conversation with Tel Aviv. At about the same time, *Time*'s attorneys were informed that Gould had notes of the main points of the evidence of the Dutch journalists.

It should be stressed that Gould and his team—like Sharon himself—were in no doubt as to their eventually receiving the original documents from the Israeli government. But at this stage the Israeli government had not yet reached its decision. Therefore Sharon campaigned discretely to persuade his colleagues to give him the vital papers.

Time applied to Judge Sofaer by way of affidavit, requesting that Gould produce the two documents forthwith: the notes on the main points of the conversation at Bikfaya and those relating to the evidence of the two Dutch journalists.

When Sharon heard about this he simply couldn't believe his ears. He was astonished to learn that under American law *Time* was entitled to receive such papers. "But these are just working papers between you and me. How can papers like this be handed over to the other side?" he protested to Gould. "And in any event, how is it that you spoke about them to the lawyers of the other side? What made you volunteer such information?"

Weissglas too was shocked by Gould's statement. Here was Sharon in the midst of a struggle to obtain the original documents from the Israeli government—in particular the notes the Mossad officer had made of the conversation at Bikfaya—and along came another uncalled-for complication.

A tricky situation had arisen. On the one hand, as former minister of defense, Sharon had the right, although not the power, to hand over the minutes of the meeting at Bikfaya to his attorneys in New York. But on the other hand, he was liable to be in serious breach of the secrecy laws were he to agree to allow "Weissglas' paper" to be handed over to *Time*'s attorneys without the prior consent of the Israeli government.

Consequently, when his outrage and consternation had cooled down, he instructed them not to "discover" these papers to *Time,* which instruction Gould carried out on the ground that American law forbids such discovery if it might constitute an offense in another country—in this case, Israel.

The whole incident cast a shadow on the relationship between Sharon and Gould's office for many months. "What did we need

73

this for?" Sharon demanded of them constantly. "Instead of concentrating on the main problem of proving *Time*'s lie, we have to defend ourselves on a side issue of no importance—two scraps of paper that *Time* has turned into 'important documents.' "

Gould's office tried to play down the importance of the incident, claiming that it was only a technicality. But Sharon was correct in surmising that *Time* would turn the "episode of the secret documents" into another weapon with which to attack him.

Sharon's lawyers in New York likewise couldn't understand that the Israeli government did not want to help Sharon in his suit against *Time*. They couldn't accept the bottom line, that the Israeli government simply wasn't interested in seeing Sharon win his case. A few ministers unquestionably were prepared to help Sharon, but the government as a whole was opposed to offering him any assistance. To Prime Minister Yitzhak Shamir, his deputy, David Levy, and others, Sharon's potential as a political rival within their own Herut party outweighed all other considerations. His success in winning his suit, so they apparently thought, would improve his chances in the jousting for the premiership.

In actual fact, Sharon had embarked on the suit without any assurance of help from the Israeli government. One day, shortly after leaving the Defense Ministry, he simply went to Prime Minister Begin and told him he had decided to sue *Time* for libel. It was a courtesy to a prime minister from one of his cabinet ministers. In that official framework Begin had no objections. Then Begin resigned, and Yitzhak Shamir took his place, with Sharon's open and direct support. It would have been a happy gesture from one colleague to another if Shamir had given Sharon a hand and helped him in the libel suit. But that was asking too much of Shamir and his friends. They were motivated only by narrow political and personal concerns and were focused exclusively on their determination to prevent Sharon's return to the center of the political stage.

"It's true that I filed a private suit," Sharon protested later. "But it was also a golden opportunity for the State of Israel to denounce *Time* for all the derogatory things it has written about Israel for so many years, for all the lies that are published about Israel in the international media."

Richard Goldstein and particularly Arnold Forster, who became Gould's emissaries to Israel, made numerous attempts to plead their case at the government offices in Jerusalem—at Shamir's office, at the office of Attorney General Yitzhak Zamir, at Dan Meridor's office. Meridor was the cabinet secretary, forever righteously rolling his eyes heavenward, forever trying to please everyone, forever the good old boy. But the lawyers had no luck. They got no help from any of these people.

Disappointed but resolved to fight them, Sharon forcefully intervened. Nevertheless, at a stormy meeting in early April 1984, the Israeli Government reached a formal decision not to make available to him the official documents that Arik needed.

This may have been the toughest cabinet meeting since Shamir had taken over from Begin. The decision was ostensibly based on "reasons of state security and foreign relations."

When Sharon heard this he confronted his government colleagues. "This is a continuation of your policy of trying to turn me over to my rivals and opponents. You handed me over to them during the inquiry and you're doing it again now. You make it very easy for yourselves by using me as the fall guy." It did no good. The government shielded itself behind formal claims of secrecy. No one in the cabinet seemed to take heed. In fact, the government's position had already been adopted in response to a letter written on March 11, 1984, by Forster, who had gone to Israel confident that he would be able to obtain the documents and notes relating to Sharon's conversations at Bikfaya and Karantina. He had addressed his letter to Dan Meridor.

The letter was sent around to all the security agencies—the Ministry of Defense, Mossad, the security service, the IDF—for their professional opinions. But even before their answers had been received, the contents of the letter were leaked to the press. Clearly this was done in order to create a negative atmosphere, so that Sharon would have a hard time getting the documents. Sharon blamed the leak on Meridor, but he was wrong. The cabinet secretary reported to Prime Minister Shamir that he had checked the leak and had discovered that—according to accepted practice in American law—a copy of the letter had been sent from Gould's New York office to *Time*'s lawyers. From *Time* the letter had somehow found its way to Israel radio. Articles in the Israeli press followed, righteously insisting that Sharon should not be given any documents. Security experts were unanimous in their refusal to hand over the documents to the New York court "because of Israel's traditional policy of secrecy regarding official documents."

And there the matter might have rested had it not been for Judge Sofaer, who himself then took the initiative, suggesting that someone such as former Chief Justice Yitzhak Kahan check the documents and inform the court whether they bore any resemblance to *Time*'s version of events.

Sharon meanwhile had taken into account the possibility that he might lose his suit solely because he couldn't present the documents required to prove his case. According to U.S. libel law, the burden of proof rested on him. And so Sharon set himself a clear plan of action.

"If I lose the case because the State of Israel refuses to provide me with the documents I need, I'll go back to Jerusalem and go public with the whole affair. I'll let the people be the judge of who acted right and who acted wrong."

The American lawyers believed in promises. Sharon too had at first believed his government would allow him access to the documents required to prove *Time*'s lie—or at least to those documents that were no longer state secrets, if, indeed, they had ever been thus classified.

But soon Sharon came down to earth. He lost his illusions as he sadly watched Arnold Forster make his endless, fruitless journeys to Jerusalem.

Forster was puzzled and so were the other lawyers in his office, particularly Gould. They were especially puzzled when, during the deposition process, they discovered the extent of *Time*'s carelessness and irresponsibility.

But Sharon by then was not confused by the unfairness of the contest. "I felt bad about Forster," he said later. "I knew that he would be met at the government offices in Jerusalem only by cynicism, deception, and lies. I considered the trial a personal matter and yet also a national issue. But my government colleagues wanted to run and hide from the war in Lebanon—especially from the Sabra and Shatilla affair. The easiest thing for them was to hide behind my back. 'Okay, here he is. We've found someone who's guilty. His name is Sharon.' And then they could wash their hands of the whole thing.

"Naturally the opposition—the Labor party—would use any possible political weapon against me," Sharon continued. "And so they wanted to make it as hard as they could for me at the trial in New York. They have always cooperated in the most abhorrent deeds. I expect nothing from them.

"But my own colleagues in the government, in the Likud—they knew all the facts. They knew there wasn't a word of truth in what *Time* had published. They had all the documents. They could have read them. I explained to Shamir and to the other ministers how important the case was—quite beyond my own personal interests. It was important at a national and an international level, for all of them as Israelis and as Jews. It was in this light that I considered their refusal to help me to be behavior of the lowest kind.

"The American lawyers like Forster and Gould," Sharon concluded, "realized right from the beginning how important the case was from a Jewish and Israeli ethical and moral point of view. This was why they were prepared to join so wholeheartedly in the struggle, and all without fee. They felt that failure to wipe out *Time*'s lie would have meant a serious danger. That is why they couldn't comprehend the behavior of the Israeli government. They couldn't understand that when things concern the top echelons of party and government, when political and personal struggles are involved, then 'national interest' becomes secondary. Their failure to understand this affected the whole trial, it was like a dark cloud. I was bothered by the fact that my lawyers couldn't understand the Jerusalem mentality—and this affected the way they ran the entire case."

THE NEXT ROUND OF THE PRETRIAL SPARRING
went to Sharon. Richard Goldstein presented *Time*'s correspondence file to the general in the spring of 1984. Sharon had returned to the United States to give some lectures in the New York area. Now, seated with Milton Gould and Goldstein at the circular mahogany table in the attorneys' offices, he examined the discovered documents.

"It's amazing," Goldstein said, his voice betraying a justifiable tone of victory, "how those people wrote and edited the paragraph."

It was Sharon's first glimpse of how *Time* had engineered its infamous canard.

As for Gould, Goldstein, and their associates, it was the first evidence that supported their belief in the negligence, laxity, and unscrupulousness implicit in *Time*'s bizarre system of group journalism. The news reporting and editing method followed by the world's largest newsmagazine would become one of the first weapons from *Time*'s own arsenal with which Gould was eventually to shatter *Time*'s defense.

Time's editorial policy remains faithful to the dictum of its founder, Henry Luce. In his *In Search of History* journalist and presidential chronicler Theodore H. White, who had been in and out of sync with *Time* for some fifty years, demonstrated that the founding father cast a long shadow. Luce brooked no nonsense about who controlled his magazines and what they said; he did. The facts were important, but in New York those facts were assembled by his editors to his design. He held, says White, that freedom of the press ran two ways. His reporters were free to report what they wished, but Luce was free to have it rewritten as he wished.

When the wishes of reporter and writer are identical, as they were in the case of David Halevy and Jerusalem bureau chief Harry Kelly, I believe you get a positively incestuous journalistic orgy.

The first document was Halevy's December 6, 1982, Telex from Jerusalem. The Kahan Commission wasn't even near completion of its investigations into the Sabra and Shatilla massacre, but

Halevy already had a scoop. He hurried to file it for the weekly Worldwide Memo, one of *Time*'s in-house peculiarities.

The Worldwide Memo is *Time*'s sugarplum. Printed supposedly as received, it's where the immediate scoops go, the delectable tidbits—and, most important, the reporter's name appears in solitary grandeur in big, bold capitals at the top.

Publishing a memo carries a lot of prestige. The weekly memos are circulated among *Time*'s top editorial echelons and among its bureau chiefs all over the world. *Time* has a big world, and the reporters vie furiously to get their memos publicized in it. Worldwide Memos are marked confidential, which only serves to make them all the more carefully read. The managers and editors, the writers and researchers, that vast army at the New York headquarters in Rockefeller Center all keep a close eye on the weekly collection of Worldwide Memos. If an item seems particularly newsworthy, they ask the reporter for clearance. Can it be used, they want to know, for a story in the magazine? Can it be quoted or was it genuinely off the record? Even *Time* apparently takes for granted the accuracy of the Worldwide Memo, so when the reporter gives clearance, *Time* holds the succulent bit for use whenever appropriate.

The malevolent indictment leveled against Sharon was spawned in Halevy's Worldwide Memo, which was called "Green Light for Revenge?" adding a question mark as a measure of prudence. It was the last prudence *Time* would demonstrate.

> The most crucial findings of the state inquiry commission investigating the Sabra and Shatilla massacre might turn out to be the newly discovered notes which were taken during a conversation between Israel's Defense Minister Arik Sharon and leaders of the Gemayel clan. Sharon came to the Gemayels' home village, Bikfaya, the morning after Bashir Gemayel was assassinated. He came actually to convey his and the Begin Government's condolences. When Sharon landed at Bikfaya he had with him only one senior Israeli intelligence officer, who went with Sharon to the meeting and took notes during the private session.
>
> According to a highly reliable source who told us about that meeting, present were not only Pierre and Amin Gemayel but also Fadi Frem, the Phalange chief of staff who is married to Bashir's

sister. Sharon indicated in advance to the Gemayels that the Israeli army was moving into West Beirut and that he expected them, the Force Lebanese, to go into all the Palestinian refugee camps. He also gave them the feeling after the Gemayels' questioning, that he understood their need to take revenge for the assassination of Bashir and assured them that the Israeli army would neither hinder them, nor stop them.

These minutes will not be published at all, in any form whatsoever, as they indicate a direct involvement and advanced planning by the Gemayel family, including Lebanon's president, Amin Gemayel.

The lie eventually to become the crux of the libel suit was hatched in a single sentence; that Sharon "also gave them the feeling . . . that he understood their need to take revenge . . ."

Those few words at the end—"these minutes will not be published at all, in any form whatsoever"—served a dual purpose. They meant that only David Halevy had the information. They also served as a great cover if Sharon or anyone else should ever issue a denial. They weren't going to be published, right? So they obviously must conceal some hideous crime; and equally obviously, Halevy's work couldn't be checked.

The countdown on the *Time* libel bomb started ticking with that Telex.

Two days after Halevy had filed his memo the New York researcher asked for clearance. On December 9 Halevy's assurance whipped over the wires: "Memo item, Green Light, cleared."

Time's cover stories run into many thousands of words. *Time* works it on a line count: 900 to 1000 is average for a cover, but the article is longer if the presiding cabal at Rockefeller Center decides there's more juice in the lemon. But the reporters at the regional bureaus file at least twice as much, sometimes three times. If they can inundate New York with a tidal wave of verbiage, it makes an even better impression. So when they send in their material, it pours through in great billows, divided into numbered "takes"—chapters—to facilitate editing.

Newly appointed Jerusalem bureau chief Harry Kelly filed "Take 9." He didn't know the Middle East, he didn't know Israel, he didn't know Hebrew. For all of this he depended on Halevy, which was a pity, because he didn't really know Halevy either. So his Take 9 had a chancy foundation. Kelly wrote:

> Part of the Report which is called Appendix B, was not published "since in our opinion," the Commission said, "non-publication of this material is essential in the interest of protecting the nation's security or foreign relations."
>
> Some of that unpublished report simply gives the names of agents identified only by single letters in the published report and secret testimony. And some of it, we understand, was published in *Time*'s Worldwide Memo, an item by Halevy, Dec. 6, for which we gave clearance, dealing with Sharon's visit to the Gemayel family to pay condolences. Certainly in reading the report there is a feeling that at least part of the Commission's case against Sharon is between the lines, presumably in the secret portion.
>
> It is clear that the Commission believed that there were so many red flags flying that practically anyone should have known what would happen if the Phalangists were allowed in the refugee camps. The Report mentions that hidden in Appendix B is testimony by an intelligence officer on "the liquidation of Palestinians.". . .

The red flags should have been flying for Kelly. His words had an extraordinary implication. The commission had decided Appendix B was not to be published, and yet Kelly confirmed part of it was contained in Halevy's memo. He also confirmed that Halevy's memo was accurate—"we gave clearance." And the memo itself accused Sharon. *Time* magazine's kangaroo court had already decided on the verdict and passed sentence two months before the commission presented its official findings.

Halevy knew nothing. He admitted in the Foley Square courtroom that he only inferred that the information was in Appendix B. Nevertheless he had sent clearance for his memo without any reservations. The request for clearance was a compliment. It meant his scoop was halfway there; it meant the big boys in New York were impressed with it.

Then *Time*'s senior writer, the smooth-faced William Smith, sat down to his task of making a single coherent story of all those takes. But he too was a member of the kangaroo court. This was

Halevy's raw reporting: Smith's job was to transform it into slick professional writing.

Smith's *Time*-style professionalism can't be faulted. In slicking up the writing he intensified the charge. It was Smith who said bluntly that Sharon had talked about revenge, that he had discussed it with the Gemayels. Smith must have gone to some trouble before he selected the incriminating phrase. The word "discussed" wasn't his first choice. There were several conspicuous erasures before he finally selected the damning "discussed." Finally he gave a last deft polish to Halevy's green-light scoop, and the infamous paragraph was done. So was the libel.

Back in the conference room of Shea and Gould's New York offices, Richard Goldstein showed Sharon a photocopy of the original paragraph typed by Smith, with the additional word "discussed." In the exact words of Smith, then, Sharon had "discussed the need to take revenge"—which meant contemplating cold-blooded murder in Sabra and Shatilla.

Somehow the libel seemed compounded by presenting as a scoop Halevy's two-month-old memo. One lie led from another—because Smith's paragraph emphasized that *"Time* has learned . . ."—only *Time*; only now; no slow-witted rival could match *Time*'s pace.

Goldstein's excitement was wholly justified. It was our first actual knowledge of *Time*'s news-gathering technique. More would follow. Since the Israeli government hadn't been at all helpful, obtaining the file had been a major achievement for Gould and his team. The elderly attorney was in fine fettle. Not only had he recovered from recent coronary bypass surgery but as an eminent litigator for many a long year, the war-horse had caught the smell of battle. More important, his wide experience told him he had entered the lists on the right side.

Sharon was curious about the techniques revealed by the file but not at all surprised. "I've been claiming from the very beginning that *Time* lied," he said.

The last document in the file was a press release, freed for publication at 3:00 P.M. EST, Sunday, February 13, 1983. One of *Time*'s publicity stunts is to announce on Sunday what special stories the magazine will carry the next day, Monday, when it hits the newsstands in the States. As the last knave in the pack, *Time*'s press agent had outdone himself. His copy for *Time*'s issue of February 21, 1983, was a tour de force. It was also a source of libel.

> "Sharon Said to Have Urged Lebanese to Send Phalangists Into Camps" [blazoned the banner headline]. An unpublished passage in the report of the Israeli Commission on the Beirut Massacre discloses that Israeli Defense Minister Sharon met with the Gemayel family on the day after Lebanon's President-elect Bashir Gemayel was assassinated, *Time* magazine reports this week.
>
> *Time* says: "Sharon reportedly told the Gemayels that the Israeli army would be moving into West Beirut and that he expected the Christian forces to go into the Palestinian refugee camps. Sharon also reportedly discussed with the Gemayels the need for the Phalangists to take revenge for the assassination of Bashir, but the details of the conversation are not known."
>
> The Israeli Commission recommended the removal of Sharon as Defense Minister. Sharon later resigned his position, though *Time* speculates that he may remain in the Cabinet as a minister without portfolio. . . .

Time was condemned out of its own mouth. It drew a clear distinction between speculation—"he may remain in the Cabinet" —and affirmation—"*Time* says . . . Sharon reportedly discussed . . . the need . . . to take revenge . . ."

It is not easy to match *Time* in its perfunctory destruction of human beings. At best, that multimillion-dollar, seven-month marathon of a trial defense can be described as a desperate groping to cover the magazine's reporting and editing system, which is not and never has been fail-safe.

WHILE HALEVY POSTURED IN JERUSALEM AS BOTH
an ardent Israeli patriot and a hard-hitting reporter, his behavior
in contacts with his *Time* magazine employers was completely different. To them he confided his disenchantment with Israel,
which he compared with Nazi Germany. Halevy made this in-
credible comparison in a "personal and confidential" letter sent
from Jerusalem to Dick Duncan in New York on May 17, 1984,
several weeks after Sharon proved to be making a solid comeback
on the political scene in Israel.

The Israeli security services had arrested some twenty Jewish
settlers who carried out antiterror operations of killings, shoot-
ings, and bombings against Arabs. During the summer of 1980,
Halevy had claimed in a story he published in the U.S. that
Prime Minister Begin was impeding the investigation. That new
anti-Begin story raised a storm of protest in Israel, since Begin
hadn't done anything of the kind. In fact, the arrest of the "Jewish terrorist underground" in April 1984, long after Begin's resignation, could still be traced directly back to Begin's orders when,
as prime minister, he had instructed the secret service to carry out
a thorough investigation in order to run the terrorists to ground.

Halevy was almost certainly confident that his letter to Duncan
would remain forever in his personal and confidential file in the
upper reaches of Rockefeller Center. It is singularly important,
therefore, to read his letter to understand just how Halevy really
regarded his native country, how he treated Sharon, and, not
least, how he depicted himself to his boss, Duncan, in New York.

Whenever I feel like writing or even when I am forced to write, I
seem to have some kind of problem with the opening lines. So, in
order to make it simple, basically there are two reasons for this
note: one, I felt like writing to you and sharing some of my personal feelings, and two, there are practical reasons.

I have to admit that the last two weeks taught me a lesson. Apparently journalistic "victories" only leave a sour taste. Almost
four years after publishing the story on the Jewish terror network,
after telling the story of Begin halting the investigation, etc., the
facts are finally proving the accuracy of the story published in the
Washington Star on August 7, 1980.

And while saying this I don't mean *Time*. Being right or wrong in our profession has little meaning. It is the personal professionalism, self-integrity and self-confidence that counts. The rest is actually irrelevant and this includes all the rough times—you know—that I went through, the names and the suspicion. Aside from the personal point of view, there are some developments—to which Jewish terrorism should be attached—that seem to me very worrying. These are the actual vindication of Arik Sharon, the cabinet minister's statement justifying the bombing of the West Bank mayors [Professor Yuval Ne'eman] and other signs of mysticism, fascism and radicalism. I don't want to draw historical analogies but it seems to me that the difficulty in recording these trends is as complicated as it was in the twenties and thirties in Europe and mainly Germany.

One thing is clear and this is that the deteriorating economic fabric, which will only become really clear after the general elections on July 23, will only add to the frightening reality.

Without being explicit, Halevy was sending up smoke signals to Duncan. He knew that the libel suit was getting closer and that his professional mask would be shattered, so here he was saying in effect: Dick, old pal, you see I was right about Jewish terrorism, so you should also believe me about Sharon's revenge story. And if I can't prove that the story is right and mentioned in that Secret Appendix B, it's only because Israel has become like Nazi Germany in regard to "the difficulty in recording these trends" that, once again, only eagle-eyed Halevy is capable of discerning.

Here is a reporter who courageously gives *Time* the scoops from the new Third Reich—in Israel.

Halevy continued his self-revelations—if, indeed, the letter honestly reflected his views and wasn't written in nervous anticipation of the trial.

The involvement of IDF soldiers and officers is another factor leading to a general feeling that someone has pulled the rug from under my feet. As far as I know the facts, I wonder whether the investigation will actually dig to the end. A few days ago when Harry [Kelly] interviewed Amos Oz, the writer, he said that he does not feel an exile in his own land. The fact that he used this phrase speaks for itself. Yet, I cannot share his feelings. The gap

85

between my generation's dreams and the day to day reality is too big.

Strange as it may sound, the result of all this is boredom. There is nothing here to cause enthusiasm, nothing rates as a challenge anymore. The political developments are running in a pattern that is easy to predict. The military-defense establishment is taking a route that at best will lead nowhere. And the intelligentzia is taking such a non-ideological approach that no sparks are lighting up the darkness that is engulfing us all.

If these statements lead you to believe that I have lost my senses, am pessimistic or have lost the ability to analyze, you will be wrong. I know this country and its people. I was once part of it and them. This tunnel is going nowhere and there is no light at the end. I might be wrong from A to Z, but I may also be right.

Whatever the case my own personal point of view is irrelevant. Someone else has to sort it out. Harry and others should find the answers and make the judgment. I managed to survive Mrs. Meir and Mr. Begin. I have done it all. I had my victorious moments and weaks [weak ones]. I had my first-rate stories and I had a bigger share of suffering for being first, for spelling it all out. I have established my reputation from here and whatever is here I have already done it. I want to spend some time in a place where the level of my personal involvement will be less acute.

I can no longer become enthusiastic over here and I will not regret what I have written, nor have I said it all because I am in a bad mood. I will not change my decision, when the weather improves or when Shimon Peres will (if at all) become Prime Minister. Cutting a long story short, I'll stay as long as it suits you, Harry, and the magazine. I would love to hear from you about the timing of my next assignment.

Halevy is clearly distressed. He feels exiled in his own land. He was once part of the country and the people of Israel—but he is not anymore. Even the IDF, which Halevy would still boast about belonging to, and it belonging to him, is not what it used to be. So he begs Duncan to get him out of Israel, to "a place where the level of my personal involvement will be less acute." Halevy just hadn't specified that it meant involvement against Sharon, against Begin.

I suggest that in his astonishing letter Halevy was paving his way out of Israel because he knew just how much dirt he would throw not only at Sharon but inevitably also at Israel once he had to stand up and defend his lie in the federal court. I suggest too that Halevy was aware that Sharon might expose his lie in *Time*'s paragraph. So Halevy prepared his escape from Israel—an escape to a secure exile, protected by his bosses at *Time* magazine. Halevy industriously let it be known around Israel that *Time* was assigning him to Washington, there to use his expertise as a roving military correspondent who would simultaneously be "covering the Pentagon," prying out its secrets.

Duncan was kind enough in a quick response to assure "Dear Dudu" that he had a timetable for Halevy's departure from Israel. He also had some consoling words: "Perhaps you could come to the States and rub elbows with all the nice, liberal, intelligent, devout Jews here and pick up a little much-needed rosy nostalgia for Israel. You know, singing songs down on the Kibbutz, that sort of thing."

Duncan's extraordinary remarks about the "nice Jews" were prefaced by a more cautious warning:

> I can certainly see how you must feel let down that justification doesn't really come in kind, for the story that got you into so much trouble. On the other hand, I have always felt that the trouble you were in was not so much a matter of truth or falsehood; plenty of stories can be half-wrong. The heart of the trouble was politics. And even when the facts now tend to vindicate you, the politics are the same. Perhaps not quite in the Begin sense, but the politico-cultural atmosphere which makes an outcast—or worse—of those who dare to criticize the Central Myths of Israel (some of them the finest myths in the West, some pretty damn debased and self-serving recently); that atmosphere is unchanged and seems to be stifling you. As it must stifle many.
>
> Your German analogies frighten me. I know what you mean, I think, but I hope you are not proved right. . . .

With an eye to the libel suit, Duncan's letter ended with a sly warning to Halevy. "Lie low on Sharon" he wrote, "you will be rewarded."

The advice was clear. At that stage *Time*'s bigwigs probably were very much afraid that any rash move by Halevy in Jerusalem might help Sharon prove actual malice. Halevy wasn't very careful when stating in his letter that "the actual vindication of Arik Sharon" was "very worrying" to him.

Later, when Halevy hit the headlines with some particularly wild insinuations about Sharon, Duncan sent an irate Telex. "Is there no Hebrew equivalent for 'No comment'?"

SHARON'S LACK OF SUCCESS IN HIS FIRST NEW
York deposition proceeding, on Friday, June 15, 1984, left him
bitter. *Time*'s attorneys took him by surprise and frustrated him.
The hostility of the Israeli press was to be expected but still made
itself felt. "No one said 'hello' when I came into that room,"
Sharon pointed out. It was the first time Sharon had felt the impact of the interrogation he would go through at the trial and the
antagonistic and distorted way at least some of the Israeli press
would present it.

Sharon's deposition was taken at the offices of Cravath, Swaine
and Moore. He arrived there in the company of Richard Goldstein and Adam Gilbert. *Time*'s principal counsel was Thomas D.
Barr, a fifty-five-year-old Missouri-born Yale graduate and corpo-
rate biggie. He had swept IBM to success in its fight against a federal antitrust action. This was his first meeting with Sharon.

In retrospect one could say that Barr played it wrong. His feet
up on his desk, he greeted Sharon abrasively, "You're forty minutes late, General, so the session will continue until seven-forty tonight." Not quite the thing to say to a man whom you know to
have arrived from Israel the same day. Not the thing to say to
Sharon at any time.

The deposition process was routine procedure for libel suits—to
enable *Time* to examine the documents connected with the trial
that were in Sharon's possession, and vice versa.

"What are the documents in your possession, custody, or under
your control?" Barr asked Sharon over and over again.

As he admitted later, Sharon was totally unprepared. "Where I
come from, at Kfar Malal, everybody knows that when you're
talking about a document, you mean a birth certificate, an identity card, or land-registration papers." Sharon's knowledge of
American legal terminology was also extremely sketchy. Asked by
Barr what documents he was holding, "to the best of his recollec-
tion," Sharon caught only part of the question and answered that
he had a collection of press clips.

Dissatisfied with the deposition taken at his office, Barr demanded a continuation in the presence of Judge Sofaer. Ultimately, because he came to believe that things would proceed

more smoothly in front of the judge, Goldstein too insisted that the deposition continue in Judge Sofaer's presence.

Sharon was aware that he was partly to blame for his lack of preparation for the deposition meeting. His attorneys had insisted that he arrive in New York a few days in advance, precisely to give him a chance to prepare. But Sharon had left the matter to the last moment. He had flown from Israel on a Thursday night, and by 3:30 Friday afternoon he was already in the thick of it. Arie Genger, a young Israeli who had studied in the United States and become an extremely successful businessman, had recognized the danger and asked Sharon's attorneys to postpone the session, but by then it was too late.

Not only was Sharon unprepared, he was dead tired. He had come to New York from the pressures of one of the toughest election campaigns in Israeli history. This was the first time the Likud had ever fought an election without its traditional leader, Menachem Begin. Begin was a vote getter, and the Likud knew it. So did the Labor party, and they threw the book at the Likud. Every problem in Israel was laid at the Likud's door. The economy, the start of the Lebanon war, its alleged failure. They disgustingly exploited the war casualties, who "had died in vain." They omitted to mention that not a single shell had fallen in the Galilee region since the beginning of the war. And in all these attacks Sharon was their number-one target. The Israeli media identified so completely and cooperated so fully with Labor that they seemed like good party members.

The hostility to Sharon was so strong that it blurred the facts. TV, radio, and press attacked Sharon every way possible but forgot to show the large crowds he was drawing in his barnstorming campaign. The more the media put him down the more enthusiastically Sharon's audiences roared their support for him. Labor concentrated on surveys and opinion polls, which promised a gratifyingly decisive victory for the Labor alignment. They forgot that the votes come from the grass-roots level and not from the pollsters.

Sharon knew what reaction he was getting among the people. He worked harder and harder. He was well aware that his success would be helping a few Likud cabinet ministers who were only too anxious to get rid of him—colleagues who gave him no support and, in addition refused to let him have the Bikfaya minutes he so desperately needed for the *Time* libel suit. But Sharon has always understood the priorities. He disregarded his personal situation because he saw the return of the Labor party to power as the greater evil. And the more he traveled the country the more Sharon was convinced that Labor's optimistic polls were meaningless. The real feeling was in the streets of Jerusalem and Petah Tikva, in Tel Aviv and Kiryat Shmona. He intensified his campaign.

Whether his colleagues liked it or not, Sharon emerged as the most charismatic leader in the party, perhaps among all the parties. For the first time, it seemed there was someone who could fill, even partially, the vacuum left by the leaders of the founding generation and their successors, Ben-Gurion, Golda Meir, Menachem Begin, Moshe Dayan. Controversy has always been charismatic for the argumentative Israelis.

Sharon had been propelled from this battlefield to New York like a missile that had overshot its target. It was a significant lesson for the remainder of his suit: prepare thoroughly for every hearing.

Judge Sofaer's agreement to continue the deposition proceeding in his chambers was a departure from standard practice, but he complied with the parties' request. Aware that Sharon had to return to Israel for the wrap-up of the election campaign, he determined that the deposition should continue through Sunday.

Sharon carefully made ready for the second meeting. He started preparing the next day, Saturday, and kept it up throughout the trial. And the person who helped him most was Arie Genger. Genger knew Americans and American ways. All that long Saturday he explained to Sharon what was expected of him. He also explained to the American attorneys what Sharon was trying to achieve.

When the deposition reopened before Judge Sofaer, Barr renewed his attack. What kind of clippings did Sharon have in his office and at his house? Had he taken home any documents after his military service or after he'd left the Defense Ministry? Barr's questions were based on distorted reports in the Israeli press

claiming that the Israel state archivist, Dr. Paul Alsberg, had said
Sharon took home documents from the Defense Ministry.

Sharon explained patiently. Press clippings are routinely collected for almost all public figures in Israel. The documents he
had in his office dated from his tenure as minister without portfolio. No, he never had had secret or military documents connected
with his service. These were routinely kept in a vault at the Israeli
Army Museum. This was standard procedure for people serving
in key positions in the defense establishment. (Later Barr also
questioned Dr. Alsberg in Israel, finding, presumably to his disappointment, that Sharon had told the truth.)

Barr was particularly interested in two "documents" that Milton Gould had stated were in his possession: the working papers of
the minutes of the Bikfaya meeting and the testimony of the
Dutch journalists. Barr kept insisting that Sharon "disclose" how
these documents had come into Gould's possession. When
Weissglas tried to explain, Barr waved him aside. He wanted a
disclosure, not an explanation. Or perhaps the real issue was that
Weissglas and Sharon had transferred these documents to Gould.
Were they authorized to do that? Who had given permission?

Time, of course, was trying for something more. They wanted
every document, minute, or record of talks between Sharon and
the Phalangists, hoping that among the papers they would find
something tangible with which to bolster their false report. While
they didn't achieve their ends, then or later, Barr and company
did succeed in giving credence to rumors that Sharon's libel suit
posed a risk to Israel's confidential state documents. Here was
Sharon making trouble for the state only because of his egocentric
insistence on suing *Time*.

These suspicions floated by Barr turned into a major issue. Israeli reporters immediately sent back lurid stories describing
Sharon's "illegal transfer of secret documents" to his attorneys.
The furor was very convenient for the defense. It became an inte-
gral part of an aggressive press campaign against Sharon, especially before the trial, perhaps in order to induce him to withdraw
his suit. Dudu Halevy and *Time*'s attorneys would later maintain
in court that their information came from Israeli secret documents, from sources including intelligence personnel in the top
echelons of the IDF and the Mossad.

When Weissglas returned to Israel with Sharon after the deposition proceeding, he was bombarded with urgent calls from Attorney General Yitzhak Zamir demanding an unequivocal clarification of the "secret documents" affair. Zamir couldn't rest until he had a written, detailed explanation.

Israel's laws of secrecy regarding matters of state are no less stringent than those of the United States. Unless they are so authorized, public figures and officials are forbidden to reveal publicly the records or minutes of confidential political and military meetings. This includes the records of meetings and discussions with representatives of foreign powers.

Sharon thus encountered an unmovable obstacle in proving what had been said at the meeting with the Gemayel family in Bikfaya. The government of Israel certainly could have helped by letting him use the Bikfaya minutes, but *Time*'s legal approach was so contorted that it's doubtful whether even the actual minutes would have stopped their juggernaut campaign. They could always take refuge in the possible existence of still other documents.

Israel's refusal to cooperate with Sharon fed the implication of *Time*'s defense that the entire hierarchy of Israel—judges, cabinet ministers, and army generals—were all involved in some hideous conspiracy of silence.

In Israel, as in the United States, political secrets reach the media with amazing speed. But Israel differs from America in two respects. First, almost nothing *remains* secret. Military or political agreements, minutes, cables, intelligence reports—all are leaked so freely they form a deluge. However, only rarely is this information published in its entirety. The informer or the informant publishes only those parts that suit the particular axe being ground, regardless of who is hurt in the process. So it's possible that, over the years following the outbreak of the war in Lebanon, portions of reports were published, even in books, aimed specifically at harming Menachem Begin and Ariel Sharon—a highly selective leaking. Thus when it came to fighting his case in New York, Sharon's hands were tied by the secrecy laws on one hand and the selective leaking on the other. So much material had already appeared in the press or in books that Sharon had to weigh every word.

Blood Libel

Gould, Goldstein, and Forster didn't quite see it that way. Not disclosing the official content of his meeting in Bikfaya would damage Sharon's chances in the courtroom, they said. "The jury won't like it," they warned him. "Even the American media are likely to use it against you." The American public, accustomed as it is to the Freedom of Information Act and not at all used to military censorship, which does exist in Israel, would most probably suspect Sharon of hiding behind the shield of the secrecy laws.

It's possible that Sharon himself underestimated the extent of this difficulty at the beginning of the battle. But he certainly never got his lawyers to understand the problem, and it caused constant friction. But by then, on the eve of the trial, Sharon was emphatic. "We will not produce any document in the courtroom if the government of Israel hasn't permitted it. And I will not say a word that would violate the laws of secrecy in Israel. Even if it leads to the case being dismissed—even if it means that I lose."

ABOUT A WEEK AFTER SHARON'S DEPOSITION IN
New York, Judge Sofaer acceded to Tom Barr's demand that
Sharon make available his files in his ministerial office, and a day
later Barr arrived for his raid in Jerusalem. He was accompanied
by two Israeli lawyers. One was Joshua Rotenstreich, appointed
by *Time* to deal with the Israeli aspects of the trial. The other was
Israel Leshem, an Israeli who had started working with Messrs.
Cravath, Swaine and Moore shortly before Sharon filed his suit.
Now his familiarity with the Israel scene and the Hebrew language had put him on Barr's team.

They began digging into the files of documents. That there
would be no state documents dating from Sharon's tenure as
minister of defense didn't disturb them. There were press clips
and a lot of private correspondence.

In the months after he left the Defense Ministry Sharon had
received thousands of cables and letters of support from people in
Israel and all over the world. Most of the senders were complete
strangers to him. In addition to those from Israel and the United
States, messages came from countries behind the Iron Curtain,
from Arab countries, and from the Far East. From Jews and non-
Jews. From anonymous supporters and from well known personalities such as author Leon Uris. Other than direct words of
sympathy and support, one main theme was conspicuous: the
feeling that Sharon's ouster from the Ministry of Defense had
weakened Israel and strengthened her enemies; that the personal
campaign against Sharon would eventually boomerang against
Israel itself. It would be found, the letter writers said, that it was
not that Sharon had led a war without a consensus but rather
that the personal attack on him was dividing the people and preventing a consensus.

Sharon had answered all the letters personally. The deluge of
support had encouraged him. It was hard evidence that he didn't
stand alone. There was a vast audience of strangers out there so
strongly opposed to the lies and defamation that they wanted to
identify personally with him in his struggle.

Sharon asked that the signatories be kept anonymous. Publishing their names would be an invasion of their privacy and danger-

ous for writers from Eastern bloc and Arab countries. Judge Sofaer accepted Sharon's request.

But there wasn't a single document in Sharon's office that had any legal value. Nor did common sense indicate that there would have been. This, however, didn't deter Tom Barr.

Rotenstreich was sensitive enough to work quietly, sitting alone in a corner. Leshem, on the other hand, would scurry eagerly to Barr every time he found a letter or clipping that seemed interesting. They asked if they could annotate Sharon's files to help catalogue them. Weissglas, present in the office as Sharon's legal counsel, agreed.

Sharon stayed on his farm.

All Barr's industry in the end led to nothing—nothing, that is, except Sharon's humiliation. But he was prepared to swallow even this if necessary in his determination to break the back of *Time.* Barr said he would be back to photocopy the so-called documents. He never returned. And not one of the documents was ever used as part of the court evidence against Sharon.

Perhaps precisely because his search had proved fruitless, Barr continued insisting that Sharon was hiding documents from him, while even the judge rebuked Sharon's lawyers for not producing the material more quickly. The pointless and disgusting exercise, whose only practical result was a lot of wasted time and effort, stopped only when Bernie Fischman arrived in Israel.

Fischman is a special person—a senior member of the firm of Shea and Gould, a scholar, a deeply committed Jew and devoted friend of Israel. His professional standing is high. He understood Sharon's battle better than anyone else in Gould's office except perhaps Arnold Forster. He understood every one of its aspects: the Jewish, the Israeli, and the personal one of Sharon himself. Both he and Forster had grasped from the beginning the historical significance of the suit: that it was as much on behalf of the Jews and of Israel as of Sharon himself.

This tall American, with his graying hair and pleasant manner, had believed from the outset that Sharon was telling the truth, the complete truth. Occasionally he had participated in meetings with Sharon to determine strategy for the trial. Sometimes he had had to rush off to Judge Sofaer to clarify a legal point. Always patient, always polite, and with an unfailingly ready smile, he asked his questions and presented his replies with the incisive logic of a Talmudic scholar.

When it had seemed that the issue of producing case-related documents would never end, Bernie Fischman went to Israel to settle the matter once and for all. He and Weissglas had arrived at Sharon's farm. There he listened to Sharon's open and detailed description of the scores of press-clipping files he kept at home. Infinitely patient, Fischman explained the technicalities of the American legal process which necessitated Sharon's answering the hundreds of questions posed by *Time*. Finally, convinced that Sharon had supplied all the requisite data, he returned to Judge Sofaer in New York with Sharon's detailed report.

The judge decided that since Sharon was being so completely cooperative, his report to Fischman was acceptable. So the judge's verdict ended the great document hunt. On this issue, at least, *Time* couldn't come up with any more demands. Nevertheless, by the end of June 1984 Sharon was on the point of withdrawing the suit in New York. It wasn't so much the election campaign for the Knesset, although that did take up almost all of his time, but rather the trauma he'd experienced in New York the same month—with his own lawyers as well as *Time*'s.

He was angry at Milton Gould for not having come with him for Barr's deposition. Sharon had sat facing Barr, watching how he tried to degrade Gould's partner, Goldstein, and Gilbert as if he thought they were "frightened Jewish children." This had made Arik boil. Finally Gilbert himself hadn't been able to stand it any longer and had shouted at Barr, "Don't shake your finger at me!" But above all Sharon was angry with himself, angry that he'd gone to the deposition unprepared—both because he had arrived in New York so late and because his lawyers hadn't given him any warning of what he was likely to face. The reason, however, was irrelevant. Gould and his assistants should know and understand they had a difficult client on their hands.

Arik had had no idea what a deposition was all about. He had sat there with fists clenched because he hadn't known the routine; it was the most formal of question-and-answer techniques. And a squabble had broken out almost immediately, which of course

Barr and the Israeli press had used to their advantage. The Israeli press saw this as a first installment of the "mincemeat *Time* would make of Sharon." With a note of glee they remarked to Weissglas, "Here [New York] this isn't the Israeli government. What does Sharon think, that this is the Defense and Foreign Affairs Committee? Here he's dealing with professionals. With Barr!"

Sharon's replies hadn't flowed during the deposition. His speech at times had been hesitant and tired. He had had difficulty mentally translating terms from English to Hebrew. All that didn't inspire confidence and trust. He hadn't been convincing— even though everything he said, as it later transpired during the trial, was the truth. His reactions may have been hesitant, but his replies were totally accurate.

Then, when Sharon had returned to Israel, he had seen what a mountain the press had made of a molehill, how they had exaggerated the whole matter of "the disclosure of the secret documents." Arguing that the documents were secret, they had accused him of having handed them over to his New York lawyers without permission. Sharon's enemies in Israel pressed the attorney general to take steps against him and his lawyers. All these stories added fuel to the election fire.

Sharon, who had returned home on the Monday following the deposition, called Dubi Weissglas: "Do two things: one, take back all the papers that are in the hands of our lawyers, and, two, tell them if the judge demands those documents from us, the suit against *Time* must be withdrawn."

One month later Richard Goldstein, who had returned to Israel for preliminary work on the trial, approached Sharon in his room at the Tel Aviv Hilton with a proposal for a settlement, which Arik firmly turned down. Goldstein tried to conceal his disappointment. "Look, Arik," he said, "we think this is a proposal that would be seen as a victory for you, and it's one that we think Judge Sofaer would encourage the parties to accept."

Sharon's smile was sardonic. "How can I accept this proposal? All it actually says is that I, Sharon, don't understand English because *Time* never meant to imply that I had encouraged the Phalangists to take revenge on the Palestinians. In other words, what *Time* has written is fine. It's only with me that things are wrong—

I simply don't understand the English language. Forget it. I didn't go to court to get an ambiguous piece of paper."

The phone rang. Sharon picked it up. "Yes, Reb Avrom, I wanted to call you before the beginning of the Sabbath. I'm sure you'll take care of the agreement between Agudat Yisrael and the Likud. Whom are you going to join in a coalition? Shimon Peres? The Labor party? No, I'm sure you wouldn't do that."

The context of the conversation related to the formation of the new Israeli government. Elections had been held only a few days previously, on July 23. Prior to the elections Shimon Peres and his followers had been convinced they would win a landslide victory, sweeping the Likud out of power. But the results had been different. The Likud lost only a little ground, and both major parties won an almost identical number of seats in the Knesset. Neither commanded enough votes alone to form a government.

Both big blocs realized they had to win over the smaller religious parties, which have traditionally held the balance of power. Sharon was held in high regard by the leaders of these parties. Only Menachem Begin commanded greater respect.

A close personal friendship had developed between Sharon and Rabbi Avraham Shapira, leader of Agudat Yisrael, the ultra-Orthodox party. Shapira and Sharon are the two heavyweights in the Knesset. A popular joke has it that during discussion Sharon and Shapira have to stand side by side, their corpulence making face-to-face conversation too awkward.

From the moment the election outcome had become clear, all of Sharon's energy and attention had been concentrated on maintaining the alliance between the Likud and the religious parties. Outgoing premier Yitzhak Shamir, Begin's successor as leader of the Likud, relied almost completely on Sharon to handle this vital matter. With both the Likud and Labor vying for an alliance with the religious parties, it was necessary to be close to the action, so Sharon occasionally stayed over at the Tel Aviv Hilton, where Rabbi Shapira called him on that hot midsummer Friday afternoon.

Shapira assured the general that his party would not join any coalition with Shimon Peres.

Earlier that day Sharon had lunched with William Safire, who

was covering the postelection period for *The New York Times.*
"Let's not discuss your suit against *Time*," Safire had said. "You
know my position." He objected in principle to libel suits against
the media. There was an inherent danger that they could harm
and even restrict press freedom. Safire would state his case in his
Times column during the trial.

"There's a difference between freedom of the press and freedom
to lie," Sharon said to him firmly. "*Time* lied, and I intend to
prove it."

The conversation turned to other things—politics, much more
to Sharon's liking. Sharon's analysis of the postelection situation
was pragmatic. "As things stand now, I can't see any way of establishing a stable government in Israel other than through a national unity government."

Safire did seem convinced. But the whole of Israel had the idea
that Labor had won on the strength of its bare plurality. Labor
party leader Shimon Peres and top level party members had met
with Safire previously. They had all been very sure that, with
Ezer Weizman, ex-Minister of Defense, head of a minuscule
party, a government could be formed immediately and the Likud
consigned to the wilderness of the opposition.

Sharon wasn't convinced by this argument. It served only to
strengthen his determination to prevent Peres from becoming un-
trammeled leader of Israel. From the moment the dust had
cleared and showed the stalemate produced by the election re-
turns, pragmatic Sharon had been promoting the idea of a national unity government. "I can see no other way of coping with
the economic problems facing Israel in the next few years," he
told Safire in their two-hour interview.

"Do you have any plan?" asked the American columnist.

"I've done a lot of thinking about it," Sharon responded. "One
thing I do know: we must do everything to avoid unemployment.
Israel has to continue drawing Jewish immigration. We're still absorbing hundreds of thousands of people who came here several
years ago. Unemployment would lead to despair and consequent
emigration. We can't afford that."

"Who will hold Finance?" Safire asked.

"I don't want to go into the matter of appointments," Sharon answered. "Right now the essential thing is to put across the idea of a national unity government."

At that point I interjected, "Some people say Sharon would be an excellent minister of finance, especially in the current economic situation."

Safire grinned. Sharon hadn't held an active appointment in the seventeen months since leaving the Defense Ministry. Any idea of his receiving an operational portfolio seemed totally unrealistic, particularly because Labor preelection propaganda had claimed a sweeping power takeover. Labor was especially keen, of course, to get rid of Sharon, who was regarded as the most significant and dangerous adversary.

A few days later echoes of this conversation appeared under Safire's by-line in the *Times*. Some of Sharon's political opponents, Safire wrote, were hoping that the general would be saddled with the Finance portfolio, a double-edged sword in the ailing economic climate. That would be the best way to guarantee his total political eclipse.

To be sure, Sharon *was* in trouble. In August 1984 he was inextricably involved with negotiations for a national unity government, and accordingly he had asked his attorneys to apply to Judge Sofaer for a further postponement of the deposition demanded by *Time*. The newsmagazine was well aware of Sharon's key role in the crucial political negotiations in Israel, although probably underestimating his chances.

Judge Sofaer had decided to grant Sharon one more postponement, but only on condition that Sharon accept the proposition that if he did not appear for the preliminary interrogation, his suit against *Time* would be dismissed. Sharon had also heard that *Time* and its counsel were claiming he had no intention of appearing for the deposition.

Right down to the deadline Sharon remained in Jerusalem, mired in the negotiations for a national unity government which had started at a meeting with Shimon Peres in Savyon and had peaked on Thursday, August 30, 1984.

With no inkling of the secret meeting in Savyon between Sharon and Peres, the media continued circulating their favorite story that "Sharon was trying to sabotage the formation of a national unity government." The reporters explained very knowledgeably that because such a government obviously would have no place in it for Sharon, he was making a desperate attempt to upset the delicate and arduously achieved negotiations.

Sharon, a member of the small team selected by Yitzhak Shamir and Shimon Peres to settle the ground rules for the new government, was adamant that there be a rotation agreement. Shamir should serve first as premier for one year, Sharon argued, and only then should Peres replace him. Sharon was convinced of the need because, as he explained to Shamir, "If Peres serves as first prime minister, there is a danger he will not observe the rotation agreement on some pretext or other—even if it means going to new elections."

A politician of long experience, Peres had noticed that Sharon wasn't going to be easily moved from these principles and had begun separate negotiations with Shamir. Shamir, who was delighted to assume the leading role on his own, had never been particularly good at holding firmly to a decision, especially through the inevitable give and take of negotiations. This required strong nerves. Then suddenly, and without prior consultation with any of the other negotiators, Shamir conceded. Peres would be first prime minister and would hold the post for two years.

It is possible that if Sharon could have remained in Israel, unfettered by the demands of the libel suit, he might have succeeded in preventing this last-minute error. Shimon Peres' overriding desire was to be prime minister, and as he had no practical means of achieving this goal other than by acceding to Shamir's demand, he would have agreed that Shamir be first in the rotation round. But Sharon had to leave for New York and the deposition demanded by *Time*.

At five o'clock on the afternoon of August 30 Sharon spoke to Yitzhak Shamir, still head of the Likud government. He had come to take his formal leave before flying to New York. Sharon was pleased about the success of the negotiations, but he told Shamir frankly that he "was giving in to Peres all along the line" in their private meetings. "What will my position be in the new government?" Sharon then asked.

"What would interest you?" Shamir replied.

"I can handle anything," Sharon said jovially. "Foreign minister, Defense, Finance—"

Shamir had lost his sense of humor. "Foreign affairs and the vice premiership are reserved for me," he answered frigidly. "Yitzhak Rabin will get Defense, Yitzhak Moda'i, Finance. As far as you're concerned, we'll look for something; we'll discuss it and see what happens."

Arik raised an eyebrow. So there was no firm decision yet about his portfolio.

"But you were the one who wanted a national unity government," Shamir said defensively.

Sharon wasn't particularly taken aback. He'd half anticipated this. And so he decided that if he weren't given an active role in the government, he would not join it. He'd had enough of being a minister without portfolio.

AFTER ONLY TWO HOURS' SLEEP ON HIS EL AL
flight, Sharon appeared at the offices of Shea and Gould on the
fifteenth floor of 330 Madison Avenue on Friday, August 31. He
gave no indication that he'd just come from exhausting discussions in Jerusalem, from phone calls throughout the night, from
workdays starting between five and six in the morning. The curtain had come down on all this in the conference room near
Gould's own office as everyone sat down on leather chairs around
the circular table: Milton Gould, Bernie Fischman, Richard
Goldstein, Arnold Forster, Adam Gilbert, and Andrea Feller, an
associate attorney.

"Tom Barr isn't in the best of health," Sharon was surprised to
hear from his lawyers. "They will probably decide to have your
deposition postponed until he recovers."

"Not a chance," Sharon replied. "I've promised Prime Minister
Shamir that I'll be back in Jerusalem within four or five days.
You yourselves told me the deposition wouldn't take longer than
two or three days."

Richard Goldstein leaned forward to explain. "*Time*'s lawyers
insist that won't be enough."

"I'm very sorry, gentlemen." Sharon was firm. "You have to
understand—they're simply trying to drag out the case; that's
why they want to prolong all the preliminary proceedings. It's not
only a question of costs. It's impossible for me to be away from Israel for any length of time, especially right now. I refuse to give in
to these obvious tactics of theirs. You said you had arranged with
them that I would come for three or four days. Here I am. Longer
than that I can't stay."

"Is there any chance that the new government might allow
scrutiny of the Secret Appendix B?" Gould asked.

"I haven't any idea," Sharon replied. "The end result is that all
the politicians, both Likud and Labor, are quite happy to let me
bear the mark of Cain. Why should they give me the document?
But I'll have another try at getting it."

"If you don't manage to get it, we're in trouble," Gould
warned. "They're going to ask you about it in the deposition,
especially the content of the conversation at Bikfaya."

"I've got no problem telling them what was *not* mentioned in the conversation," said Sharon. "I can tell them unequivocally that the subject of revenge didn't come up at all, in any way at all."

"But what about your conversation with Bashir three days earlier, on September twelfth?" Gould had done his homework.

"That was a political discussion. I can talk about it only if it has been published in the press." Sharon stopped short. "What do the September twelfth talks have to do with the case? Bashir was still alive then, and *Time* published that I tried to encourage his family to avenge his death."

"They'll try anything," Gould warned.

"Let them try." Sharon wasn't put out. "They'll find nothing, because nothing like that ever was said on any occasion."

Before the deposition, one more attempt at a settlement came and went. At noon on September 4, along with Sharon and his wife, Lily, the whole team was gathered in a first-floor room of the Foley Square courthouse. A battle had been raging since early morning over two typed sheets, the judge's proposal for ending the suit by making a settlement. "Settlement" was the key word. Judge Sofaer was sparing no effort to end the suit peacefully even before the trial began. We had with us the full text of his proposal:

> In February and June of 1983, Ariel Sharon, the former Minister of Defense of the State of Israel, commenced libel actions in Israel and the United States, respectively, against *Time* based upon a portion of an article it published concerning the Report of the Israeli Commission of Inquiry into the events at the Sabra and Shatilla refugee camps in West Beirut. The portion sued upon stated:
>
> One section of the Report, known as Appendix B, was not published at all, mainly for security reasons. That section contains the names of several intelligence agents referred to elsewhere in the report. *Time* has learned that it also contains further details about Sharon's visit to the Gemayel family on the day after Bashir Gemayel's assassination. Sharon reportedly told the Gemayels that the Israeli army would be moving into West Beirut and that he expected the Christian forces to go into the Palestinian refugee camps. Sharon also reportedly discussed with the Gemayels the

105

need for the Phalangists to take revenge for the assassination of Bashir, but the details of the conversation are not known.

The cases have been settled on the basis of the following statements:

Time never intended to suggest by the article that General Sharon or anyone else representing the military or political echelons of the State of Israel encouraged, instigated, or condoned the massacres of Palestinian civilians in West Beirut. *Time* had no information that General Sharon or anyone else acting on behalf of Israel knew in advance of the massacres or that they would in fact take place. *Time* has always believed that nothing in its article could reasonably be read to have conveyed such conclusions. If any of its readers did draw such conclusions from the article, *Time* did not intend to convey them.

Time never had access to the secret appendices to the Commission's Report, and it has no reason to believe that there is anything in these appendices which differs from the public findings of the Commission, including its conclusion that neither General Sharon nor anyone else representing the military or political echelons of the State of Israel incurred direct responsibility by encouraging, instigating, or condoning the massacres. As the article stated, the Kahan Commission Report was "hailed in the U.S. and Western Europe as a remarkable example of self-criticism by a democratic society."

"No! Absolutely no!" Sharon snapped indignantly after reading the proposed draft. There was a tremor of anger in his voice. "What does it really say in actual fact? That I don't know English and that I didn't understand that *Time* in no way intended what I claim it published. What everyone understood? A scrap of paper like this! Is that what I sued for?" He looked at it contemptuously with a dry laugh to soften his reaction. "I won't accept it—no way!"

Sitting at the long table opposite Sharon, Gould's associate Bernie Fischman eyed him worriedly.

Sharon thrust the typed sheets forward. "Look—give this back to the judge and tell him you're not prepared to show it to your client. The answer is no—*n o!*" Sharon's voice was harsh.

Everyone looked anxious—Lily, Genger, Richard Goldstein, Adam Gilbert, and Andrea Feller.

Gould made another try. He wanted to persuade Arik to go over the text once again and indicate the specific points he disagreed with.

"Milton." Sharon's voice softened. "Look, don't tell me you don't know there's dirty work going on here. We don't even know if *Time* has agreed to the text."

Goldstein broke in cautiously. "The judge said if we agreed to wording acceptable to him, he would make it his business to lean on *Time*, on their attorneys, to come to a settlement. Bob Rifkind's here for *Time*."

Sharon gave him a level glance. "I'm prepared to assure you here and now that won't happen. We'll agree, and *Time* will reject. And then we'll make another concession. And they'll leak it to the press, as if we're on the defensive. They'll make it look as if *we* came here looking to settle and *they* refused. Who needs it? We came here to fight," Sharon said emphatically, "and this proposal won't lead to any kind of settlement. All it will do is slow down our momentum."

The atmosphere was tense. It was reflected by Gould and Goldstein. They looked cold and steely.

"There's nothing lost in just reading the thing," Genger said tentatively. He agreed with Sharon, but he wanted to ease the tension.

There followed a linguistic battle for several hours. We went over every sentence—sometimes every word. Eventually Gould, Fischman, and Goldstein went off to the judge's chambers and returned with an amended draft.

With unmistakable misgivings and occasional open anger, Sharon went over the new draft. Someone brought in coffee, soft drinks, and sandwiches from the coffee shop in the building.

"Is it okay with you?" Gould would ask Arik each time he corrected the text.

When we'd finished, Arik suddenly recoiled. "The whole thing doesn't seem right to me. Instead of the judge leaning on *Time* and pulling a retraction and an apology out of them, something with fair and reasonable wording, we have this thrust at us. It's not a pleasant situation. *Time* accused me of murder. *Time* ought to be punished."

Blood Libel

Meanwhile, in the courtroom the reporters were waiting to hear Sharon's deposition. They'd been told things were running late because of "procedural clarifications."

The amended settlement was typed up and given to Sharon once again. Gould, the ubiquitous pipe angled from his mouth, tried to explain. "In my time I've experienced hundreds of settlement discussions. But this time the judge is more involved than I've ever known a judge to be. I've never seen anything like it. That's why I want to give it a try."

Sharon looked at the retype. His face flushed. "No!" The exclamation was abrupt. "I won't agree to this. There's no retraction here. There's no apology." His voice dropped. There was infinite pain in his low tone. "*Time* published a blood libel about me. How the hell do you *settle* a matter like this? A blood libel. A blood libel you *fight!*"

Gould paled. His anger had risen too. He turned to me and Genger and asked us to come to another room with him. Outside, he spoke vehemently. "The judge's attitude carries weight. It's not at all a bad proposal. *Time* will be admitting that it had no information whatsoever in regard to what it published about Sharon. I think Arik should agree to it."

Only after another marathon analysis, with a lot of additional amendments, did Sharon finally agree to sign the proposed settlement. But he was still patently reluctant.

Their faces bright with satisfaction, the lawyers hurried off to the judge. Sharon had made some far-reaching concessions.

Arie Genger read the amended version out loud.

> In February and June of 1983, Ariel Sharon, the former Minister of Defense of the State of Israel, commenced libel actions in Israel and the United States respectively, against *Time* based upon a portion of an article it published concerning the Report of the Commission of Inquiry into the events of Sabra and Shatilla Refugee Camps in West Beirut.
>
> The cases had been closed on the basis of the following statements:
>
> *Time* states that it never intended to suggest by the article that General Sharon encouraged, instigated, or condoned the massacres of Palestinian civilians in West Beirut. *Time* had no information

that General Sharon knew in advance of the massacres or that they would in fact take place. *Time* believes that nothing in its article could reasonably be read to have conveyed such conclusions. If any of its readers did draw such conclusions from the article, *Time* did not intend to convey them.

Time also confirms that it never had access to the secret appendices in the Commission's Report.

Only one word still remained controversial. Sharon insisted that the statement should say "The cases have been settled" and not "closed."

Before they broke up, Sharon said emphatically, "You'll come to realize it was all a waste of time. Those *Time* lawyers who're here in the building now, they don't have authority to conclude anything. They'll have to go back to the editors for approval."

And that, indeed, was what happened. Later, on the evening of the same day, Goldstein and Weissglas arrived at the Regency Hotel with yellow legal pads scribbled full. It was the text of a settlement as dictated by *Time*'s lawyers.

Sitting behind a desk, with his back to the window overlooking Park Avenue, Sharon glanced briefly at the sheaves of paper. He gave a sardonic laugh. After all the effort at the courthouse there was virtually no resemblance at all to the text that Sharon had accepted so reluctantly.

Sharon's patience was wearing out. His tone was abrupt, with only a veneer of politeness as a gesture of respect to his own legal team. This time, unquestionably, it was General Sharon speaking. "Tell them," he said, "tell the people at *Time* you didn't even bother to show me this document. They don't want a settlement. They're conducting a war of attrition. *Time* wants war, and that's what they'll get—as of tomorrow morning in court."

Time's machinations had enabled Sharon to profit in at least one respect. One day of the days set aside for his deposition had fallen away. For itself *Time* had achieved nothing.

TOM BARR DIDN'T APPEAR IN COURT TO EXAMINE
Sharon at the deposition proceeding. In his place was one of
Barr's assistants, Stuart Gold. Young, Jewish, bearded and bespectacled, Gold tried to attack Sharon. But Sharon reiterated
one simple sentence. "What *Time* published was not merely a lie
but a blood libel against the Jewish people, the State of Israel,
and against myself." Sharon used the public deposition at the federal district court to attack *Time* over and over again. Deposition
sessions are usually held in private.

As Sharon and his lawyers had anticipated, the judge didn't
stop questions that in Sharon's opinion were irrelevant to the suit.
In the preliminary consultations with his lawyers, they had promised to object every time such a question came up.

During recess Sharon complained. "You fellows are asleep. You
don't move fast enough to object, and even when you do, the
judge overrules you." For the first time Sharon had to learn the
meaning of such words as "sustained," "overruled," and "stipula-
tion." They were terms the judge was using a lot.

Gold insisted that Sharon explain why he had filed the libel
suit in New York. Sharon's answer was unfailingly the same. "I
am a Jew, a member of a nation that knows the meaning of blood
libel. I decided *Time*'s publication could not be left unanswered.
What was published in *Time* was a blood libel against the Jewish
nation, the State of Israel, and myself. Could there be a worse defamation than being accused of instigating murder?" Sharon's
voice resounded through the courtroom. He seemed angry and
stabbed a finger at Gold. Someone in the courtroom began to ap-
plaud. The judge called for order.

Sharon had used his military expertise to launch a frontal attack on *Time*. His charge that the publication constituted a blood
libel was picked up by the media all over the world. *Time*, not interested in a settlement, began to see how Sharon would react at
the trial.

Time spokesman Michael Luftman responded immediately.
Talking to the press he described Sharon's charges against the
magazine as "unsupported, unsupportable, and outrageous."
Luftman continued, "He is a politician. He's using the witness

stand as a bully pulpit to say a lot of things that are not germane to the case."

The first hearings were held in a small chamber on the first floor of the courthouse. Only a few people attended. But when the story got around that Sharon was in court the audience swelled. The judge transferred the proceedings to a larger chamber on an upper floor.

Sharon was especially sensitive on the issue of secrecy. Yes, he said, he had read Secret Appendix B of the Kahan Report, but, no, he had no intention of divulging what was in it. "What I *can* say is that it doesn't include what *Time* published. I never discussed revenge with the Gemayel family or with anyone else in the Lebanese forces."

Gold wanted to know how he was financing the trial. "I sold my house in Zahala," Sharon responded simply.

A ripple went through the courtroom. Even Sharon's lawyers were surprised.

What Sharon did not tell the court was what the simple white house held for him. Zahala was established in the fifties as a residential area for regular army officers. It was a pretty Tel Aviv suburb, with modest detached houses and lawns and trees. Lieutenant Colonel Sharon lived there with his first wife, Margalit, near the home of then Chief of Staff Moshe Dayan. His next-door neighbor was Colonel Motti Hod, later to become CO of Israel's air force, the victors of the Six-Day War.

It was here, between military campaigns, that Sharon had raised his first child. The same house saw Sharon suffer two terrible personal tragedies. Margalit was killed in a traffic accident while driving to Jerusalem in her small blue car. Gur, their only child, was fatally wounded near the house when another boy accidentally shot him. It was in the same house that Sharon overcame the double tragedy. He married Lily, Margalit's sister, and built a new family. His two sons, Omri and Gilad, were born there.

When he became CO Southern Command and commander of the Suez front in December 1969, Sharon moved to an army apartment in Be'er Sheva. He never returned to the house in Zahala. Later his permanent home became the spacious house surrounded with lawns and flowers that he built on his farm in the south.

In answer to Gold's questions Sharon described Israel's sensitivity to casualties, both military and civilian. "I was particularly offended by *Time* magazine because as a Jew I don't know of any other people in the world more sensitive than Jews when it comes to human life."

Saguy, Arie Genger's son, who had asked permission to come to the hearing with his father, had tears in his eyes. A sensitive lad with beautiful eyes, Saguy was about to celebrate his bar mitzvah in Israel. "It kind of hit me when Arik said that," the boy said later.

Even on that fifth day of September 1984 one could sense some of the drama that would unfold in the courtroom later. Sharon was getting a more practical idea of what he could expect there.

The *Time* attorneys wanted him to remain for a few additional days of deposing that week, but Sharon was reluctant to do so. He was prepared to call outgoing Prime Minister Shamir and ask for approval to stay only an extra day. It was 5:00 P.M. in New York, 11:00 P.M. in Israel, when, with Judge Sofaer's permission, Sharon called Shamir's home in Jerusalem from the Foley Square courthouse. The premier's wife, Shulamit Shamir, answered the phone. "I hope I'm not disturbing you, calling so late," said Sharon. "Not at all," she said graciously, "Yitzhak is still awake."

Sharon explained the situation to Shamir, who was understanding and approved his staying in New York for the additional day. He also had news for Sharon. The Industry and Trade portfolio had been earmarked for Sharon and was awaiting his return.

"I'm very glad," Sharon said. "I'll be back in Israel before the end of the week."

For Sharon the appointment was added proof of his ability to conduct a multifront battle. Here he was fighting a civil suit in New York, and back home across the world, in Jerusalem, they were aware he had to be counted and had given him the post he wanted—minister of industry and trade.

Time's attorneys had their extra time to question Sharon on Thursday morning. Sharon left the courthouse at noon on his way to the Regency Hotel and thence to Kennedy Airport and his flight back to Israel. Richard Goldstein and Dubi Weissglas spoke briefly with him in front of the heavy pillars of the courthouse entrance.

"*Time* is going to propose a new settlement," Goldstein said. "Maybe we'll be able to call you about it even before you leave the hotel."

By then Sharon knew where he stood. "Nothing but a complete retraction and an apology," he said firmly. "I won't go along with their games anymore. I'll see them in court."

ABOUT A WEEK AFTER RETURNING FROM HIS DEPO-
sition in New York on Friday, September 14, Sharon was invited
to the presidential residence together with all of the other cabinet
members for the formal meeting of the president of Israel, Chaim
Herzog, and his new government. The Israeli public had great
hopes for the National Unity government. While the ministers
were lining up for the traditional photograph, Shimon Peres and
Sharon spoke briefly.

"In essence, the government has been formed in accordance
with what we planned that night in Savyon," said Prime Minister
Peres with obvious satisfaction. He invited the new minister of industry to meet with him privately.

Thereafter Sharon threw himself into work at his ministry with
his usual zeal. He scheduled round-the-clock appointments with
the heads of Israeli industry and toured industrial plants.

He asked his attorneys in New York to delay the opening of the
trial for as long as possible in order to enable him to participate to
the maximum in the economic efforts that the government had
undertaken. *Time* wanted Sharon for an additional deposition in
October, about a week before the opening of the trial. Sharon told
his attorneys unequivocally that he'd had enough. He wouldn't
permit the *Time* legal team to give him the runaround any longer.
Too much time had already been wasted on their spurious attempts at settlement. Sharon would be at their disposal for another deposition only a couple of days before the opening of the
trial. He asked too that the trial should not begin before November.

Meanwhile Richard Goldstein made an excited call to Dubi
Weissglas in Israel. "I couldn't fall asleep last night. I read the
documents in Dudu Halevy's personal file. I'm absolutely
stunned."

At his home in Tel Aviv, Weissglas learned that Goldstein was
stunned for two reasons: first, because the documents would help
prove in court who Halevy really was; and second, Goldstein was
shocked as a Jew. There was the letter Halevy had written to
Duncan, *Time*'s chief of correspondents, in which he compared
events in Israel to those in Nazi Germany.

Through painstaking work Goldstein and his colleagues had managed to make a significant breakthrough in September 1984. Systematically and stubbornly, Gould's team had carried out a thorough investigation of certain employees at *Time*. During routine questioning about work procedures, Goldstein and Adam Gilbert had discovered that each *Time* reporter had a personal file in which confidential letters were kept. Goldstein had demanded Dudu Halevy's personal file.

Then a bitter wrangle over the file had begun. *Time*'s attorneys of course knew what the file contained, and they were apprehensive. They didn't want to hand it over to Gould. It would create a dangerous precedent, they claimed, an unwarranted invasion of privacy.

Judge Sofaer ordered them to produce the file, which was to be viewed only by Sharon's attorneys. When they later got the file, they knew they had found a potential powder keg. For the first time, perhaps, they realized how right Sharon had been in claiming that Halevy was a dubious character. Everything came out in his file—including the fact that Halevy had been put on probation by the magazine for an untrue story published about Menachem Begin.

Now the lawyers fought for the judge's permission to show the file to their client. When Judge Sofaer decided in their favor over the objections of *Time*'s attorneys, Goldstein excitedly called Weissglas. He promised to send Halevy's file by special mail. And in the meantime, Goldstein promised, they would fight for use of the file as evidence in open court and for any other requirements.

Time's lawyers pulled out every stop to prevent this. They understood the file was dynamite. Sharon too realized the significance of the documents. But he didn't get particularly excited, because he wasn't surprised. He knew who Halevy was, at least from what the reporter had published about him.

The contents of Halevy's file were not similar to the Telex traffic *Time* had had to submit to Gould in accordance with the "discovery of documents" procedure, although those Telexes were damaging enough in themselves. Here, in this personal file, were letters from Halevy to his editors in New York, and from them to him. They were letters the writers had never envisaged becoming

115

public, and they revealed the true nature and character of this Israeli who reported from Jerusalem for the world's largest weekly newsmagazine. They showed who he was professionally—a very important point for the trial. They also showed who he was as a Jew and an Israeli, a point still important to some Jews in Israel and in the rest of the world. The Telex traffic on the defamatory story was a battering ram for Gould to begin the assault on *Time*'s legal defense at the trial. These letters were to be the charge with which he would break down the walls.

Despite his heavy work schedule in Israel, Sharon himself was obliged to find the time to follow the developments of the case in New York. On Tuesday, September 25, between a meeting with an investor from Brazil and negotiations with the directors of a large Israeli industrial concern, he managed to dictate a number of questions for Morris Draper to his New York attorneys.

Time had summoned Draper to the deposition. Draper had replaced Philip Habib as special U.S. envoy for the Middle East. Draper had commuted on his own and with Habib between Beirut and Jerusalem during the days of the Sabra and Shatilla tragedy. *Time* had insisted that Draper testify in court. The State Department objected, because it doesn't permit its employees to divulge official secrets in open court.

The deposition was to be held in the judge's chambers in Washington on September 26, the eve of the Jewish New Year. It was two years to the day after a meeting between Sharon and Draper in Israel, immediately after the Sabra and Shatilla tragedy. *Time* hoped to extract incriminating information from Draper that could be used against Sharon. *Time*'s attorneys told Gould's team in New York that they were hoping to hear Draper say that he had warned Sharon against sending the Phalangists into the Palestinian camps. *Time* considered Draper a very important witness.

Sharon knew that he had never heard any such warning from Draper. So the day before the deposition, calling from Tel Aviv, Sharon instructed his attorneys to ask Draper certain questions. These were some of them.

- When did the U.S. intelligence community first know about the massacre?

- When had the U.S. Embassy in Beirut first become aware of the massacre at the camps? Was it the same night? Or had they received a warning before that?
- Was it true that the Embassy had intercepted cables and had already received news of the massacre on Friday, September 17, 1982, while the Israeli government became aware of it only on the following day, a Saturday?
- What was done about the information? What action was taken in Beirut to prevent the possibility of further slaughter?

Sharon told Richard Goldstein that there was no substance to the entire *Time* insinuation campaign of Draper stories. "It's just another trial balloon," he said.

As soon as Sharon had replaced the phone there was another call. This time it was his friend Armand Hammer, from his office in Los Angeles. Hammer had visited Israel a few days previously, and both Sharon and Prime Minister Peres had attended the opening of an exhibition of paintings from Hammer's important collection. Now Sharon told Hammer on the phone that he had spoken to Peres after their talks in Israel and that both he and Peres would do their best to enable Hammer to go into business in Israel.

When Dov Weissglas arrived, Sharon had to ask him to wait while he tried to find the time to formulate appropriate answers to additional questions from *Time*'s lawyers.

That evening Sharon squeezed in another call, this one to Foreign Minister Shamir, who was attending the United Nations annual assembly in New York. Sharon explained that he foresaw great danger in Prime Minister Peres' approach to the Taba-area conflict between Israel and Egypt.

"Peres wants to meet the Egyptian president, Hosni Mubarak. In return the Egyptians want us to give them Taba," Sharon told Shamir. "Why should we make any concessions to them? Why should we have to pay for his agreement to meet Peres?" Shamir promised to take care of the matter.

The next day, the eve of Rosh Hashana—the Jewish new year—Sharon returned home late. In the early hours of the morning Gould's office called. Barr had made a new settlement

117

proposal. Gould had rejected it out of hand, saying that *Time* could sign only one statement, the one they had rejected the last time Sharon was in New York. He wasn't even prepared to submit it to Sharon, Gould said.

Sharon was quite happy—he'd had his fill of *Time* magazine and its games.

Gould's office had still more news that Rosh Hashana eve. In spite of *Time*'s objection, Judge Sofaer had instructed that Sharon be informed of the contents of Halevy's letters in his personal file at *Time*. The attorneys told Sharon the letters contained sensational information about the standard of Halevy's reporting and his personal and professional bias. They were sending Sharon copies by special delivery.

Two years to the day after the tragedy of Sabra and Shatilla— on the eve of Rosh Hashana in 1982—from which Halevy and *Time* magazine had constructed their false and defamatory statement about Sharon, he began to feel that he could see light at the end of the very long and dark tunnel.

THE NEXT BLOW *TIME* RECEIVED WAS SELF-
inflicted. If *Time*'s Jerusalem bureau chief Kelly hadn't mentioned that he had spoken with Ehud Olmert about the story concerning Sharon, no one would have known about it. The court would not have discovered that just two weeks after publication of the story, *Time* was told it had no foundation. Or to put it another way, Harry Kelly, head of the *Time* bureau in Jerusalem was told twenty months before the trial that what had been published was incorrect, and yet *Time* had not seen fit to retract the statement.

This discovery was also the result of patient investigation by Gould's office. In his quiet, thorough manner, Richard Goldstein had cross-examined Kelly during his deposition in New York. *Time*'s Jerusalem bureau chief said that in the second half of February 1983 he had met Knesset member Ehud Olmert at a dinner given in Israel for New York's mayor, Edward Koch. They had never met before. The discussion moved to the Sharon-*Time* affair. Olmert is a member of the Likud, Sharon's party, but is no close friend of Sharon.

Olmert told Kelly that in his capacity as a member of the Knesset Foreign Affairs and Defense Committee, he had studied the Secret Appendix. There was nothing in it that gave substance to *Time*'s claim about Sharon. In his deposition Kelly averred that he had asked Olmert to read the appendix again and clarify precisely what was there. Olmert, eager to maintain good relations with the foreign and Israeli press, allegedly reexamined the appendix and called Kelly, saying, "There is nothing there that resembles your story." Nevertheless, at his deposition, Kelly admitted that he did not report this startling information to New York because he did not know how much credibility he could attribute to Olmert's statements. (At trial, however, Kelly appeared to change his testimony and say he did not report Olmert's information to New York.)

This disclosure by *Time* caused a sensation and raised a lot of questions. As a matter of principle, how could an Israeli Knesset member be willing to probe into highly classified state documents in order to pass on information to *Time* or to any other member of the media? It is as though a senator in the United States might volunteer to check a highly classified federal document for *Time*'s Washington bureau chief.

The Kahan Commission's Secret Appendix B was kept deep in a government safe in Jerusalem. Olmert could study it only by virtue of his special status as a member of the Knesset's Foreign Affairs and Defense Committee. Committee members who get reports on confidential state affairs were permitted to read the Secret Appendix whenever they wished. It rather seems, from the story told by *Time*'s Jerusalem bureau chief, that Olmert became a *Time* stringer.

Another Knesset member who took advantage of his privileged position was left-wing, Palestinian supporter, professional Sharon-hater Yossi Sarid. He also rushed to read the Kahan Commission's Secret Appendix B. One may assume that had he found even a hint of what *Time* reported, he himself would have used it in his public declarations against Sharon. He might even have volunteered to appear as a witness for *Time*. But Sarid beat Olmert to the punch by releasing a public statement. What *Time* had published about Sharon, he said, was not present in the confidential appendix.

Sharon was amazed at Olmert. After all, this Knesset member was a member of Sharon's own political party, the Likud. During Sharon's term of office as defense minister Olmert had never missed a chance to visit or talk with Sharon and to support him, Begin, and the Lebanon war publicly. And now that Sharon was suing *Time*, Olmert had not felt obliged to say a single word to Sharon about *Time*'s request. Olmert had seen Sharon on innumerable occasions at the Knesset and elsewhere and had never said a word.

At the time Kelly was having his deposition taken, Olmert was in New York and heard about Kelly's testimony. Immediately on his return to Israel, Olmert hurried to Sharon and explained what had happened. He offered to give sworn testimony in New York.

"Do as you see fit," Sharon replied. "I will not interfere."

FIVE HOURS BEFORE MY SCHEDULED DEPARTURE
for New York for my deposition before *Time*'s attorneys, I received
a call from the Ministry of Defense. I was not to testify on what
had been said between Sharon and the Phalangists at the meeting
at Bikfaya. It was the senior legal counsel of the Ministry of Defense speaking. If I acted otherwise, I would be in violation of the
law.

But Sharon had already told the court in New York exactly
what had happened at Bikfaya, I argued. There was no secret of
any kind. The deputy legal adviser of the Defense Ministry, Brigadier General (Res.) Dov Shefi, disagreed. "As a former civil servant, you must not testify in a New York court concerning the
war in Lebanon." He quoted sections of the law under which I
could be charged if I went ahead with my testimony. "If you do
otherwise, you will do so on your own responsibility."

"You are creating an absurd situation," I retorted angrily.
"*Time* and Dudu Halevy are spreading the lie that Israel's former
minister of defense encouraged the Phalangists to take revenge on
the Palestinians. I, who happened to attend that meeting, am not
permitted to tell the court in New York that the *Time* story was a
complete fabrication?"

It was no use. The mechanism of justice has its own twisted
logic. I canceled my trip to New York.

There was a great deal of justifiable anger at Milton Gould's
office. The documents they had hoped to get from Israel through
Sharon had not materialized. Now they would have to do without
a witness who had actually been present at the talks between
Sharon and the Phalangists.

It was a last-minute development. I had been certain I would
be permitted to testify on the Bikfaya discussion, not only because
Sharon had already testified on the subject in court during his
deposition three weeks earlier. I also sincerely believed there was
no security or operational secret involved—not at the time of the
discussion and certainly not now, more than two years later.

That was why, when a young man approached me in court at
the time of Sharon's deposition and handed me a piece of paper,
everything had seemed quite straightforward. It was the sub-

poena ordering me to appear for a deposition by the attorneys at *Time*. It had never occurred to me or, for that matter, to Sharon that the Israeli authorities would forbid me to testify. I had resigned from the Israeli civil service in July 1983 and gone back to journalism. As a private Israeli citizen and a friend of Sharon's, I considered it my duty to testify in court to what I had heard at Bikfaya.

For several days Sharon tried everything to change the ruling. I tried from my end. But it was no use. Milton Gould called. Angrily he told me that if I didn't testify, *Time* would use this as additional leverage to obtain dismissal of the suit. In addition, my failure to observe the subpoena put me in violation of the laws of the state of New York.

Trying to steer a middle course, I decided to go to New York and attend the deposition but to act in accordance with the Official Secrets Act. On the eve of Yom Kippur I managed to reach Shefi. "It's all on your own responsibility," he said. "You can't afford to do some of the things that cabinet ministers and Knesset members permit themselves. Try not to get into trouble with the law."

I was worried on my trip to New York. I was walking a very thin line between not wanting to violate any secrecy laws and wanting to testify for Sharon. And I was aware that the slightest slip on my part would put the entire blame on him.

Dubi Weissglas called me from Tel Aviv to say the Defense Ministry had now sent an official warning by registered letter not to mention anything at all I had learned during my service at the ministry.

The deposition in New York at the offices of Cravath, Swaine and Moore took nineteen hours and extended over three days. My principal interrogator was Robert Rifkind, but big gun Tom Barr sat in from time to time. Their Israeli adviser Israel Leshem was there also, to help with the Hebrew and scurry back and forth.

Fortunately I hadn't agreed to accept their English translations of anything I'd written in Hebrew. So they were nicely disconcerted when I found several errors in a single passage of an article on the Kahan Commission.

Their main emphasis was on Sharon. They wanted me to tell them all about him. How many times I had seen him recently and how often we had talked on the phone. What he had said and what I had said. And, of course, what was discussed at Bikfaya. This last question was flung at me several times and in all kinds of phrasing.

"I was at Bikfaya, and I also attended the talks between Sharon and the Phalangists at the Karantina. The subject of revenge was never discussed directly or indirectly either by Sharon or by any-body else." I repeated this until they were obviously sick of hear-ing me talk about what *hadn't* been said at that meeting. Even the attorneys from Gould's office tried to get me to be a little more forthcoming, in view of the pressure from *Time's* counsel. I stub-bornly refused to say more. They knew of the warnings I'd re-ceived from the Israeli authorities. This skirmishing went on for a number of the nineteen hours.

Apparently having decided to throw in his hand, Rifkind blandly asked about the subject of the next book I would write. It was a great opening. "It will be about a media empire that persists in a lie, even though it is aware of the truth. The title will be 'The Rise and Fall of the Liars' Empire.' It will be a story larger than life and wider than truth." This was the gist of my reply.

Rifkind was taken aback. Hesitantly he asked where I was going to place this empire?

"I haven't decided yet. Maybe I'll write it in the form of a novel—but it's possible that it will be nonfiction."

The title hadn't just come off the top of my head. Sharon's at-torneys had told me about Halevy's deposition, specifically his re-sponse to a simple question about what he'd been reading the night before his deposition—*The Rise and Fall of the Third Reich*. It was in accord with his letter to Duncan and his comments about Israel.

The last line of my role as active witness in the suit was deposed on the witness stand in courtroom 110 on the first floor of the Foley Street courthouse. "The question of revenge was never dis-cussed at Bikfaya," I said. In view of the Israeli secrecy laws, I could not go beyond it. Therefore the judge ordered it stricken out.

Dudu Halevy was delighted. "That's great. They wouldn't ac-cept your testimony."

AS THE DATE OF TRIAL DREW CLOSER IT BECAME
apparent to *Time* that Sharon was not giving in. The various and
curious attempts to deter him at the last minute, including is-
suance of subpoenas to high Israeli government officials, were intensified. The campaign to frighten Sharon off was conducted in
all sorts of ways and through all sorts of channels. At the Regency
Hotel in New York a number of well known and prominent Jewish people came to visit Prime Minister Shimon Peres and his al-
ternate, Foreign Minister Itzhak Shamir. The two of them had
come to the United States to meet with Ronald Reagan on the
first official visit after the formation of the new Israeli government.

The self-appointed Jewish dignitaries asked Peres and Shamir
to influence Sharon to withdraw his suit against *Time*. Their reason: the trial could only hurt Israel—because the atrocities of
Sabra and Shatilla would be rehashed just when they had been
forgotten by the public. These people also maintained that Israel's opponents would pounce on the case in their regular smear
campaigns by again accusing the Israelis of killing innocent
Arabs. They concluded their argument by asserting that Israel
could not afford to enter into a war with as powerful an organization as *Time*.

All this was immediately leaked to a number of Israeli newspa-
permen, who took pains to explain "what enormous damage this
private trial of Sharon's will cause to the State of Israel" and how,
"because of his ego, the entire State of Israel will suffer again."

Now that the outcome of the trial is known, it is safe to say that
all of these reasons were groundless. But they revealed one of the
worst aspects of this whole affair, namely, that a number of prominent Jews, as well as the Israeli press, were ready to go on living
with these lies and defamation—as long as it was Sharon who had
to bear the brunt. This was a very dubious moral approach—the
approach of frightened ghetto Jews.

It should be said in Peres' defense that he did not try in any
way to influence Sharon. He probably knew that it would be use-
less. Shamir mentioned to Sharon that a number of eminent Jews
had approached him and asked him to try to have the suit with-

drawn. But he, Shamir, was not prepared in any way to interfere with Sharon's decision.

The intimidation campaign also included publication of false reports in the Israeli press: "In the trial Sharon will be asked how he killed Egyptian prisoners in the Sinai desert in the Six Day War," one of the Tel Aviv papers reported. "Sharon will be cross-examined on the murder of Palestinian citizens at Kibiye," warned another. "Sharon will be asked in the trial against *Time* why he refused to carry out orders in the Yom Kippur War," a third newspaper disclosed. *The Jerusalem Post* stated that *"Time's* lawyers want to run Sharon through the gutter . . . they plan to bring out before the jury as much dirt about him as possible."

One sensational fabrication followed another. A press report from Washington intimated that in the forthcoming trial, secret recordings kept by the National Security Council in the United States would be played to the court, and these—so it was alleged—would show that "Sharon knew in advance of the massacres at Sabra and Shatilla." The truth is that the CIA does tap the private telephones of political leaders in various foreign countries—including Israel—in all sorts of ways. It is reasonable to assume that there were those who really hoped that official Washington did indeed have recordings of some of Sharon's telephone conversations that were totally incriminating. Perhaps too they hoped that because of the political hostility to Sharon of a number of high-ups in the Reagan administration, these tapes would be made available to *Time's* lawyers.

Sharon, however, knew that it was not possible that such tapes existed—because he had never been involved in any discussions that preceded the massacre at Sabra and Shatilla.

THE TRIAL BEGINS

MILTON GOULD WANTED A JURY TRIAL. SHARON

had no objection. "I see no advantage to a trial before a single judge rather than a jury," he said. "On the contrary, the jury system seems to have proved itself."

The jury system does not exist in Israel. A system of a judge sitting with assessors is followed. Sharon was aware of this and curious to see the other system in action. He has always been curious, has always wanted to probe the unknown, even when as a boy in Kfar Malal he dreamily stared at the distant hills of Samaria, wondering what lay beyond them.

But there were other significantly practical reasons for Sharon's decision. He was unhappy that the judge appointed to hear the case was a Jew. It could even be said that he was somewhat worried about it. Anything remotely connected with Israel aroused the large American Jewish community; and something as controversial as the war in Lebanon and Sharon's role in it would certainly arouse tempestuous reactions.

Sharon knew too that Judge Sofaer had close ties with Israel. The judge had been eminently fair in actually pointing this out. Even before the trial began he had explained in detail to counsel for both sides that his association with Israel was tangible as well as emotional. Indeed, it was already known in Jerusalem that some of Judge Sofaer's personal friends in Israel belonged to the camp opposing Sharon, that among them were two former senior IDF officers who favored full concessions to the Palestinians. Sofaer's aspiration to rise to the very top of the American judiciary was also common knowledge.

None of this had deterred either counsel. Not for one moment did they doubt his total objectivity.

While the lawyers had no doubts, all these factors did make Sharon watch the judge very closely and analyze particular aspects of his attitude toward the trial. Sharon felt that the judge repeatedly tried to distinguish between the team from *Time*'s Jerusalem bureau, with special emphasis on its Israeli reporter Dudu Halevy, and the top echelons of Time, Inc., in New York's Rockefeller Center. He seemed to want to identify the Israeli reporter as the root culprit, while absolving the New York editorial office from responsibility.

Blood Libel

The lack, as far as Sharon knew, of a single Jew in the six-member jury (plus the six alternates) selected in New York City, known to have the largest Jewish population of any city in the world, although seeming singularly odd to Sharon, was more than acceptable. He realized that the process of selection entailed a careful investigation of prejudice. It would have been very difficult to find a New York Jew who was wholly neutral on the questions to be resolved, thus eliminating the city's entire Jewish population as a pool for jury selection.

With the jury impaneled and ready to go, there appeared to be no other problem. But a storm broke on November 7. In a telephone call from Israel, Sharon learned to his consternation that a report had appeared in the Israeli daily *Davar* implying that Milton Gould had objected to there being black people on the jury, that he had said that blacks on the jury would reduce his client's chances of success. "There is nothing we can do about it," Judge Sofaer reportedly had told Gould. "This is due process the American way," *Davar* reported.

For Sharon the possible consequences of the story were clear. He might be labeled a racist.

He reached Gould at his office late in the morning. "You know as well as I do that I never said one word about the jury," Sharon exclaimed. "I never mentioned either blacks or whites—I was never even consulted on picking the jury. As you know well enough, I don't care who sits on it." Sharon was hardly able to control himself.

Gould had clearly been shaken by the false report. "I never said any such thing. We were talking in the judge's chambers about the makeup of the jury, in the presence of *Time*'s lawyers," he said. "We were discussing the jury in the usual way. This sort of thing is off the record. And now this paper has maliciously misstated what was said."

The report on Gould's comments about black members of the jury prompted some of Sharon's friends in New York to try to persuade him either to dismiss Gould or, at the very least, to demand that a new jury be chosen. Troubled, Sharon ordered Gould to report to the judge what had come out in the Israeli press and might come to the ears of the jury, so that the judge, at least, would be aware of this serious situation.

130

Judge Sofaer saw nothing necessarily prejudicial in it. He was certainly not going to choose a new jury at this juncture, he said. And should the jury happen to learn about the *Davar* article, he said, he himself would see that they were put right.

Sharon had arrived in New York on November 6, a week before the opening of the trial, to prepare for it properly, but, following the first day of Arik's arrival, when the *Davar* article had caused such a contretemps, Gould was not to be found. He had gone off for the whole long weekend. His associates at the office said he had shut himself up at home to prepare his opening address to the jury in the best traditions of a star rehearsing for his premiere. But Sharon wanted Gould and only Gould.

In order to fight this war, General Sharon needed General Gould. Up to that point Sharon had not really prepared properly for the trial as far as his own evidence was concerned. He, and he alone, had to be prepared for questioning on many minute details of his life—things that he had done and things that he had not done but that the newspapers had "reported." True, the lawyers had promised him that every time something came up that was not relevant to the case, they would jump up and object. However, in the deposition proceedings Sharon had already had a taste of *Time*'s lawyers' managing to introduce all sorts of things that had no direct, or even indirect, bearing on the case—and getting away with it.

Now Gould was at home and had sent his associates and assistants to help Sharon in the trial preparation. Sharon wasn't the only one who found this behavior somewhat odd and even impolite. "At the end of it all, Gould has to lead me in the direct examination," Sharon pondered aloud. "And he has to be on the complete alert during Barr's cross-examination of me. How will he be able to do all this without our devoting a few days to going over all the abundance of material there is?"

Despite the pleadings of the other lawyers Sharon refused to work at Gould's office when Gould himself was not there. It seemed that things had gotten off to a bad start; once again there had been a communications breakdown between Gould and Sharon. Sharon therefore decided to prepare for the case on his own.

He studied the Kahan Report again—this time in depth—

going over his own testimony given in open court before the commission as well as the text of his speech in the Knesset six days after the tragic events of Sabra and Shatilla. These were things he had said from a public platform, and to repeat them in court in New York was permissible and would therefore not be a violation of the secrecy laws—a factor that had worried Sharon from the moment "the secret documents" issue had become blown out of all proportion.

Dubi Weissglas was busy explaining to the American lawyers that Gould simply had to appear for the preparation stage. In the meanwhile Sharon went to see a good friend of his, a well known American lawyer, and in the course of their chat they discussed a number of aspects of the trial. The most important thing, the American lawyer told him, was that "you have to appear the way you are. You must tell the story of your life to the jury. In the eyes of the jury you are first and foremost General Sharon, an Israeli minister. You belong to the Establishment, which is not always that well liked by simple folk. To them you are part of the administration, to which people in America relate with automatic suspicion—even more so than in Israel."

In order to get the truth across and convince the jury of it, the lawyer continued, "you have to make it plain to them that you were not born a general and that you were not born a minister; that you are, as you so often boast, simply a farmer; that you were born on a farm and that you have gotten where you are through all sorts of trials and tribulations—a human story that every American will not only understand but might identify with, because America loves success stories like that."

Gould's office was next informed that *Time* intended applying for a postponement of the trial. The reason given for this was that Tom Barr was ill. He had, in fact, not recovered properly from the moment he had become ill at the time of Sharon's deposition. *Time*'s contention was that they were relying on Barr's representing them. On account of his being indisposed, they wanted a deferral of the trial date.

It was not impossible to accept the fact of Barr's being ill. But Sharon felt that *Time* was taking advantage of Barr's illness to make things even more difficult for himself, who obviously could not be out of Israel indefinitely just to pursue his libel suit. Perhaps *Time* also was using the opportunity to make things more difficult for him and for Gould's office by increasing the costs of the case.

Fortunately Judge Sofaer rejected *Time*'s request on the simple ground that there were other sufficiently eminent lawyers at the firm of Cravath, Swaine and Moore who could step into Barr's shoes. As for Barr himself, he announced that he would go for a medical checkup and then consult with his doctor and his wife as to whether he would continue in the trial.

After three days Gould finally appeared at his office. He and Sharon exchanged chilly glances. But when Gould immediately began to display a phenomenal knowledge and familiarity with all the facts, dates, and details of the case, it became perfectly evident that he had not stayed at home for nothing—and the ice was broken. Gould had studied an enormous amount of material—documents and books—that enabled him to guide Sharon in his description of the circumstances surrounding Sabra and Shatilla down to their most minute details. In this way he could prepare Sharon for the manner in which his evidence should be given.

The night before the trial opened, Sharon did not leave his hotel. He preferred being with Lily and Gilad and watching television. One of the programs that evening was part of the long and celebrated television series *Heritage,* in which Abba Eban starred: the history of the Jewish people and of Israel. The episode shown that night was not to Sharon's liking. "Just look how Abba Eban depicts us," Sharon said before he went off to sleep. "As a nation always needing to justify its existence, as a nation in need of sympathy, always requiring to explain why it has the right to defend itself."

Sharon did not just say these things—he believed and felt them. In his mind he kept coming back to his resolve that in his own testimony in court he would take the opportunity to present Israel's history the way he saw it—the way he had lived it and the way it ought to be shown.

FINALLY SEATED ON NOVEMBER 13, THE JURORS
listened attentively to Judge Sofaer as he outlined the issues of the
case.

"The word 'libel' may be unfamiliar to you," he said. "In general, a libel is committed when someone publishes a false and defamatory statement about someone else."

Sofaer addressed the jury like a patient teacher. He said that
Sharon bore the burden of proving to them that *Time* had libeled
him. Moreover, in order to prove that he was libeled, Sharon
must show several things. First, he must prove that the statements
Time made about him were defamatory. Second, he must establish that they were false. And, third, since Sharon was a public
figure, he must show that *Time* had published the statements with
actual malice—that is, knew that they were false or published
them with reckless disregard as to whether they were true or false.

Sharon followed the judge's remarks intently.

"What do I mean when I say that Minister Sharon must prove
that the statements as made by *Time* were defamatory? The word
'defamatory' has a special meaning. A statement is defamatory if
it tends to injure an individual in his trade, profession or community standing; if it tends to diminish the esteemed respect, good
will or confidence in which the individual is held, or if it tends to
expose him to scorn, ridicule, shame, contempt, or embarrassment. A defamatory statement is one that excites adverse and derogatory feelings about a person or that prejudices him in the eyes
of the average members of the community who read that statement.

"In deciding whether the statements made by *Time* are defamatory, the first thing you have to decide is what message was conveyed by the words in the allegedly offending paragraph. In
making this determination, you must not consider the words or
even the sentences in isolation, but must consider them in the
context of the article as a whole.

"You must decide what meaning to give the statements on the
basis of how you conclude the publication was understood by the
average reader.

"To state that a minister of defense charged with the conduct of the war condoned a massacre of innocent civilians or that he lied to a public commission about his role in such a massacre is to defame him. If, however, you agree with the defendant that the statements have none of the defamatory meanings I earlier described, then you must find that plaintiff was not defamed by *Time*."

The judge went on to discuss the second element Minister Sharon must prove to establish his claim of libel—falsity. Sharon must prove that the statements are false, the judge said. If he is unable to prove that the statements are false, the jury must return a verdict for *Time*. "No matter how harmful and defamatory a statement may be, a plaintiff cannot prevail in a claim of libel unless he proves the statement to be false. But if the jury finds the statements *Time* made are substantially true, although inaccurate in certain relatively insignificant details, then you must find for the defendant," the judge said.

Judge Sofaer interrupted himself and remarked to the jury, "I see you are taking notes. I don't permit note-taking by jurors, and I will explain to you why. I think if you pay attention you will catch everything I say, whereas if you take notes you may miss something I am saying while you are writing. I prefer that you listen to me and then listen to the lawyers and then listen to me at the end of the case again.

"We have now come to the third element," he continued. "We have talked about the first two elements, ladies and gentlemen, that are in dispute here, meaning was it defamatory and was it false. We are assuming that the plaintiff has proved to you that the statement was defamatory and false. He must still prove a third element, and that is that the statements were published with actual malice."

The judge went on to explain that actual malice has a very special meaning in the context of the case. "It doesn't mean malice in the conventional everyday sense of ill will, hatefulness or spitefulness. Rather, to publish a statement with actual malice means to publish it with knowledge that the statement is false or with a reckless disregard as to whether or not it is false. This element puts into issue 'the state of mind' with which *Time* magazine through its employees published the statements involved. It is not enough to find that *Time* should have known that the statements were false. The jury must inquire into *Time*'s state of mind at the time of publication as evidenced by what *Time*'s employees knew and intended, and determine whether *Time* published the statements with knowledge that they were false or with a reckless disregard to whether they were false."

Judge Sofaer made it clear that if Sharon failed to prove this element, publication of the statement with actual malice, then he had not proved libel.

Following the judge's opening remarks, Milton Gould addressed the jury, summarizing the plaintiff's case. His opening statement was a classic indictment of *Time* in general and its story in particular. It combined cynicism, an incisive wit, and an unassailable analysis of what *Time* had done to Sharon. Gould stood facing the jury and talked to them about the lie *Time* had published about Sharon, "the esteemed war hero and the well known Israeli leader." They were expressionless. A window shade in the courtroom rattled continually as the first biting winter wind battered the walls.

Every now and then Gould turned, walked forward toward Judge Sofaer, or confronted his own battery of aides—three poker-faced secretaries. Then he would turn again, profile to the jury, and face the packed courtroom. To the right were the lucky ones who had found seats. They included Jews (who rushed forward to shake Sharon's hand during recess). To the left, on the front bench, sat Sharon, dark-suited, unmoving, his arms folded across his chest—a posture he was to maintain throughout the trial. Lily sat next to him, successfully concealing her inner turmoil. Behind them was the press, conspicuous for the constant movement of reporters in and out of the courtroom to file their stories.

Gould's voice cut through the silence. Here, to be sure, were the nuances. When he was indicting *Time* his voice would rise. When describing what had led Sharon to bring his suit to New York, to *Time*'s home ground, his voice deepened as he indicted the nemesis of Jewish history. Gould was playing his role to the hilt. Here was a member of that vanishing breed, the great American lawyer in the tradition of Clarence Darrow who knew the importance of unfolding a drama before a jury in a courtroom.

Sitting next to me in jeans and leather jacket was Gilad, Arik and Lily's younger son. "Listen," he said, "the old guy's good." Gilad would be going into the army soon. He used the last few weeks of his freedom to be by his father's side.

Gould's team—his young partner Richard Goldstein, and their associates Adam Gilbert, and Andrea Feller—sat at a table closer to the judge's bench. The latter two were ready to hand Gould any document he might need during his opening speech. And woe betide them if they made a mistake or took too long.

Behind them sat *Time*'s legal counsel, with their backs to the audience—Tom Barr, Saunders, and Rifkind. Two other people sat at the same table: William Smith, a senior writer for *Time* in New York, and David Halevy.

Gould had now arrived at the summary of his case. Leading into it with a flourish, he promised the jury that at the end of the trial they would learn how the "seed of the lie" had grown at *Time*. He elaborated on his theme, and his sonorous voice echoed throughout the courtroom as he said that at Sharon's September 12, 1982, meeting with Bashir Gemayel they had discussed the part the Phalangists would play in the plan to take over West Beirut.

Sharon was stunned. "Why did he say that?" he said, exploding. Sharon couldn't believe his ears. Not only was Gould's peroration completely untrue, it also went diametrically against the entire legal framework Sharon had so carefully constructed from hard, verifiable facts ever since the Kahan Commission Inquiry.

In June 1982 the Israeli government had approved a contingency plan whereby the Christian Phalangists would enter West Beirut when necessary. This basic principle had been accepted unanimously. The IDF's entry into West Beirut and the auxiliary role allotted to the Phalangists were part of just such a contingency. It had been a precautionary measure taken immediately after the murder of Bashir Gemayel on September 14. Indeed, Chief of Staff Eitan had discussed it with the Phalangists only in the early hours of September 15. Sharon could hardly have discussed with Bashir Gemayel before his death a measure taken as a precaution after his death.

In one sentence Gould had demolished the entire structure. Even if what Gould had said didn't approximate *Time*'s allegation, it was a providential chance for Barr. Going up to the bench, he moved that the case be dismissed. Judge Sofaer denied the motion, but he did permit Barr to depose Sharon again, during the trial, on the September 12 meeting.

Sharon was livid. Here he was, condemned as a liar out of the mouth of his own counsel. Although aware that Gould had only made a slip of the tongue, Sharon also recognized that it was a serious tactical error and that it could yet be the source of a lot of trouble.

During the recess following Gould's address Sharon went to a room on an upper floor of the courthouse. He was finding it difficult to calm down. He asked Dubi Weissglas to bring Milton Gould in.

Sharon was still edgy when Gould entered the room. "It's too bad you said that, Milton. Didn't I explain to you that I never discussed that with Bashir?"

Momentarily Gould couldn't understand Sharon's anger. Then too he was obviously ruffled by Sharon's public criticism—there had been quite a few people in the room. Gould's assistants were visibly taken aback as they got the full impact of Sharon's anger.

"We'll have to correct what you said," Sharon continued. "Otherwise Mr. Barr will take it up and make a big thing of it. They will cross-examine me on it, and I have nothing to say but the truth—that it never happened."

Sharon soon persuaded Gould to correct his error. After the recess and before Gould had concluded his opening speech he approached the bench and said, "About that meeting at Bikfaya. I misspoke. Sharon never said that to me. I was wrong. I saw it in one of the books I'd read about the war in Lebanon."

Then Sharon relaxed.

But Milton Gould was very angry that day. He left the courtroom right after his opening speech. He was fuming. Arnold Forster said to me, "Arik has to restrain himself. I've never seen Milton so angry. He barely stayed—he wanted to quit altogether. He almost had a heart attack. Arik has to have more faith in him. Milton knows what he's doing."

TOM BARR BEGAN HIS OPENING ADDRESS TO THE
jury that afternoon. After months of work with his powerful war
machine scavenging for the slightest bit of dirt about Sharon, he
now stood face to face with the real Arik Sharon. It wasn't the
most favorable time to give the impression of not being in the best
of health.

Lily was the first to notice it. "Tom Barr is really ill," she whispered from her place on the front bench alongside her husband.
Although only a dim wintry light filtered through the high windows of the courtroom, Barr's face was visibly pale. Every now
and then *Time*'s counsel rubbed his chest. He didn't raise his
voice, just stood there with his back to the crowd, his tilted nose
profiled when he turned to face jury or judge. The stocky frame in
pinstripe three-piece suit, the thick-rimmed glasses, all oozed self-
confidence.

Barr's files were heavy with thousands of documents, all
superbly ordered and catalogued. Everything had been kept confidential. He would make mincemeat of Sharon. That, anyway,
was the feeling conveyed by the expression of his associates in the
courtroom and the smug look on David Halevy's face.

His voice pitched low, Barr turned to face the jury.

"This is an important case for *Time*," he said. "*Time*, as you
know, is a weekly newsmagazine which is delivered throughout
most of the free world every Monday, containing a weekly analysis of news events throughout the world." He then presented the
principals involved in writing the story that was the subject of the
libel suit.

"Harry Kelly, who was the bureau chief in Jerusalem at the
time the story was written, is a veteran journalist who for more
than 30 years was at the Associated Press, the *Chicago Tribune*. He
covered the Watergate affair in Washington for the *Chicago Tribune*. He was assistant editor for the *Washington Star*. *Time* magazine at one time owned that newspaper, subsequently sold it in
1981, and he went to work for *Time*. He is now the bureau chief in
Mexico City.

"William Smith, sitting at counsel's table is another veteran of
30 years, mostly with *Time* magazine. He has been bureau chief in

Anchorage, Alaska, in Nairobi, Kenya, and in New Delhi, India. Since 1976 he has been a senior writer in the world section, and he has written 20 to 30 major stories on the Middle East, 20 in 1982 alone. Not only did he write the cover story that is at issue here but he wrote 20 other stories covering the Lebanese war, the massacre itself, the investigation of the massacre, the testimony before the Kahan Commission. So by the time he came to write this story, he knew a very great deal, and I am going to tell you in my opening, most of which will come tomorrow, a great deal more about what he knew.

"David Halevy was born in Jerusalem. He is an Israeli, and he has had fundamentally two careers: he has been a soldier and a journalist. He joined the Israeli Defense Forces in 1958 at the age of 17. As a soldier he has fought in three major wars: the Six-Day War in 1967, the War of Attrition in 1970, and the Yom Kippur War in 1973 and '74. He has fought in addition in a lot of skirmishes and battles. He has been wounded four times, was a paratrooper, a commander, intelligence officer, tank battalion commander, and is now a lieutenant colonel in the Israeli Defense Forces.

"For the last 15 years when he wasn't fighting, he was working for *Time* in the Jerusalem bureau, for the *Washington Star* briefly in Nicaragua. He reported many important stories, and many of those stories, a significant number of them, were based on important confidential sources."

To show the jury he meant business, Barr had his assistants hang in the courtroom maps of Beirut and the area of the Sabra and Shatilla refugee camps. A projector was ready at hand so Barr could at any moment demonstrate to the jury who Sharon really was. Barr's assistants projected, one after the other, blown-up slides of poisonous articles about Sharon that had been collected from newspapers around the world. Kibiye, Mitla, and Gaza were names that repeatedly cropped up. They were very strange to the jury at the beginning.

As Sharon expected, Barr immediately began building Sharon's negative image for the jury by concentrating on the negative press reports. The Israeli media's long-standing fear of Sharon had ensured that enough had accumulated over the years.

"Let's look briefly at the reputation that Ariel Sharon had long before February of 1983, when *Time* published this story," said Barr. "There actually are hundreds of articles to choose from, in the United States, in Israel, in Western Europe. I'm sure there must be articles in the Arab countries, in Russia. I haven't even attempted to look at those.

"I am not even going to suggest to you that I am presenting to you all of the newspaper articles that have been written about the plaintiff. If I did, we would be here until next summer, because there are indeed thousands of them all over the world. I am going to try and select, though, important articles from major newspapers in the United States and Israel, and major magazines, which wrote about General Sharon roughly during the period of time when he became Defense Minister in August 1981, up to the time when the *Time* article was published."

Sharon sat quietly, his arms folded across his chest, while the "selected" articles were projected on a screen for the jury.

Barr read them aloud: "This is an article published in the *Financial Times* of London on June 12, 1982. It is headed 'Bloody and Daring Warrior.' Let me just read the first paragraph—'The architect of the Israeli blitzkrieg on Lebanon, General Ariel Sharon, is either a military genius or bloodthirsty megalomaniac, depending on who you talk to in Israel. The former paratroop officer who last year fulfilled one of his dreams by becoming Israeli Defense Minister has been described as a war looking for a place to happen.'"

Gould objected, but the judge permitted Barr to continue.

Focusing on another article, Barr went on with his harangue. "I am trying to show not what is the truth. I don't have the slightest intention of trying to demonstrate to you what happened in 1953, which is what this paragraph is all about. What I am trying to show is not the truth of these things but what his reputation was at the time the *Time* article was published."

Then Barr continued reading from the article: "'Sharon first came to prominence as founder and commander of the notorious 101st Unit which specialized in cross-border retaliation raids against Palestinian guerrillas (then known as fedayeen) in the Gaza Strip and on the West Bank then under Jordanian control.

In one such raid his unit killed 69 Jordanians, half of them women and children . . .' "

Barr's third contribution came from *The Washington Post* of June 11, 1982. " 'Israel's Controversial Defense Minister: Architect of the Strike into Lebanon,' " Barr quoted. "Here you will see much of this same material appearing: 'To his admirers, Sharon is one of Israel's most brilliant and inspiring field commanders, unconventional perhaps, but brave beyond question and not afraid to put his own career on the line if it means engaging the enemy. To his critics, Sharon is a petulant, undisciplined, and insubordinate militarist whose enormous personal ambition skates at the very edge of psychosis.' " Barr continued. "And you will see here the stories repeated, as they frequently are, about Unit 101, the guerrilla attacks, the raid in Kibiye, the killing of 69 civilians, half of them women and children, and so forth."

Barr's next presentation came from *Newsweek* of June 21, 1982. He read several selected paragraphs: " 'Sharon doesn't exactly look like George Patton. At age 54, he has a mop of silver hair and the girth of a southern sheriff. But like Patton he is a relentless warrior, daring to the point of recklessness, impatient with caution and commanders other than himself.' "

Only then did Barr get to his point. "You see in the middle paragraph, in 1953 we go through the Kibiye event, the killing of the women and children, blowing up the Arabs, and so forth." Barr wasn't being very subtle. He was not only showing the jury Sharon's unsavory reputation but was trying to brainwash them into believing that Sharon was a longtime killer of innocent Palestinian women and children. In other words, it was only a single step from Kibiye to Sabra and Shatilla.

Gould's repeated objections were to no avail. Barr brusquely continued with his parade of clippings.

Despite his outward calm Sharon was very tense. He could read *Time*'s game precisely. Barr wouldn't need more words to reinforce the image of this bloodthirsty general who came seeking redress from an American court. He was reinforcing *Time*'s claim that Sharon was "libel-proof." And if this shock tactic didn't work, *Time* had an alternative line of defense: Whether *Time*'s story was or was not drawn in part from Appendix B, whether Sharon's conversation had taken place at Bikfaya or somewhere else, *Time*'s story was "substantially true." Barr spelled this out very distinctly.

"General Sharon, I think, will testify that he has seen Appendix B, and he will testify to some extent about what he recalls is in Appendix B, or rather what he says is not in Appendix B. *Time* had very good reasons for believing and continuing to believe, unless and until we see otherwise, that the material we said was in Appendix B is in Appendix B. But I tell you again we have not seen it, and I tell you also that whether or not the information, the precise information is or is not in this particular secret part of Appendix B, we believe and we think the evidence will show to you that the article is nevertheless in substance true. That is, the things that happened, that are described in the article, happened. Whether they actually happened at the precise time and the precise place and whether Appendix B contains exactly what we say it contains is neither here nor there. Substantially what we say and what the proof here will show is that the events we say happened, happened."

The press clippings had their effect. A chilly, almost frightening atmosphere pervaded the courtroom, which was full of Americans far removed from the events being related. Judge Sofaer, it is true, was aware of this and frequently warned the jury not to take the newspaper stories into account insofar as their veracity was concerned. Almost paternally, the judge explained to them, "The newspaper reporters who wrote those articles are not the people who are before this court for examination to confirm or refute what they wrote." But it was impossible not to relate to these exhibits, even though they couldn't be authenticated.

Barr even enlisted the aid of the Israeli press and read extracts from their material, which had long since successfully demonized Sharon. He read an article from *Al Hamishmar:* " 'An Image in the News. Arik, King of Israel. Arik Sharon's lies have become famous, but it seems that the forgiveness demonstrated by this country towards Moshe Dayan is being repeated for Sharon. Everybody knows who he is but they silently and forgivingly ignore his deeds. This week Menachem Begin compared Sharon's actions to those of Hannibal. But let's hope that we will not end up like the commander from Carthage.' "

Barr paused, and turned to the jury. "You will remember from

143

your history that the commander from Carthage ultimately was badly defeated by the Romans."

While Barr kindly refreshed the jury on their ancient history, he did not enlighten them on current events—that *Al Hamishmar* is a small daily, with a circulation of about five thousand. It is the mouthpiece of an equally small leftist party, Mapam, which has always violently opposed the Likud, Begin, and Sharon. Many Israelis, let alone a New York jury, have never heard of it.

Barr continued with more of the *Al Hamishmar* special: " 'Sharon has always been different and his differences have always been paid for with many victims and much pain.' "

One item that Barr quoted was headlined "Revenge as Principle: That generation of fighters has forgotten Arik's part in the horrible military action in Kibiye in 1953. Sharon was authorized to perform a partial bombing of houses, but the operation turned into a destruction of many houses and a killing of women, children, and the elderly." Aside from branding Sharon as a killer, Barr also wanted to indicate to the jury that "the state of mind" of *Time*'s writers also was affected by articles such as these, which they read in Jerusalem and in New York.

Despite his signs of illness, Barr overlooked nothing. He made his opening address with all the ferocity of a religious zealot calling for a holy war. His presence in court also was an indication of the importance he attached to this case; even though ill, he was prepared to sacrifice himself. His appearance also indicated the importance *Time* attached to the case. *Time* also was prepared to sacrifice him. His long opening went into a second day in court.

Barr's armory was limitless. Hundreds of documents had been collected from the media, which at that stage were all mainly predisposed against Sharon and in favor of *Time*.

Leaving nothing unsaid, Barr drew a lurid picture of Sharon's partners in the war in Lebanon. "Pierre Gemayel died about a month ago," he said. "He was the founder of the Phalange in the 1930s. He founded it after returning from the Berlin Olympics. He liked what he saw in Germany. He liked the Nazis and the Fascists in Germany and Italy and the Phalange in Spain, and this organization, you will hear from the evidence, was essentially a right-wing or perhaps even a fascist organization right from the beginning. Bashir Gemayel was one of his sons. He was elected president of the state of Lebanon in the middle of August 1982, and was assassinated by being blown to bits in a house in September 1982.

"Amin Gemayel was his brother, still is his brother. He is now the president of the state of Lebanon. Fadi Frem was the head of the national staff of the Phalange and he was married to the granddaughter [sic] of Pierre Gemayel.

"Eli Hobeika was the head of a very special group of Phalange. He had a reputation throughout the Middle East as a killer, a murderer, a person who had participated in a number of massacres with this special unit of his troops. This was well known. Everybody in the Middle East knew it. And Hobeika was the man, and that special unit was the group, that was sent into those camps on the night of the 16th. Mr. Gould, in his opening, suggested that the Phalange were sort of gentlemanly soldiers, doctors, lawyers who picked up the sword when it was necessary. Our evidence will suggest something quite different. Our evidence will suggest that the Phalange were really a gang, a gang of murderers, rapists, who destroyed as a way of life, who were well known to destroy as a way of life, who massacred civilian populations almost routinely.

"It was common. It was repeated. It was well known. Revenge, blood for blood, is as common to this group, as ordinary and as expected as that the sun will rise.

"Bashir Gemayel himself, with whom Mr. Gould told you the plaintiff met on the 12th of September to plan the entry into West Beirut to take care of the Palestinians, Bashir himself reputedly participated in a number of these massacres, not only of the Phalangist—I am sorry, not only among the Palestinians but also of his rivals among the Christians."

Except for one tiny slip showing he'd learned by rote and not by meaning, Barr had prepared his lecture well. He brought blood into the courtroom. Revenge and blood—this mixture, repeated by Barr and later by *Time* personnel in the courtroom, was used to project the idea that *Time*'s paragraph was written innocently and factually.

But violent emotions weren't restricted to history lessons. There was hatred in that courtroom, hatred toward Sharon on the part of the *Time* people.

145

MILTON GOULD WASN'T AT ALL PLEASED TO HEAR
next day of Sharon's determination to divert his testimony to the
Kibiye affair. He preferred their original plan of action, in which
Gould by his own questioning guided Sharon in telling the story
of his life, and emphasized the crucial role he had played in Israel
in the war against Arab terrorism, as well as in major campaigns.
It was to be a short history of Israel, taken chronologically, from
the War of Independence to Lebanon and included specifics and
available published documentation.

"What's actually going on here?" Sharon inquired coldly. "As I
said, *Time* wants to present me as bloodthirsty, as though my entire army career was stained with the blood of innocent victims,
starting from Kibiye and right up to Sabra and Shatilla." He insisted on his plan.

Gould reluctantly explained to Sharon that Tom Barr was entitled to ask for any note or document that Sharon might hold in
his hands while on the stand, so he advised Sharon to take along
only notes in his own handwriting and official military publica-
tions.

"I'll be happy to hand them over to Barr," Sharon said. In fact,
he had asked his lawyers to make copies of parts of the publica-
tions, specifically those relating to the growth of Palestinian terrorism and the number of victims terrorism had claimed in Israel
and worldwide. "Let's use *Time*'s own projector and screen,"
Sharon suggested.

Sharon was looking forward to telling the real story of the raid
at Kibiye. It was almost noon on Thursday, November 15, just
before the court recessed for the weekend, when Gould began his
examination. "Were there occasions during your life when you
were accused of killing Palestinian or Arab civilians?" he asked.

Sharon: "I heard—yesterday I heard the story of Kibiye something like ten times here."

Q: "Story of what?"

A: "Of Kibiye."

Q: "Spell it, sir. In English how would you spell it? How is K y
b i a, phonetic? Let's try that."

A: "I know it is very hard. We are speaking about foreign
names and a foreign language—Kibiye."

Q: "We are satisfied. Kibiye is the name of a place which figures, as I understand it, in accusation against you for murdering
civilians, right? You tell us what happened at Kibiye. What is
Kibiye all about?"

In a calm, quiet voice Sharon went back more than thirty
years. "Kibiye is about 20 miles northwest of Jerusalem and
about a mile and a half, maybe, from Israel's 1967 borders. It is a
village, a few miles away from a small Israeli town called Yahud.
Between the 10th and the 15th of October of '53, Arab terrorists
who came from Kibiye went into this small town of Yahud and
threw hand grenades into the bedroom of an ordinary civilian
family. It was a deliberate attack. A mother and two small children were killed. One of them was a girl. Her name was Shoshana."

The court was silent as Sharon continued. "I would like to emphasize now, just to give you the atmosphere in Israel of those
years in the '50s. In March, 1954, at a place called Scorpion Pass,
on the road from Be'er Sheva, twelve people, women, children,
were killed, massacred. Arab terrorists broke into their bus and
killed them.

"In April 1954, near Tel Aviv—maybe about ten minutes'
drive from Tel Aviv—at a place called Shafrir, eight boys, maybe
around ten years old, were praying. Hand grenades were thrown
into their room. They were saying their evening prayers. Four
were killed, three wounded.

"In April 1955, in a village called Patish, in the Negev, in the
southern part of the country, close to the Gaza district, a wedding
was being held. Hand grenades were thrown into the group of
celebrating people. A 22-year-old girl was killed.

"In October 1956, at a place called Kadima—it's not far from
the place where I was born—two laborers working in an orange
grove were killed and their ears were cut off and taken.

"In 1955, in order to travel from a place called Gedera, about
20 miles from Tel Aviv, the traffic was organized in convoys. I was
stationed there then. I was commander of the Israeli paratroopers.
I remember this from my own experience, that you had to go
there in convoys. There were nights when you couldn't go to
Jerusalem, the capital of Israel, which is 40 miles from Tel Aviv."

Having drawn the background, Sharon now moved on to the

main issue. "Now I would like to come to Kibiye. I was then commander of the 101st Unit, a special unit formed to fight terrorists. One of the purposes of forming this unit was that terrorists in those days, like later in Lebanon, used to find shelter among the civilian population. The special 101st Unit was created in order to go and hit terrorist targets, in order not to harm the rest of the population.

"I was ordered to carry out a raid on Kibiye where we knew, first from tracks that led us to the border, in the direction of this place, and from other intelligence sources, that those terrorists came from Kibiye.

"Kibiye, a village on a hill, held several dozen, maybe 30 or 40 or 50 armed men. They were part of what used to be called the Jordanian Home Guard. I myself commanded this operation. About 70 of my people participated in this operation in Kibiye itself. There were three roadblocks. We had a small decoy operation because the Jordanians used to protect the terrorists. They used to come out and act against our forces. Altogether, we were about 100 soldiers."

Standing before the jury, Sharon was clearly trying to remember every detail.

"I led those forces. The action took place at night. We came into this place. We were armed with light weapons. We had one section of two mortars. We intended to surprise them. It was a very hard operation; I can tell you this from my own experience. First we broke into and captured the defensive positions that were protected with thick, high barbed-wire fences and trenches. I believe about eight people were killed in the fighting in those trenches. They were all armed men.

"Another four were killed when a Jordanian reinforcement unit managed to get into the village in the middle of the operation. We went into Kibiye. It was at night. And we found the place empty. We didn't hear anything; we didn't see anything, except in two places. In one place we found a boy, a child. So we took him to a safe place. In another place, after we had fused the explosives, I was standing there with the officer who had placed the fuses. They were already lit, and he moved in. He found a girl, maybe between eight and ten years old. We took her out."

Sharon made his first point by admitting openly, "We checked as much as we could have checked. If you ask me if we could check every hole, every cave, every cellar, my answer will be 'no.' It was impossible. It was a war. We were in an area occupied by the Jordanian forces since 1948. We made every effort. I don't know if anybody else would have done it.

"I remember this officer taking this girl out. Believe me, we took all possible precautions. We endangered ourselves by staying several hours. After blowing up the houses we left. When I came back, I was met at the border by a representative of the central command. I reported to him that we accomplished this mission and that I myself saw between 10 and 12 enemy casualties.

"Only later did I hear on the Jordanian radio that they were talking about 69 people killed. We did not see them."

Then Sharon took a printed page out of his pocket. "I now want to read the story from *Time* magazine about the night of Kibiye."

Gould: "You mean it was reported in *Time* magazine? When?"

Sharon: "It was reported in *Time* magazine on October 26, 1953."

Time's article, under the headline "Massacre at Kibya," gave a different description of the raid:

> . . . At 9:30 one night, most of the people were just going to bed in the Jordanian village of Kibya, 20 miles northwest of Jerusalem and a mile and a half beyond the Israeli frontier. A light still burned in the village coffee house, where a few villagers were preparing to depart; on this quiet night as usual, everyone put his trust in the U.N. "truce" and 30 skimpily armed Jordanian national guardsmen. Suddenly, Israeli artillery, previously zeroed into the target, opened up, and a 600-man battalion of uniformed Israeli soldiers swept across the border to encircle the village. For the next 2½ hours the town shuddered under shell bursts and small-arms fire; villagers, screaming and milling, rushed out to the surrounding fields and olive groves. Then the guardsmen's ammo (25 rounds per man) gave out, and the Israelis moved into Kibya with rifles and Sten guns. They shot every man, woman and child they could find, then turned their fire on the cattle. After that, they dynamited 42 houses, a school and a mosque. The cries of the

149

dying could be heard amid the explosions. The villagers huddled in the grass could see Israeli soldiers slouching in the doorways of their homes, smoking and joking, their young faces illuminated by the flames. By 3 A.M., the Israelis' work was done, and they leisurely withdrew. . . .

Judge Sofaer interrupted. "I think the discussion about Kibiye is appropriate in light of the anticipated evidence through newspaper articles about it, and I think since we are talking about newspaper articles a *Time* article is not inappropriate."

Gould: "It says here in this paper, the *Time* magazine, that: 'Israeli artillery . . . zeroed on to this target Kibiye and a 600-man battalion of uniformed Israeli regulars swept across the border to encircle the village.' Was there any artillery zeroed on the village?"

Sharon: "Never."

Gould: "Were there 600 Israeli regulars?"

Sharon: "No."

Judge Sofaer was now beginning to get annoyed and told Sharon that he was going too far in the use of the Kibiye story.

Gould: "It says here that 'for the next two and half hours the town shuddered under shell bursts.' Were there any shell bursts?"

Sharon: "No."

A harsh discussion ensued between the judge and Gould, which almost prevented Sharon from getting in his well prepared punch line. He raised his voice as he turned to the jury: "I want to say a sentence about what could have happened. If I could have sued *Time* magazine then, believe me, I would not have been here today."

EVEN BEFORE THE START OF HIS CROSS-EXAMINA-
tion Barr had tried to upset Sharon's credibility with the jury.
The press cuttings *Time*'s lawyers had assembled, some in English
and others translated from Hebrew into English, shown on a
screen in the court, had said in effect—in one case in so many
words—"Sharon Lied to Ben-Gurion." Barr's purpose was clear.
By using a press report accusing Sharon of lying to David Ben-
Gurion, Israel's first prime minister and defense minister, Barr
was insinuating that Sharon was a liar, period. Barr also wanted
to prove that this was the *Time* correspondents' "state of mind"
while writing the paragraph about Sharon. Having seen the accusation leveled at Sharon repeatedly in the press, they, and obviously Dudu Halevy, tended to disbelieve anything Sharon said.

The reports had been written by Sharon's political adversaries—people who for the most part had never had the privilege
of talking to Ben-Gurion. Sharon, however, had had close contact
with the "old man" from 1953 till Ben-Gurion's death in 1973.

It was Sharon himself who often frankly told the press, Knesset
members, and ministers in the government about his sole brush
with Ben-Gurion, something for which the great Israeli leader
had long since forgiven him. It had happened in 1955 while
Sharon was commander of the paratroopers. Sharon's best
fighter, Lieutenant Meir Harzion, had asked to be released from
the army after his seventeen-year-old sister, Shoshana, had been
cruelly murdered by Bedouins in the Judean Desert, in Jordanian
territory, while hiking with her boyfriend, who had also been
killed. Harzion got back the dismembered body of his sister in a
sack from the Jordanian authorities. Harzion and some of his
friends then went into the Judean Desert and killed the five Bedouins who had murdered the two youngsters.

Lieutenant Colonel Sharon reported this to Prime Minister and
Defense Minister Ben-Gurion. However, he left out one detail in
his report, namely that Chief of Staff Moshe Dayan had also had
knowledge of the incident. Sharon had learned too late that Meir
Harzion was already on his way to the Judean Desert to avenge
his sister's murder, and when he reported this to Dayan, the chief
of staff had told him, "Do everything to stop them. But if they

have crossed the border, do everything to bring them back safe!"

Sharon greatly respected Dayan and had wanted to protect him from the "old man's" anger over Harzion's private punitive raid. Later Sharon felt that he had been wrong in giving Ben-Gurion an incomplete report. So when he had next met Ben-Gurion he made a point of giving him a full and detailed account. Ben-Gurion's immediate reaction was one of great anger toward both Sharon and Dayan. Later, however, particularly because of his frankness over this affair, Sharon's relationship with Ben-Gurion grew even closer. Many years afterward, when Sharon had become a general, he received the warmest of congratulations from Ben-Gurion. In spite of this, in the courtroom in New York, Barr quoted a headline from the politicized Israeli media: " 'Have you stopped lying?' asked Ben-Gurion of Sharon?"

The days during which Sharon was questioned in the courtroom in New York, and especially when he was under cross-examination by Tom Barr, were grueling for him. Barr, trying to shake Sharon's credibility, relied on things Sharon had said or that had been said about him throughout the stormy years, on many occasions. However, Barr did not succeed, because in one respect the ordeal was easy for Sharon. He did not have to alter his words or his evidence. For better or worse, Sharon had stuck to the facts throughout the years—and someone who does not alter facts cannot be caught lying.

In his cross-examination Barr used specially prepared colored maps of Beirut and the Palestinian camps. Directing one to be displayed, he asked Sharon to tell the court about his discussion with Chief of Staff Lieutenant General Rafael Eitan at the forward command post overlooking West Beirut on the morning of September 15, 1982. Barr turned from the map to Sharon. "The forward command post Mr. Gold will point out to you, General, that is the forward command post being referred to, isn't it?"

Barr and Sharon were arguing about the Phalangists' entry into Sabra and Shatilla, but Gold wasn't keeping pace with them. He couldn't find his way around the map. Sharon tried to help from the witness stand, but even that didn't work, so the judge gave him permission to step down.

It was odd. Here were Barr's carefully prepared maps, and his team didn't know how to read them. So Sharon took over. The map and the scene came to life.

"In our area the sea—this will make it easier because I noticed Mr. Gold had that problem before—the sea is always in the west. And north is up there, always up. In our area it's easier—we don't have seas on both sides; we have the sea only on one side, and that is always in the west. So that might be easier to follow." Sharon spoke with the understanding and patience of a good teacher.

"That is south. That is north, south, west and east. This point here is southwest." Sharon pointed at the southwest part of the Sabra and Shatilla camps.

Sharon was in no hurry to return to his seat. He had sensed Barr's discomfort and continued leisurely and authoritatively using the map to elucidate the situation in West Beirut in those fateful days of Sabra and Shatilla. An American newspaperman described Sharon's performance best: "When Sharon stood next to the map and started his explanations, I felt for a moment as though I were participating in a meeting of the General Staff in which Sharon explains how best to attack Beirut."

The jury, the judge, the entire press corps could now see for themselves what at least some of them must certainly at times have tried to imagine: the image of Sharon as a military commander and his formidable record of combat experience. It was like a legend come to life: a man who knew precisely what he was talking about and who said it succinctly and authoritatively. When it came to maps and map reading, Barr simply didn't know or understand, or perhaps wasn't prepared to understand, his opponent. Sharon and maps are an old love. When he sees a map it comes alive to him—the mountains, the rivers, and the valleys all spring into relief. A map to Sharon is like a musical score to the conductor of an orchestra. It's also another weapon in his hands.

The courtroom became completely silent the moment Sharon faced the map of Beirut. Everyone's gaze was fixed on him and on the map, as though the two had fused into a single unit.

After establishing his authority as the reader *par excellence* of *Time*'s maps, Sharon returned to the witness box, holding the Kahan Report in its original Hebrew version in his hands. There-

153

after, whenever Barr asked him a question based on the English translation, Sharon referred to his copy, assisted when necessary by his counsel Dubi Weissglas.

In response to Barr's questions Sharon testified that on September 15 he was told by the chief of staff in the forward command post in Beirut that he had instructed the Phalangists to enter the camps. "I approved his decision," Sharon acknowledged. "And if the chief of staff had come to me earlier I would have approved his decision, because I think that was the right decision to be taken."

Barr was increasingly impatient with Sharon's leafing again and again through the Kahan Report. Sharon remained adamant. "I've already found differences between the Hebrew and English versions. And because the matter is so important for me, so important for the State of Israel, so important for the moral values of all of us, because of all this I think it is important, Mr. Barr, that I am able to see the Hebrew version." When Sharon said "Mr. Barr," he enunciated the words with care. "Mr. Barr" became a sort of battle cry among us. Gilad was the best at imitating his father roaring "Mr. Baarrrrr"—the *r* reverberating through the courtroom.

Barr insistently asked why Sharon had sent in only 150 fighters to deal with the 2000 terrorists reportedly in the buildings of Sabra and Shatilla.

"We did not instruct the Lebanese forces how many people to send there," Sharon explained. "I learned later that what they could have sent there was about 150 people. A war was going on. Attention to the war was focused on this corner because it produced tragic, regrettable events which all of us were very sorry about. But divisions participated in this battle. It had to be done very fast. Our forces were entering Beirut from other directions."

Sharon described West Beirut as a town of more than 24,000 buildings. It's an Oriental town. Some quarters are modern and some are very old. The town is built on two levels, surface level and underground, where there are 600,000 residents. The Israeli operation was aimed at capturing key points. There was no chance or even possibility of encircling every building or street or quarter. But to take control of main road junctions, as in any

154

town, "like here in New York," Sharon said, "it's simpler, because of the avenues and the streets. There in West Beirut it's entirely different.

"The second part of the operation was to seek out and find terrorists—2000 terrorists who took shelter in the buildings and used the civilian population as hostages. They did this in all the wars, in Tyre, in Sidon. Before coming to West Beirut they used to force the civilians, the women and children, to stay at the windows.

"It was a different kind of war," Sharon continued, "not a mobile war where tanks are moving in the open. Not a war in trenches. It was a search for PLO terrorists who were hiding among the civilian population."

Barr asked whether there were hundreds of casualties in Sabra and Shatilla.

"I think it's very important to know the truth. We came here for the truth," Sharon began. There were several reports, he said—early reports by Israeli sources, saying 700 to 800 people had been killed. Then came a joint report by the Lebanese attorney general and the International Red Cross, and they spoke of about 460 killed.

"Every life is human life," Sharon said, "so numbers don't make any difference here. But I think it's important to know that among those 460 killed there were 35 women and children, half of them Lebanese, half of them Palestinians, more or less. Maybe more Lebanese than Palestinians. The rest of the casualties, males, 425, were divided. There were about 300 Palestinians, about 100 Lebanese. And the remainder were from other countries, Iranians and Syrians and so on. In point of fact, the terrorists who came there and stayed weren't only Palestinians but also volunteers who came from all around the world to help the PLO terrorists."

At recess that day, and later, Arik presided in a back room at the courthouse, listening to comments from his attorneys and friends. He listened especially closely on this occasion to comments from his wife, Lily, and from Gilad, his son. His other son, Omri, remained in Israel. While still in New York they heard that Omri had joined the Israeli units in Lebanon. Lily couldn't hide her concern. Arik didn't say a word.

Sometimes, when Arik saw the anxiety of his friends during his long cross-examination, he would say, "Don't worry so. Laugh, just laugh. Take it easy. I've seen more serious things in my life." Lily smiled obediently every time, but inside she was tight with anxiety. Sharon didn't need to say a word—she was very conscious of her husband's agony during this war in New York.

The attorneys and Genger often concentrated on the English phrases Sharon had used. He would mentally translate from Hebrew to English, and the result wasn't always clear to the jury, so they'd explain and rephrase. Sharon would laugh. "In the papers they say I'm a controversial figure and intransigent." He enjoyed rolling out those words. "Is that good or bad? Are those words positive or negative?" was a frequent question. Sharon would carefully note any corrections he had to make, repeating the words and phrases, sometimes even writing them down. Once, during such a discussion of language, he told us about the first stage fright he remembered from his childhood.

"At the end of the first grade we were rehearsing for the annual school play at our village, Kfar Malal. I got the part of chalk, and I had only one line. The day of the play arrived. The hall was full of teachers and parents, including mine." As Sharon continued telling his story in the back room of the New York courthouse he seemed to blush, very much as he'd undoubtedly done fifty years earlier at the village school in Kfar Malal. "I found myself standing on the stage with a piece of chalk in my hand, and I was paralyzed. I looked at the chalk, but I'd forgotten my line. I didn't say a single thing."

When the cross-examination resumed, Barr tried again to make Sharon stumble. "General Sharon, you have seen the transcript of the minutes that were taken in the Karantina meeting?"

Sharon, rather puzzled: "I am sorry. Can you raise your voice, please?"

Barr enunciated slowly and clearly. "Have you seen the minutes or transcript of the Karantina meeting?"

Sharon: "Yes."

Barr, still enunciating carefully: "Can you make that available to us so we can read it?"

Sharon, unhelpfully: "No."

Barr, closing in: "There were notes taken at that meeting also, weren't there? There were notes of the meeting taken at Bikfaya?"

Sharon, aloofly, teasingly: "There is something wrong with your voice, Mr. Barr."

Judge Sofaer, trying to accommodate: "There is an echo. Turn it down, please."

Barr, very slowly and clearly: "There were notes taken at the meeting of Bikfaya?"

Sharon, very unhelpful: "Notes?"

Barr tries for the third time: "There were notes, a transcript of the meeting at Bikfaya?"

"Yes," Sharon says flatly.

Barr gets excited. "Have you seen those notes?"

"Yes."

This is the moment of truth, thinks Barr. "Can you make those notes available to us?"

Sharon doesn't show it, but he's sighing. "No."

Barr: "You described, General, your entire conversation with the Gemayels at Bikfaya yesterday, did you not?"

Sharon watches him. "Yes, I did."

Barr: "How many copies of these minutes or transcripts were made, to your knowledge?"

"I don't know," Sharon says. Observing them I wondered whether *Time*'s counsel thought that he was questioning a records clerk.

Barr tries to help him. "More than one?"

"I believe more than one, but I don't know how many."

Barr: "Did you get a copy?"

Sharon, wearily: "I got a copy when I was Minister of Defense. I was one of the people who got those copies."

Barr: "And there were other people in positions of responsibility within the Israeli government who got copies at the same time also, correct?"

Sharon was still in his stride. "A small number."

Barr: "When was the last time you saw the minutes?"

Sharon: "Months and months ago."

Barr had a look of triumph about him. Here was the ditch he'd so carefully prepared. "You described yesterday to us the conver-

157

sation that you say took place between you and Pierre and Amin Gemayel. What I want to ask you is, taking, assuming, that conversation, you described that conversation accurately—I am assuming that for this question—" Sharon's expression was tight, but he let Barr continue despite the gratuitous insult "—is there anything in that conversation that in your judgment should have led the Israeli government to withhold that document, those minutes from the lawyers in this case and from the court? Is there any subject among the ones that you described to us?"

Sharon answered with ease. "That is not for me to decide. Israel is a democracy, a state of law. There is a law. There are regulations. I tried very hard to make these papers, these documents, available. I tried, and you know I did."

Barr's another would-be trap concerned the Kahan Commission Report. Sharon, unafraid, advanced into it.

Milton Gould had explained to Sharon that *Time*'s lawyers would do everything to take advantage of Sharon's having attacked the report of the Kahan Commission, notwithstanding the fact it was the official report of a commission comprising three eminent public figures, two of them Israeli Supreme Court judges. *Time* would likely use this to show that Sharon's brazenness was simply par for the course, the implication being that if Sharon had objected to the august Kahan Commission's findings, it wasn't surprising that he was out to get *Time* on the same issue.

Sharon had soothed Gould's anxiety. It was all a matter of logic. "I certainly accept all the facts set out in the commission's report. But there is no way I can accept its conclusions."

This distinctive reasoning became one of the pivotal issues in the trial. *Time*'s lawyers made much of the fact that all their clients had done was to write about Sharon precisely what had been written about him in the Kahan Report. They hammered this line so hard that eventually it seemed as though the Kahan Commission was established for the sole purpose of allowing *Time* to write its story.

Time actually agreed with Sharon that the conclusions of the report did not jibe with its description of the facts. But *Time* went one better than the commission. It did not agree with Sharon's having been found indirectly responsible for Sabra and Shatilla.

Had *Time*'s reasoning been applied, he would have been found directly responsible.

It was an astonishing abuse of an authoritative body established by a sovereign country. Unlike Halevy, Sharon defended both his own honor and that of his country. "I will not let you turn this suit into a new version of the Kahan Commission," he said angrily. "I have never agreed with the conclusions of the Kahan Commission. But I have respected them, and the Commission, as is only proper in a democratic country run by the rule of law. I left the Defense Ministry. I paid the price."

Sharon ordinarily doesn't like making personal declarations of this kind in public. His lawyers had to work long and hard to make him say publicly in court what he had said to them in private consultation—"Yes, I was punished for that and I have paid the price."

Barr had made an obvious and telling attempt to twist the Kahan Report to suit his own purposes. But Sharon left his declaration of honor in his interviews and in the trial records: "I did not come to sue *Time* magazine in New York in order to have a second Kahan Commission," he thundered. "This is not a second Kahan Commission."

Judge Sofaer made an effective observation on the same point. "This lawsuit is not over the Commission's findings. If *Time* magazine had published a statement that the Commission was correct in blaming General Sharon to the extent they blamed him, that would have been totally protected, and we would not have been here today.

"*Time* will have to show something in addition to this evidence in the Commission report, something that indicates an action or a discussion about revenge with the people who then went into the camps right after the discussion, either that kind of discussion or something equivalent to that kind of discussion."

CHAPTER
TWENTY-TWO

WHENEVER SHARON HAD A MINUTE TO SPARE IN
New York—and there weren't many minutes he could spare during the trial—he never forgot that he was minister of industry and
trade for the State of Israel—a senior minister in the economic
cabinet. And that the most serious economic campaign in Israel's
history was under way. The struggle was against a soaring inflation rate and dwindling foreign currency reserves, both followed
by the specter of widespread unemployment.

The government had decided on a price freeze and had
charged the Ministry of Industry and Trade with implementing
it. There were also other problems, new problems, every day. So
Sharon was in daily contact with his ministry officials. Between
5:00 and 8:00 A.M. in New York there would be a phone call from
Jerusalem, then at midday or early afternoon, for a general report
and to get guidelines and instructions. If he had forgotten anything, Sharon would call back around midnight—morning in
Jerusalem. He would take care of this after nightly discussions
with his lawyers analyzing the daily court sessions and preparing
for cross-examination of witnesses the next day.

He would pull out one of his small notebooks and diligently jot
down comments on testimony already heard and add suggestions
for the next session. He noted each point and tried to understand
every detail. This was no helplessly drifting client, his lawyers discovered.

His nightly average of sleep was about two to three hours—
slightly more than he had allowed himself in Lebanon; a vast
amount compared with what he had permitted himself during
the Yom Kippur War. Both his physical and mental capabilities
never ceased to amaze his New York attorneys. They now began
to understand the legend. Lily was worried because he was eating
too much, as he always did when under intense strain. He went
through innumerable cans of corned beef she bought at the supermarket, and finished off the cheeses and yogurt that were always in the small refrigerator. Then there were the ubiquitous
salty crackers. Next to mustard, salt is Sharon's favorite condiment. Add some hot peppers and you have a Sharon-style gourmet meal. "I'll lose weight after the trial," he promised Lily.

Still more activity was pushed into his already overloaded schedule. Sharon utilized his enforced stay in New York to meet with potential American investors. These tycoons, mostly Jews, were people Sharon had met at the hotel or during lunch recesses. It was an opportunity he used to the maximum. He explained Israel's urgent need for investment in export industries, and, anticipating the question, would promise to defend them against Israel's notorious bureaucracy, which had deterred so many investors in the past. On Saturday nights Sharon minded the store.

One Saturday he hosted a delegation of Israeli economic representatives serving in the United States, and others who were on short-term visits here. On another, Sharon's guest was an Israeli who had developed a vast business empire in the United States and Panama. He wanted to return to Israel and was looking for investment opportunities there. "All you have to do is come over," said Sharon encouragingly. "There is plenty to invest in." He explained at length what his ministry was doing to attract industrial capital investment to Israel.

On yet another Saturday Sharon called off a meeting with Gould. He felt it was more important to meet an obligation directly benefiting Israel. Industrial tycoon Armand Hammer was in Los Angeles. Sharon wanted to persuade him to buy a company in Israel Chemicals. Sharon had government approval for the sale of state-owned corporations. "Surprisingly enough, it's a socialist government that accepted this idea. It was rejected by the Likud government, which was supposed to be the standard bearer of private enterprise." The irony appealed to Sharon.

Notwithstanding his efforts, Sharon's opponents in Israel exploited to the hilt the protracted trial in New York. Critical statements and press comment intensified daily. How could he stay in New York so long at a time of economic crisis at home?

"When are you returning to Israel?" was a constant question flung at him by reporters.

"My schedule will be determined by the court," he would reply. Sharon was well aware that *Time* would prefer to have him back in Israel. "When I am in Israel," he commented acidly, "quite a lot of people want me abroad so I can't influence the government. When I'm in New York, they suddenly pine for me."

Blood Libel

His opponents tried another and more damaging line of attack—the legal expenses. The Israeli press ran wild. Amounts ranging from fifty thousand dollars to a quarter of a million were floated as representing the costs already expended on his stay in New York. To add to the implied squandering of funds, news reports would give nitpicking details such as the presence of his bodyguards. With Israel in the midst of an economic crisis, these flights of fancy added fuel to the fire.

Sharon's initial decision to ignore the accusations was a mistake. Answering them out loud right from the beginning would have blocked the damaging speculation. The trial costs weren't being borne by the government. Sharon himself was responsible for underwriting the legal expenses. As for the rest, he would return every cent Israel's treasury had spent on the matter so far— which, in fact, is what he did. The Fund for Financing Legal Expenses, established by the Law Office, was covering the cost of Sharon's stay.

WHEN THE TRIAL RESUMED AFTER THE THANKS-
giving recess, *Time* produced a new navigational hazard called
etzlenu—"among us."

Some *Time* employees said their paragraph was inspired by
Sharon's own words during his opening statement to the Kahan
Inquiry Commission in Jerusalem. In the courtroom several days
earlier, Sharon had smiled sardonically as Barr laid the foundation for his grotesque new story.

Barr spoke quietly as he faced the jury. He was quoting, he
said, from Sharon's testimony before the Kahan Commission in
Jerusalem. "This is translated from Hebrew to English by General Sharon himself. It was done at his deposition. The first part
was a question from one of the members of the Commission, Justice Barak, and the question is:

> This means that a feeling of revenge as a result of the death of
> Bashir was not a relevant consideration?

> Sharon: I would like to say a word with the permission of the
> Commission's members on the subject of revenge as I know it
> among the Arabs. Revenge as accepted among the Arabs does not
> include children, women and old people. There are certainly Arab-
> ists who are greater experts than I am. Yes. I say that in the light of
> my knowledge. In light of my experience, revenge exists, without
> doubt. . . . Amin himself at the funeral, to the best of my recollec-
> tion, at the funeral on the 15th of the month, used the word "re-
> venge." The word "revenge" also appeared, I would say, in
> discussions among ourselves [in our place].

Here Barr stopped to emphasize *Time*'s logic. "That reflects
some difficulty in translating the exact meaning of the word from
Hebrew to English, and we will have some testimony on that in
due course. But this is General Sharon's own translation."

The word at issue was the Hebrew *etzlenu*, which is understood
perfectly by anyone having only a reasonable command of Hebrew. To be sure, it does not lend itself to precise English translation, but until *Time*'s contortions a free translation of "among us"
or "among ourselves"—in the context of the report, meaning
"among the Israelis"—has always been perfectly acceptable and

not misunderstood. The members of the Kahan Commission themselves certainly didn't question it.

And now Barr tossed a totally different meaning at the jury. Those six excellent people, who had already been faced with so much that was unfamiliar, were now presented with a linguistic twist. Barr hinted to the jury that when Sharon said *etzlenu* in Hebrew, he meant that revenge was discussed between him and the Phalangists, or, at least, between the Israelis and the Lebanese. This, Barr suggested, was how the *Time* people had understood the word, so their paragraph was perfectly innocuous. Barr's air of injured innocence was perfect.

Of course, what *Time*'s counsel failed to point out to the jury was that Sharon had testified to the commission in open court a month before Halevy's Worldwide Memo scoop. How month-old news became a scoop once and then again when it already was three months old is best left to *Time* to explain.

Sharon was irritated by this sudden digression and not a little worried. He had noticed that Judge Sofaer too had taken note of *Time*'s reading of the Hebrew word *etzlenu*. So Sharon and his lawyers went about finding a Hebrew linguist who could instruct the jury precisely in the meaning of *etzlenu* in the context in which he had used it. He didn't rest until an authorized Hebrew linguist was found, someone who was both acceptable to the court and who knew enough English to explain the whole thing to the jury.

"Always new surprises," Sharon said, leaning back in his chair at the head of the table in the small back room after the court session. "Sometimes it reminds me of the stories of the Eastern European Jews. About a Jew walking in a dense forest who's confronted by a bandit on horseback. The Jew overpowers the bandit and thinks he's done with it. Then a wild beast appears. He overpowers it too—and suddenly a snake appears. . . ."

THURSDAY, NOVEMBER 29, 1984—A WINTRY DAY IN
New York and a crucial day in court. At long last, a major breakthrough occurred in Sharon's libel suit against *Time*. After many
hours in the witness box, where he squirmed and twisted to make
his story stand up, Dudu Halevy finally was forced, word by
painful word, to admit that he'd lied.

Under steady questioning by Gould, Halevy was still hanging
onto the story of his sources, those infallible sources that had
made him infallible too. But now he broke. The attentive jury
and the packed courtroom heard that *Time*'s infamous paragraph
didn't have any foundation at all. Halevy had never seen the Secret Appendix. He had never been told the story that he told
Time. His brilliant journalistic achievement was based on his personal evaluation, his personal analysis, his personal disregard for
truth, and his personal conclusions that Sharon had discussed revenge with the Phalangists in Bikfaya.

The courtroom buzzed as it absorbed the full significance of
Halevy's reluctant admission. *Time*'s representatives and attorneys looked bleak. The gargantuan efforts of the great *Time* machine over the past six months crumbled as surely as the walls of
Jericho.

Sharon sat listening in the front row, quietly making notes,
quietly watching and listening as the fraud was exposed. At
last—vindication.

Gould had been prodding steadily at Halevy. Layer by layer,
he had stripped away the lies. How did the action go, Gould demanded to know. He wanted it step by step. Laboriously, the
story emerged.

Back in Jerusalem, Halevy said, Kelly had asked him what precisely was in Appendix B. Kelly was already writing Take 9 of the
cover story. Now Halevy had to come up with the goods. "I tried
to call General Number 2. I said to Mr. Kelly, I think Appendix B
has some relationship or makes some mention of the condolence
call of the meeting at Bikfaya. You remember my memo from December 6?"

Gould: "Why did you say to him that any reference to the—
that Appendix B contained any reference to Bikfaya?"

Halevy: "The main reason for that is, of course, when you read the report it is very clear that the Commission is hiding between the lines a lot of information which is related to meetings between Minister Sharon and the commanders of the Phalangist leadership, the political leadership of the Phalangists. This is one reason. I think it is very clear from the report.

"Second reason is that at the time, I think Kelly and I talked about it, that we know that all the notetakers and the people who participated in those meetings were called to testify before the Kahan Commission. The participants of the meetings at the advance command post, at the Karantina and at Bikfaya were called to testify before the Commission. We knew that the notetakers were called to testify. Whether they testified before the Commission itself or by fact finders, I think something which I vaguely remember, but I think some of them did."

Judge Sofaer leaned forward. He had been listening to this intricate verbal choreography for a long time.

"This is all information you had in your head, in your own head?" Sofaer was driving at a specific point.

Apparently Halevy didn't recognize that. He answered like a lamb. "Sure."

Sofaer: "What did General Number 2 tell you?"

Tilting his head to one side, Halevy became very mysterious, almost poetic. "I remember one sentence from what he said, and he said, 'It all started at Bikfaya. Go back to Bikfaya and check Bikfaya.' It sounded to me then as a kind of Shakespearean line, Julius Caesar, but this is the line I remembered from my conversation with him. 'It all started at Bikfaya. Go back to Bikfaya and check Bikfaya.' "

While reading the commission report, Halevy said, he had inquired of Kelly: " 'Where is the case against General Sharon?' We obviously reached a conclusion that there was a case against Sharon between the lines."

"I said to Mr. Kelly, I think I agreed with him that we can conclude that there is a case against General Sharon or Minister Sharon between the lines, that it is probably in Appendix B and that I will check back with my sources."

Sofaer went on with the questioning. Cheerfully Gould let him do the honors. The courtroom was hushed. It isn't often the judge departs from his essential role of watching and listening.

"General Number 2 told you that it all started at Bikfaya. Did he tell you anything else?"

Halevy: "No."

"That is all he told you?" Sofaer stressed the "all."

Halevy: "Yes. But then I called another source which I think we described him here as a government official, a high-ranking government official, and I asked him."

Sofaer prodded again. Maybe he was getting tired of all these mysterious high-ranking sources. "Was this a different source from your four sources?"

"No." Halevy hastened to set the judge right. "He is one of them. He is the one that is adding the last sentence of my World Memo. He is the one saying that these minutes will not be published at all."

"He was the high-ranking official?" Sofaer sounded doubtful.

"Yes," Halevy said.

Gould decided to put in a couple of words. "What did he tell you?"

Halevy: "He said that there is a list of intelligence officers and intelligence personnel mentioned elsewhere in the report. So I specifically asked about the notetakers of the meetings which I regarded as very important based on what I knew at the time and he said, yes, they are mentioned there. The notetakers of the meetings are mentioned there."

Sofaer wanted to pull the facts out of this thicket of verbiage. "You asked him for the names of the notetakers mentioned in Appendix B?"

Halevy was finally reduced to a monosyllable. "Yes."

The judge wanted to be sure about this. "And he said, yes, they are mentioned?"

"Yes." Halevy was sure.

Those "confidential sources" were a lifeline to Halevy. He hung on desperately. "My source, the high-ranking government official, source Number 4, I think, is making very clear that Appendix B is a reference book and index, a code book, and people are mentioned there, that parts of testimony appear there."

Sofaer pounced. "Did he say to you, parts of the testimony appear there?"

Halevy hesitated. "No. He said it's a reference book. It's an index, it's a code."

Was there an unknown echo in the Foley Square courtroom? But Sofaer kept boring right in. "And he told you that the names of the notetakers are there?"

"Correct," Halevy said.

Sofaer's questions gathered momentum. "But he didn't say anything to you about parts of testimony being there, did he?"

Halevy fidgeted. "Maybe it was my understanding that he is making a reference or the names of those agents that appear there is a reference to their testimony and their documentation."

From the bench slightly above the recalcitrant testifier Sofaer's voice came over young and clear: "So you inferred that?"

The question was right on target. Halevy hesitated again, and then even his natural arrogance failed as he tried with a rush of words to get through to these people, a senior lawyer and a most able judge, who somehow didn't understand.

"Yes, I would say so . . . I knew that all the participants of the meeting, at the advance command post at the Karantina and at Bikfaya testified. I knew that the notetakers testified. Where are their notes? Where are their testimonies? In some kind of secret appendix, correct?"

Gould's comment was dry. "Nobody said that to you, did they?"

By now Halevy was very nervous. "Sir," he began. Suddenly the aggressive Mr. Halevy was being deferential. "You read it . . ."

Back to Sofaer: "That is the way *you* read it."

"Yes," Halevy admitted, "that is the way I read it. It's my evaluation, my analysis based on my 43 years of living in Israel and going through a lot of coverage of governmental official matters."

A few newsmen, not waiting for the knockout blow, hurried out of the courtroom to the nearest phones.

Gould continued. "It was your speculation that it must be there, is that right? No one told you that it was there and you simply concluded from your vast experience that it must be there?"

Gould's rhetorical question, his accusation, rang through the courtroom.

But Sofaer hadn't finished. He was going to clear this up so there wouldn't be any loose ends. He fired several more questions at Halevy, making it clear that after Halevy had checked with his sources he returned to Kelly and told his hapless bureau chief that he now could write with absolute confidence that Appendix B contained the message put across in Halevy's December 6 memo.

"You didn't say those words. You did something to communicate that message to him, did you not?" Sofaer was smarter than Kelly.

"Yes, sir."

Gould applied the pressure. "How did you do it, by words or gestures?"

Suddenly Halevy's memory failed him. "I don't recall. I think it was a gesture."

Gould helped him out. "Was it a gesture, not a word? Did you go in and put your thumb up, like that?"

"It could be," Halevy allowed.

"Didn't you testify?" asked Gould.

Halevy was unrepentant. "I testified that I don't recall exactly."

Gould sighed. This one just didn't know when to lie down. He'd have to refresh Halevy's failing memory. He read to him his testimony given two months earlier.

Not even Halevy could stall any more. "I went into Mr. Kelly's office and raised my thumb to the kind of 'Okay, all cleared.'"

THE TURNING POINT

THE ADMISSION FORCED OUT OF HALEVY—THAT
he in fact only inferred what he wrote so knowledgeably about
Sharon and about the secret Appendix B, that he had merely
"evaluated the story"—brought him personally and *Time* magazine collectively under heavy fire from American journalists. "To
do a Halevy" became synonymous with careless and negligent reporting.

Even before the verdicts were announced, Ken Auletta of the
Daily News voiced his anger: "The attorney for one of journalism's
great institutions, *Time*, advances the proposition that the next
time an editor asks a reporter to cite his sources, or prove his story,
the reporter need only respond: 'I *know* it is true, because I *think* it
is true.' Around the courthouse, reporters refer to this as 'Doing a
Halevy' in honor of *Time*'s reporter, David Halevy."

Auletta continued this theme under the headline "A Case of
Libel, a Lesson in Journalism":

> Sitting back in the press section of the ornate federal courtroom,
> an Israeli journalist turned to an American colleague and said:
> "I'm not so long at this business of journalism, but this trial is one
> of the best journalism schools." For months the reporter has
> watched lawyers for former Israeli Defense Minister Ariel Sharon
> and lawyers for Time Inc. claw at each other. . . .
>
> Now, as the trial enters its final days, and *Time* lawyers and
> spokesmen cloak themselves in sanctimony, this journalist, like
> many others who have covered this trial, is repelled by both sides.
> He knows that even if *Time* is found innocent of libel by the jury, it
> is guilty of journalistic felonies. *Time* reporters were sloppy and bi-
> ased and hungered for a scoop, all the sins *Time* warned against in
> a December 12, 1983, cover story, "Journalism Under Fire." Worst
> of all, the journalist knows, that however unattractive Sharon may
> be, *Time* is guilty of journalism's capital offence: arrogance. . . .
>
> . . . Sadly, it falls to Ariel Sharon to instruct *Time* on what it
> should have done: "retract and apologize." Then, if Sharon per-
> sisted in his libel action, *Time* could predicate its defense on the
> sound proposition that it is not guilty of malice—which is a test for
> libel—simply because it made a factual mistake. We often make
> inadvertent mistakes in journalism, *Time* could have said, and
> unlike many of those we cover, we openly admit it. Instead of

a humility defense, *Time* has hunkered down. It has refused to print a retraction. It has arrogated to itself the task of be-smirching Sharon's name, [which] has already been accomplished by an Israeli tribunal. It has pretended that its journalism is nearly infallible and that its reporter, David Halevy, is John Peter Zenger, rather than a sloppy journalist who was once placed on probation by *Time* and who has committed numerous errors in this case.

All the words and legal documents in this trial narrow down to two simple questions. First, can *Time* substantiate that single para-graph? Second, can Sharon prove malice? If the answer to both is no, as I think it is, what, then, is the trial about? The simple an-swer, I think, is: vanity and arrogance.

Time is too vain and arrogant to admit error. And Sharon is seeking vindication from an American jury for the ignominy he has properly suffered at the hands of a different kind of Israeli jury. With *Time*'s help he is succeeding.

For *Time* there are two juries in this courtroom. When its case goes to the legal jury this week, it may be found innocent of the narrowly interpreted crime of libel. I hope it is. But among a jury of their journalistic peers I sense it is already judged guilty. It has got its facts wrong and won't admit it. . . .

Halevy's admission that his conclusions about the content of Appendix B originated not from four sources, as he had claimed previously, but from his evaluation, his analysis, stirred up a lot of angry media reaction in the United States.

"Sharon's offensive puts *Time* magazine on trial," announced the *Los Angeles Times* in its "Opinion" section. As Lally Wey-mouth wrote: "With the same dedication and disregard for the odds he once reserved for fighting Arab armies, Israeli Minister Ariel Sharon has taken on *Time* magazine in a $50 million libel suit over an article it published in February 1983.

"Few here or in Israel initially believed that Sharon had a chance of winning his case, but with the trial about to enter its fifth week, knowledgeable legal observers now think that the for-mer Israeli general is close to scoring the sort of surprise victory he once won on the battlefield. . . ."

Weymouth's article emphasized that "Gould's case was strengthened last week when Halevy responded to a question by

Federal District Judge Abraham D. Sofaer by admitting that his conclusions about the contents of Appendix B originated not with the four sources he previously had claimed, but with 'my evaluation, my analysis based on my knowledge of 43 years of living in Israel.' " Minister Moshe Arens, who was described in the article as one of Sharon's major rivals for the future leadership of the Likud bloc, was quoted as saying: " 'I think the trial has already been an achievement for Israel, and it's clear to everyone that the *Time* story was false. If he wins, I think it will be great for Israel. It will be clear that some of the media reported with distortion and lack of objectivity in the Sabra and Shatilla affair. Of course Sharon didn't plan the massacre. It's an accusation against Israel and was intended as such.' "

In addition, the *Los Angeles Times* presented various opinions from experts.

> Journalists and constitutional lawyers also are divided over the implications of a Sharon victory for the American media. Floyd Abrams, a prominent First Amendment lawyer, says, "I think it is possible if Sharon . . . wins, that many editors will insist a heavy burden be met before they engage in high-risk journalism. There will be a change in the desire to cover high-risk stories."
>
> Robert Warren, a partner in the Los Angeles law firm of Gibson, Dunn and Crutcher, which sometimes litigates First Amendment cases for the *Times*, regards Sharon's suit as a dangerous precedent and suggests that if the general wins, Libya's Col. Kadafi may follow him.
>
> Steven Brill, editor and publisher of *The American Lawyer*, who says he is an "absolutist on the First Amendment," brushes these arguments aside and says of the Sharon trial, "*Time*'s conduct makes me embarrassed to be a journalist, and they are going to lose. They said they learned it was in the appendix. It's not."
>
> Military historian Edward Luttwak agrees: "*Time* accused Sharon of something he was not guilty of—instigating the massacre. It seems clear he's innocent of that accusation. A magazine that puts its words on sheets of paper that go around the world has a greater responsibility to watch its words than someone blurting out his opinion at a cocktail party."

Weymouth described two interviews she had had with Sharon.

Whatever the trial's outcome, no one could have predicted at the outset that Sharon would have done as well as he clearly has. Indeed, when he decided to bring his suit, he stood to lose at least as much as he had to gain. When asked again why he decided to push forward, Sharon hummed a tune, sang the words in Hebrew and translated what he explained was a Hassidic song, "All the world is a very narrow bridge, and most important is not to be afraid to fall."

He looked straight at me and said, "May I tell you something? I'm not afraid. I've never been afraid to say what I think, or fight for what I believe in."

IN THE WAKE OF DUDU HALEVY'S EXAMINATION

Time again was rumored to be interested in a settlement. Milton Gould had come into the back room after the morning session on Tuesday, December 4, 1984, his pipe jutting from his mouth. Arik had just finished lunch and was ready to go into court for the afternoon session. Gould seemed hesitant. It was possible, he said, that there would be no hearing that afternoon.

That certainly was a surprise to the rest of us. According to the schedule set by Judge Sofaer, hearings were held mornings and afternoons.

"Barr tells me he'd like to talk to me this afternoon," Gould said flatly.

There was a long silence. Then Sharon said, "We've seen their previous attempts at settlement."

"It was in the cards they'd come up with an offer of settlement," Richard Goldstein commented with mild satisfaction.

All sorts of rumors were by then swirling around the courthouse. One had it that Tom Barr wasn't feeling well and needed medical treatment. Another said there was a violent argument raging at Time, Inc., as to whether to allow the suit to continue when they were being harmed virtually daily by what was coming out in testimony. Others mentioned *Time*'s being in trouble about libel-insurance payments—there was some argument with the insurance company about the amount paid to the lawyers, with the costs of the case having spiraled way beyond the original estimates. Sharon was adamant. "We mustn't let them make fools of us. What I want is a full retraction and an apology."

"And payment of all the costs," Goldstein added emphatically.

"Tom told me the financial aspect is secondary," Gould explained. "We'll come to terms on that one."

Gould and Sharon left the room and talked in the corridor, moving slightly away from the security officers. In light of *Time*'s previous intransigence, Barr's attitude certainly represented a marked change.

Sharon made a last observation before we returned to the hotel. "I wouldn't put too much store in *Time*'s settlement proposals.

What they want is for us to break stride and slow down the momentum we've achieved in the last few days."

Meanwhile opposing counsels, Gould and Barr, had gone to inform the judge of developments. Judge Sofaer, who from the start had wanted the case to end in a compromise, was happy to adjourn proceedings for the day. The reporters weren't told the reason the session had ended early. For obvious reasons both sides wanted things kept quiet.

At about eight o'clock in the evening Richard Goldstein arrived at the Park Lane. He was beaming from ear to ear. "We've arrived at a very good settlement," he said happily as he took off his overcoat and dumped his heavy briefcase on the floor. After so many months of concentrated effort this was a very satisfying moment for him. "They want a settlement," he repeated.

Arik was sitting behind a desk in one corner of the room. He'd napped briefly and now, alert and refreshed, he was listening closely to every word.

Goldstein took a folded sheet of paper from the pocket of his suit, walked over and handed it to Arik, then sat down on the couch opposite him. The document was typewritten, with a few additions and amendments written in by hand.

"We spent the whole afternoon, right until now, at Barr's office, and we came to this agreement," Goldstein said. "Barr says he's got Grunwald's approval." Sharon, his glasses on his nose, studied the document. He didn't say a word, just read and reread the contents carefully.

"We told them," Goldstein continued, "that they'd have to pay all out-of-pocket expenses in an amount of between five and six hundred thousand dollars at most, as we assess them. Anyway, we undertook to give them a detailed statement. There's still some disagreement about the costs."

"About the wording of the settlement also," Sharon said, looking up from the sheet of paper.

Cautious though he was, Goldstein nevertheless had betrayed his excitement when he announced his news. Sharon now felt that he'd curbed that excitement a little and continued, "I think the wording here represents a big step forward." He read the brief text out loud.

In February and June of 1983, Ariel Sharon, the Defense Minister of the State of Israel, commenced libel actions in Israel and the United States, respectively, against *Time* based upon a portion of an article it published concerning the Report of the Israeli Commission of Inquiry into the events at the Sabra and Shatilla refugee camps in West Beirut. The cases have been terminated on the basis of the following statements:

Time did not intend to suggest by the article that General Sharon encouraged, instigated or condoned the massacre of Palestinian civilians in West Beirut, nor did it intend to say, and had no information that, General Sharon was told by the Phalangists or the Gemayel family that the Phalangists would kill innocent people if they entered the camps. *Time* regrets it if any of its readers drew such conclusions from the article.

Time believed that the portion of the article concerning the alleged details of Sharon's condolence call to the Gemayel family and the inclusion of those details in Appendix B was based upon reliable information. However, *Time* has never seen Appendix B and has concluded on the basis of information now available to it that that portion of its article was incorrect. *Time* regrets the error.

Sharon looked up. He seemed patently satisfied. Any changes he'd previously wanted to make didn't seem necessary now after he'd read it aloud. He was ready to accept it as it stood. "This is a retraction and even an apology," he murmured. "*Time* expresses its regret twice in one page."

After listening to a few more explanations from Goldstein, Sharon asked him, "Are they prepared to publish this in the magazine itself?"

"No," Goldstein replied. "Barr expressly stated that they are ready to sign the statement, but they won't publish it in *Time*."

"Why not?" Sharon asked. "Haven't they got the guts to admit on the pages of their own magazine what they did?"

The question was left hanging in the air.

"We've set up a meeting for tomorrow morning," Goldstein said, "to finalize the settlement."

It became clear that the more Sharon read the draft, the more convinced he seemed there was a measure of accomplishment in what was being offered, and he infected Lily with this satisfaction.

"So the struggle's been worth while, then?" she remarked happily.

"Most definitely! We've got what we were after." There was a distinct note of satisfaction in Goldstein's voice.

Lily disappeared into an adjoining room. Goldstein walked after her in concern. Later he told me she'd had tears in her eyes—tears of joy because the fight was over and because it had achieved what they had set out to do.

Arik put on his suit. This was a special evening for another reason also. Milton Gould had personally invited Arik to attend a banquet being held in honor of the venerable attorney, and Arik had gladly accepted. The banquet marked Gould's outstanding work for the Israel Bonds drive over many years. The guests included a number of prominent New York lawyers and judges as well as other celebrities. The party was by way of being a double celebration for Gould.

Now Sharon rushed to the Sheraton Hotel. By the time he entered the banquet hall everyone was already seated. He was recognized immediately, and the guests all broke into spontaneous applause, clapping him all the way to his seat at the head table. Sharon was seated with Robert Morgenthau, guest of honor Milton Gould, Arnold Forster, and Israel's new ambassador to the United Nations, Benyamin Netanyahu.

When Sharon was called on to speak, he focused on Israel's economic problems.

"What we want are investments, not donations," he declared. "We are entering a new era, and we will need the support of American Jewry more than ever. Israel cannot exist without the Jewish people. At the same time, the Jewish people cannot exist without Israel." He devoted a few warm words to Milton Gould, "who has stood beside me in taking on the might of the *Time* empire to wipe out the blood libel they published." He didn't omit Arnold Forster—"a courageous figure who has been identified over many years with every one of Israel's struggles." Sharon also praised Robert Morgenthau for his outspoken defense of Israel.

Goldstein had gone off in search of a public phone from which to call Barr and tell him there were a few minor amendments they'd need to discuss in the morning. They arranged to meet to wrap up the agreement and, of course, finalize the issue of the costs.

Around midnight, after the banquet, Arie Genger came up to Sharon's suite bringing with him Meshulam Riklis. Riklis was among those friends who had helped cover Sharon's expenses.

Sharon showed them the text of *Time*'s retraction and apology, and both agreed it was quite an achievement.

"But they don't want to publish it in the magazine," Sharon said.

"That's not so important. The entire American press will gladly print the whole thing. And if we want to, we could buy a full page in *The New York Times*—or in *Time* itself, for that matter—and publish the full text of the settlement."

This appealed to Sharon. "I've so much to do in Israel. There is so much we can and must push through at the Ministry for Trade and Industry. I want to get back and tackle all of that, to put all my energy into that."

"I'm dying to get home—to the farm, to Israel," Lily agreed happily. She'd invited everyone up for coffee. "I can't stand these hotels anymore. Let's hope we can finish things off soon over here and go home." She leaned over to place a platter of assorted cheeses on the table.

Arie Genger was still skeptical. "They should have signed tonight—finished it off tonight. It's a pity. Who knows what will happen tomorrow morning."

The next morning the lawyers met and—proving Arie's skepticism to be well founded—finalized nothing. *Time*'s lawyers got into a long and apparently pointless argument about the legal costs.

When it was time for the next court session to start, both sides lined up again in the courtroom to renew battle, as though nothing had happened.

At midnight that night, a well known American journalist called me. "So there's a settlement," he said, "and you people aren't telling? You're making no announcements?"

For a moment I was completely taken aback. How had the story leaked out? But I was stating the truth when I told him, "There is no settlement."

181

"What is this you're telling me—that there's no settlement? I heard from an excellent source that there is a settlement and that the whole business of a court adjournment yesterday was for nothing other than reaching a settlement. I hear Barr called Grunwald in Paris, where he was having dinner at the Tour d'Argent, and got his approval for the statement."

"There is no settlement," I repeated and, in doing so, established the actual facts of the situation.

But the newsman wouldn't be put off. "I know Grunwald returned to New York today. And he's in a meeting related to this matter which has been going on for hours at Rockefeller Center. There will be a settlement." He was adamant.

"So why don't you phone Grunwald?" I rejoined.

"I did, but he's not returning my calls."

I was obliged to disappoint the newsman. The battle in court continued. Then a few days later the judge asked *Time*'s lawyers what had transpired with the settlement negotiations. Their reply was obscure and evasive: there had supposedly been a disagreement about the costs, and that's why the settlement had fallen through.

The judge responded that *if* this was the case, he would gladly intervene to break the deadlock.

But *Time* clearly wanted to continue the war, so the question of settlement was dropped. There were those who claimed to know of differences of opinion within the portals of *Time* in which the hawks had gotten the upper hand over the doves.

"This time," Sharon remarked, "it will be a fight to the finish."

HALEVY SPENT ABOUT A WEEK ON THE WITNESS
stand, facing the examinations of Gould and also Barr. He drew
on his imagination to describe Sharon's condolence call in Bikfaya as an unadulterated blood-and-vengeance session, complete
with the complicity of the Israeli army. "I said before, and I will
say it again, that the matter of retaliation was brought up by
Sharon. Reprisal was brought up by Sharon. I said that Pierre
Gemayel, to the best of my knowledge and to the best of the
knowledge of my sources, said that the blood of Bashir Gemayel
has to be avenged, or should be avenged, something to that effect,
and that Minister Sharon, at one occasion he is saying—at one
time he is saying reprisal, retaliation, reaction to the conspiracy,
and the second time he says nothing. And these are my words that
he gave them the feeling."

Gould wisely waited until breath and imagination both failed.
Then, with a glint in his blue eyes: "Will you tell me, how does
one by a gesture or by silence give the assurance that the Israeli
army would neither hinder them nor try to stop them? What kind
of gesture is that?"

Halevy breathed deeply for the next swoop into the unknown.
"I will make it very clear to you. Please, Mr. Gould, if you come
and you tell me that—uh . . . no, if Mr. Sharon comes to the Gemayels and Pierre is making a statement of revenge or a statement
that the blood of Bashir Gemayel should be avenged and Mr.
Sharon keeps talking about the need to send the Phalangists into
the refugee camps and the fact that the IDF is moving into West
Beirut and will encircle and besiege the refugee camps, how do
you call that? It's very simple."

Gould found this anything but simple but let Halevy continue.

"You call that a coordination. You call that giving them the
feeling. You call that the IDF will neither hinder nor stop them. I
don't like to talk about it. I hate the subject. I am telling you, sir,
it's painful, but this is a very clear type of giving the feeling, a
very clear type."

Even Judge Sofaer was compelled to comment. "He didn't
have a body movement in there. He [Gould] is looking for a body
movement." Was there a hint of irony in the solemn judicial observation?

Gould, the glint now a definite piercing gleam: "Body movement or gesture that conveys to the observer that the Israeli army would neither hinder them nor try to stop them?"

The judge felt an understandable need for clarity. "Why would there need to be a body movement if 'Source 2' had told you that he had asked for a reprisal in effect, as you say, and then Pierre had said he wanted to avenge and he didn't say anything?" The judge's youthful voice was very firm and clear now. "Why would there have to be any body movement at all?"

The question the judge had tossed out and left hanging cast a logical doubt on other Halevy stories, so far fairly solid to untrained ears.

During court recesses reporter Halevy was full of complaints.

"Why do you write that I'm an Israeli reporter?" he querulously asked several American journalists. "Simply say I'm a reporter."

The journalists were mildly taken aback. They customarily referred to him in their reports as *Time*'s Israeli correspondent. It was perfectly accurate.

"But you are an Israeli, aren't you?" was the surprised response.

"I am an Israeli patriot," Halevy said pompously, "but as a journalist, there is no connection with where I come from. You can just as well write I'm from Honolulu."

During his testimony Halevy was so engrossed in his new mythology that he remained oblivious to the blatant contradictions he was putting forth. He presented himself as the fighting officer in the IDF reserves come to protect all the Israeli generals. At the same time he presented some of these same generals as eager leakers, willing to give him any and every military and political secret so he could hit the headlines first in *Time* magazine. Not only was he doing a great job for *Time,* he believed; his industry was also in the interests of those Israeli generals who knew what was best for Israel. After all, that was why they cooperated with him—for the good of Israel and against Arik Sharon, who could only harm that country.

Whatever his motives, this was the overall picture emerging from Halevy's testimony.

In Israel, as in the United States, the unapproved disclosure of classified information to a reporter by military personnel is a violation of the security laws. In Israel, as in the United States, the law lays down straightforward and specific charges and penalties for such violation.

The accuracy of the information Halevy claimed to have received was not the essence of the present argument. More important was the principle behind his receiving it. If Israeli generals indeed had given Halevy the information he claimed they had, he was presenting very senior IDF officers as an irresponsible gang of men incapable of preserving classified data. Halevy was reticent with his information because he was well aware that federal laws protected him in his refusal to identify his confidential sources. His sources would remain as secret as the contents of Appendix B, and he firmly defended them, saying only that they also included two Israeli generals, "General No. 1" and "General No. 2."

Gould nonetheless tried to sound out Halevy about some of his Israeli military contacts. "Mr. Halevy, are you acquainted with a man named General Mitzna in the Israeli Defense Forces?"

A cautious "I am" from Halevy.

Brigadier General Amiram Mitzna was a former commander of the Israeli army staff and command school. Immediately after the massacre he had called publicly for Sharon's resignation. When told by Chief of Staff Eitan that he should cease his protest or resign from the IDF, Mitzna found his job cozier than his principles.

Halevy looked distinctly worried as Gould pursued his question.

"Are you acquainted with General Ben-Gal—B e n g a l?"

"Yes, sir," Halevy answered, then added, "I would say I am acquainted with all the generals of the Israeli army."

"Is General Ben-Gal a friend of yours?" Gould persisted.

"Yes, sir," Halevy answered in a great rush. General Ben-Gal (Yanosh—Ben-Gal's nickname) was bitter about Sharon, who refused to designate him as chief of staff of the Israeli army.

Gould: "Have you had meetings with General Ben-Gal at his home in Caesarea?"

"I went to parties at his home, he went to parties at my home. We had a couple of dinners together." It sounded very innocuous the way Halevy put it, but clearly he was wary. "Meetings, when you talk about meetings, are you talking about beyond social planned meetings or something like that?" Halevy was very emphatic. "No, sir."

Gould wanted to be sure. "No meetings beyond parties, right?"

Halevy: "Social contacts, a lot. I followed General Ben-Gal during the first week of the war in Lebanon when he was a commanding officer of all the Israeli troops in the eastern sector of Lebanon, at the Lebanese Beka'a Valley when they fought against the Syrian division, sir. I was with him, I think, three days, three full days." Here the heroic posture was noticeably emphasized.

Back came Gould. "Sir" —the elderly attorney was most polite— "during the early days of the Lebanese war did you have conversations with General Ben-Gal about Arik Sharon?"

"About Arik Sharon?" Now, whom else would Halevy think Gould was interested in? The repetition was distinctly nervous. "I would assume that I had. Ariel Sharon was a very fascinating topic in those days. I would guess everybody talked about him, and especially the IDF generals."

Gould wasn't interested in other IDF generals. He had his specials to concentrate on. "How about General Mitzna? Did you have conversations with him about General Sharon?"

The usually voluble Halevy slowed down. "I think I had."

Gould wasn't going to let it go at that. "Did you have conversations with Mitzna about General Sharon?"

This time he had Halevy up against a wall. "I said before and I will repeat my answer now. I decline to answer because any indication will be a breach of the relationship—uh . . . might be a possible breach of the relationship between journalist and his source. You are now asking [about] a specific name." Halevy must have been grateful for the First Amendment.

But Gould had encountered this evasion before. Back came the question slightly differently phrased. "Was he one of your sources?"

Halevy: "I decline to answer that question as well, sir."

Now Gould prodded him again. "Was Ben-Gal one of your sources?" Halevy repeated the same answer.

Gould hadn't run out of names he could toss around. "How many private conversations did you have with Mitzna about Sharon?"

Halevy had his answer down pat. "I decline to answer for the same reason." But he did manage to enlarge a little so as to bring in his illustrious combat record. He explained that General Mitzna was chief of staff to General Ben-Gal at the Beka'a Valley. He repeated that he had spent three days there at the beginning of the war.

Gould: "Did there come a time when you spent some more time with these men and they were critical of Sharon?"

"With them and with others, and a lot of them were very highly critical of General Sharon, yes, sir."

Gould kept cool. "I just want to know about these two fellows, Mitzna and Ben-Gal."

"Be my guest."

Gould: "After September 14, did you spend any time with either or both of these generals?"

Halevy: "September 14?"

Gould: "September 14 or 15."

Halevy: "Yes, I spent time with them and with other generals, a lot of them."

Halevy, the person who in the witness box in New York boasted about "his" IDF, didn't hesitate to portray the IDF as led by generals looking for a Halevy to whom to leak their secrets.

Gould looked for the generals when he questioned Halevy about the Bikfaya meeting. "Do you know a man named Elkana Harnof?"

"Yes, sir, I do," Halevy admitted.

Gould: "Have you ever discussed this subject with Elkana Harnof?"

Halevy, heavily virtuous, replied, "I think it's improper for me, sitting in this courtroom in Manhattan, to discuss identities and my conversations with top-ranking Israeli intelligence officers."

Gould hung in. "Have you ever discussed the subject about which you are testifying in court with Elkana Harnof?"

Halevy: "I decline to answer."

Gould's monosyllabic "Why?" was very dry.

Halevy figured he had it all worked out. "Because if I did, I identify him immediately as one of my sources. If I did not, you can eliminate the number of my sources. Therefore, sir, I decline to answer that question."

Gould drew the obvious conclusion. "I understand you to be telling us then that Elkana Harnof is one of your sources."

Halevy looked harassed. "I said I decline to answer whether I discussed it. I answered that I know him."

The closest Halevy came to identifying a so-called source for his Bikfaya story was when he claimed to have met at Bikfaya the deputy chief of Israel's Mossad. Describing the funeral of Bashir Gemayel in somber and dramatic detail, Halevy said he'd met there the superior officer of the Israeli central intelligence agency.

Halevy's friendly association with IDF generals perhaps led him to his second fatal mistake during the trial. His first had been his admission of having "evaluated" his story about Appendix B. Then he had to reveal that at Bikfaya he had met a high-ranking Mossad officer.

Under questioning Halevy told the jury he'd had a conversation with the Mossad officer on the day of Bashir's funeral, on September 15, in Bikfaya.

Halevy: "I was inquiring into the political situation and I said what's going to happen now? And he said something, in substance, not in words, but he said something which—he said it's all lost, it's all gone. I mean with the death of Bashir it's all lost, Israel has lost the campaign. I spent with him very few minutes. His hands were with some bands."

Q: "Bandages?"

Halevy: "Yes. I learned later that he was digging there at the Kataeb headquarters in Ashrafiya, the Phalangist headquarters."

Q: "When you say a Mossad official, was it a high, low official?"

Halevy: "Deputy Mossad official."

Q: "A high Mossad official?"

Halevy: "Yes. I saw some more Israelis there."

This was perhaps the only time Halevy identified an Israeli senior official with whom he allegedly talked about the situation in Lebanon in the aftermath of Bashir's death: the deputy chief of the Mossad.

Later, when Sharon and his lawyers compared this statement with other vague descriptions Halevy had given about his sources, they arrived at some significant conclusions. First, it could be deduced from Halevy's testimony that the Mossad officer he had met in Bikfaya was the same person who took down the minutes of Sharon's conversation with the Gemayels. Second, this note-taker, the deputy chief of the Mossad, was allegedly the source, or at least an important source, for his memo.

Why this sudden generous cooperation in the courtroom? Why say openly that in Bikfaya he had talked to the deputy chief of the Mossad and thus blatantly incriminate the man? This led to another question. If the official indeed was the source, why had he told Halevy a lie about nonexistent minutes and a so-called revenge conversation?

Sharon arrived at the conclusion that Halevy may well have met the deputy chief of the Mossad at Bashir's funeral at Bikfaya but that all the rest of Halevy's tale was simply a lie, like the lie Halevy had written about Sharon himself. For senior Mossad officials, Halevy knew, are not permitted to testify either in U.S. or Israeli courts. At a later stage Sharon would take advantage of this mistake on Halevy's part—whether such mistake had been intentional or not.

On his last day on the witness stand Halevy pulled out all the stops. He blamed the entire Israeli defense establishment for having coordinated with the Phalangists in Lebanon, who, he said, had a plan for a "final solution" for the Palestinian problem in Lebanon. It was a great new headline for the press, this phrase that evokes only one image, the unparalleled crime of Nazi Germany.

"Just look how low a person can stoop to defend his lie," Sharon said to me quietly as we sat listening. "How rotten some people can become . . ."

Halevy's statements in the last stage of his cross-examination were reaching a new level of hyperbole. Looking firmly at the jury, he announced his knowledge now of new material making "that paragraph look totally irrelevant." "Now" meant December 6, 1984, two years to the day after Halevy had planted his bogus story by sending his Worldwide Memo.

"We are now in December," he continued, "so I think for the

last 12 months I worked for Mr. Barr and for Cravath, Swaine and Moore, and among other things, they wanted my knowledge and they asked me to brief them on Middle Eastern affairs, the situation in Lebanon, the situation in Israel. . . .

"During this process we approached, I would say, between 12 to 15 people in Israel, in Lebanon and in Europe, people that were either inside the Sabra and Shatilla camps or were involved in the planning, the coordination that was going on between the IDF and the Defense Ministry on September 15 and the Phalangists in Beirut.

"What we learned from these sources are basically, if I can put it in clear categories, and I will try, we learned, I would say, three major categories. One, the level of isolation of encircling, of besieging, of surrounding the camps and not letting anyone come out. I was not aware of it at the time. . . .

"A second category which I think we firmly established, and got a lot of confirmation, was the level of coordination between IDF field commanders and the commanders of the Phalangists. The third level or the third category as we learned a lot, and I think a lot of material, in many of those conversations we confirmed some suspicion, some facts we could not check out at the time which related to the knowledge, the broad knowledge of the IDF officers and the Defense Ministry officials regarding the atrocities of the Phalangists during Israel's invasion.

"I am talking about between June 6 and September 14, and also relating to the Phalangists' plans. I am using a word which I am very hesitant to use but 'final solution' for the Palestinian problem in Lebanon."

Gould refused to be diverted. "Now, sir, you did not learn anything more about the visit of Sharon to the Gemayel family which is referred to in the paragraph, did you? That paragraph which is in evidence."

A flattened Halevy: "No, sir."

"And," Gould said, "you did not learn any more about what was in Appendix B?"

Halevy: "No, sir." But not to be outdone, he repeated his earlier statement. "If I would have obtained that information on February 10, 11, 1983, this paragraph would have looked much harsher than it looks now."

The judge tried to pull some coherence out of the jumble of words. "That is," he said, "if you had known that the camps were more closely surrounded than you had known, that more extensive coordination existed than you had known about, and that the IDF had had more extensive knowledge of these invasion atrocities—"

Halevy, very smartly: "And the Defense Ministry."

Judge Sofaer: "And that they also knew of Phalangist plans for the 'final solution,' as you put it?"

Clearly the judge too found the phrase distasteful, but Halevy didn't bat an eye.

"Yes, Your Honor."

Judge Sofaer: "And that information would have led you to write this paragraph about General Sharon's visit to the Gemayels and his knowledge of their plans for revenge more strongly?"

Halevy wasn't even ruffled. He simply barked out one word. "Correct."

JUDGE SOFAER HIMSELF TOOK OVER THE CROSS-
examination of *Time*'s Jerusalem bureau chief, Harry Kelly. In a
rapid-fire series of sizzling questions the judge attempted to pin
down the professional standard of a *Time* reporter. Aside from
Halevy's own contribution, this turned out to be another crucial
stage in the trial.

Milton Gould had already given Kelly a thorough going-over.
It was amazing to watch the elderly attorney keep the pace day
after day, now for the third consecutive week. His team had
worked until the small hours preparing material for the next day's
session. No free weekends. A continuous state of emergency: a real
war for Gould and company, just as it was for Sharon.

Kelly described how he and Halevy had prepared the story
about Sharon at Bikfaya, and how the rewritten story, the playback, had been in Jerusalem.

Responding to Gould's demand for more details, Kelly elaborated: "Sometime between Friday night and Saturday morning
we received from New York the playback of the story. The playback being the writer's edited version of the story as it will probably appear in the magazine. We were asked for any comments
and corrections on the playback. And the procedure we used
when we received the playback from New York on the Telex—the
people who have contributed to the story sit down, we number
the paragraphs and we go through it graph by graph, to see what
comments—whether we think there is an inaccuracy, whether in
some cases they could be worded differently."

Sharon's Bikfaya story was included there, in paragraph 20. It
had been rewritten and edited in New York.

"One of us was at the typewriter," Kelly continued. "I'm not
sure who, probably me, and we went through it paragraph by
paragraph. We undoubtedly discussed this paragraph. My memory is that I said, 'Is this paragraph okay with you?' and Mr. Halevy said, 'It's okay with me,' and I said, 'It's okay with me.' "

Gould asked Kelly if he'd noticed the change in the wording. In
New York the writer—with the approval of the editors—had
eliminated the words "[Sharon] gave them the feeling" and sub-
stituted it for "Sharon discussed."

"You noticed that, did you not?" Gould urged.

Kelly: "Yes."

Sofaer moved in. "You did not think it was significant?"

Kelly didn't try to fool around. "Right."

Kelly made a strong impression of a decent guy who found himself trapped. He now faced a skirmish with Judge Sofaer.

"You knew on what basis Halevy had written his original words in the 'green light for revenge?' memo, that is, that he had had minutes, or had had minutes read to him?"

"Yes, sir," Kelly said heavily.

Now Sofaer took over completely. "That reflected simply the statement that the Gemayels had said to him they wanted to [avenge] the death of Bashir, and there were no other statements. There was no statement about how he gave a feeling or what questioning occurred. There was nothing like that in the notes, right?"

Kelly: "Yes, sir."

Sofaer was getting tough. "Yesterday you said that you regarded the 'green light' memo and that language in the 'green light' memo as an accurate reflection of those notes, the notes that didn't have any of that language. Do you regard also the final playback as an accurate reflection of the original minutes?"

Kelly tried. "I think it was to me, sir."

Sofaer, sharp as a razor: "It's still an accurate reflection?"

Kelly tried harder. "If I can quarrel with the word 'discussion' or 'discussed,' and at the time I read it I did not quarrel with it, I don't think Mr. Halevy did. It seems to me that sometimes a discussion is a communication, that people may say things and someone else—"

Sofaer simply cut him off. "Did it occur to you what had happened? The original minutes said simply that the Gemayels had said they wanted to avenge the death of Bashir. That is all they said, right?"

Kelly: "Yes, sir."

Sofaer barely waited for the acknowledgment. "And then in the first version it says he, Sharon, gave them the feeling that he wouldn't object. Now, in the second version, that original statement that the Gemayels had said 'they wanted to avenge the death of Bashir' became 'they discussed,' that Sharon discussed with the Gemayels the need for revenge. Did it occur to you that now perhaps the statement was not an accurate reflection of the original minutes?"

"Sir," Kelly replied, "I did not at the time, because if it had occurred to me I would have asked him to change it."

Sofaer: "You didn't think back to the original minutes that Halevy had explained to you?"

Kelly maneuvered. "I may not have, sir. Because, as I explained, we get a lot of material on a cover story. The playbacks, we respond to every paragraph. We get checkpoints on various questions. This was going on late at night, as I recall. We worked until late Saturday. It was going on all day Saturday also, and I don't recall focusing on that detail of discussion, but there was a discrepancy between 'gave the feeling' and 'discussion.' "

Sofaer, not to be outmaneuvered: "So for this final version you did not, but if you had thought of it, would you regard it as an inaccurate reflection of the original minutes? Is this the way you would normally report as a *Time* reporter, a *Time* correspondent? Would you pick up your typewriter and write out the words 'discussed the need for revenge' from the kind of minutes that you told us Halevy told you he had?"

Kelly flushed deeply. "Sir, at the time I didn't think it was inaccurate. I thought a discussion—"

Sofaer looked straight at this senior member of *Time*'s staff. "I realize you didn't think it was inaccurate at the time. I am asking you now. What is the standard that you would apply as a reporter if you had the minutes in your mind? Would you write the words 'discussed the need for revenge'?"

Kelly tried another tactic. "Sir, I didn't have the minutes in my mind."

The judge's voice was icy. "I gather you didn't, but will you answer my question? I am asking you if you did today, if you had the minutes here and the article here side by side and the minutes said the Gemayels said they wanted to avenge the death of Bashir, and the article said that Sharon discussed the need for revenge with the Gemayels, would you write that article from those minutes?"

This was Kelly's Alamo. He faced it. "I may not, sir, particularly after this." He gave a sigh of relief. The press corps smiled, some with sympathy, some with irony. Most of them rushed off to the phones.

Gould put in a question. "You mean you have learned to be more careful?"

Time's counsel Stuart Gold leaped up with an objection. Gould looked innocent. "That is a perfectly proper question. He said 'particularly after this' and I asked him whether the reason is not to be more careful."

Sofaer ruled hastily. "Sustained." He wasn't going to allow this skirmish to deflect him. "I do think that I would like to have an answer to my question about your standard of reporting as a reporter. You have an important position as a chief correspondent in a bureau there and you have had many years of experience, I gather. Would you, as a reporter, if someone else wrote that story from those minutes, would you consider that an accurate story?"

You couldn't fault Kelly for trying. "Sir, I did not read the minutes. I understood from reading Mr.—"

Sofaer didn't want to know. His voice was knife-edged. "Assuming that you were told only what you said yesterday you were told, and assuming that is all the minutes contained, would you regard the story that appeared in *Time* as an accurate story based on those minutes? Would you regard the story as inaccurate based on those minutes that said—"

Kelly didn't even let the judge complete his question. It was easier this way. No more messing around. "I would not use the word 'discussed.' "

More of the reporters in the courtroom shot out to break the story of Kelly's admission of defeat.

Sofaer had got just about all he needed. He had one more question, rather a leading one. "Smith wouldn't know anything about this, would he? Smith in New York who wrote that word 'discussed,' he wouldn't have known that the original words had been based on minutes that were somewhat being interpreted?"

Kelly gave credit where it was due. "No, sir, he wouldn't."

Here was Gould again. "And it was Smith in New York who put in the word 'discussed'?"

"I assume it was Smith in New York," Kelly answered. "It could have been someone else, but I think it was Smith."

Judge Sofaer had operated on Kelly with the same razor-sharp precision he had used on Halevy. It was a masterpiece of cross-examination. The judge had forced major admissions from two major witnesses. The only material difference lay in the reaction of those two witnesses. When Halevy realized he was cornered, he looked flustered, put out. He'd been caught. Clearly he'd grasped too late that his admission in court was something he had tried to cover up for a long time. Kelly, on the other hand, took it on the chin. He was a journalist, and he wanted to be at peace with his professional standards, to be done with all this furtive hiding behind words.

A MAN HAS TO BE EITHER A BORN OPTIMIST OR EN-
duringly stubborn to do what Judge Sofaer did during the *Sharon
v. Time* trial. The Israeli government's suggestion about the documents was merely lip service and would make no legal impact. It
did, however, give the judge an idea. He asked both parties if they
were willing to have him appeal personally to the Israeli government in an attempt to find a viable legal method of obtaining
either the documents or their contents.

Milton Gould agreed instantly. Finally the *Time* lawyers also
agreed, despite hedging with legal formalities.

Judge Sofaer's offer, first made in the early stages of the legal
proceedings, showed his awareness that the entire case hinged on
examination of the documents. This was the only possible explanation for his continued dogged efforts in this regard, for the
beautifully worded, lucid, and precise letters he sent to Jerusalem.

My personal conjecture, supported by the suppositions of several New York friends and outside lawyers, is that Judge Sofaer's
persistence can have been due only to his conviction that the documents contained nothing attributed to them by *Time*. Apparently his impeccable logic had led him to the simple
conclusion that Sharon would not have dared bring a libel suit in
New York if there had been even a grain of incriminating evidence in the documents. Moved by his sense of justice and duty to
his high office, the judge wanted to bring the truth to light.

Initially Sofaer's letters went unanswered. They found their
way to the government secretariat, where they quietly collected
dust. No one had any idea what to do with them, especially as
there had been a government decision not to assist Sharon in his
problem with the documents. Quite by chance one day the Jerusalem bureaucracy forwarded Judge Sofaer's letters to a diligent
and fair-minded man, Dennis Gouldman, head of the International Department at the Ministry of Justice. He, at least, had the
courtesy to send the judge a reply, although he stated that Sofaer's request to examine the secret Appendix B of the Kahan
Commission Report was not feasible. He outlined Israel's rules of
secrecy, explaining that they were particularly binding for inquiry commissions on security matters.

This was the judge's chance. Now there was at any rate a specific person for him to turn to, who had answered him, albeit negatively. Negotiations began to take shape. Each letter written by Sofaer was approved by the litigants. The judge familiarized himself with Israel's secrecy laws. He began to pare down his requests, and finally he put the question on the bottom line. Was the government prepared or was it not to give the minimal assistance required to help uncover the truth in a matter of such basic importance? There was massacre involved and honor.

Judge Sofaer accelerated his one-man crusade while Sharon was still on the stand. On November 7 and 14 he sent off two additional letters emphasizing that the matter was becoming urgent. Like the attorneys, the judge had realized that legally acceptable documents would very soon become central to the entire case. His efforts had progressed to the point where an examination had theoretically been approved. The question was how to conduct the examination. The judge suggested that the former chairman of the inquiry commission, Justice Kahan, be the examiner. *Time*'s legal team agreed, on condition that the lawyers representing both parties be allowed to study the documents.

Sharon had misgivings about this condition. He knew just how vital the documents were to his case, but what if their contents should be leaked to the press? Especially Appendix B; he knew what it contained. From his point of view he was perfectly willing to have the entire appendix made public—it could only help him, he felt. But this was a state document and should remain top secret. As a former army officer and as a government minister he knew that if the documents were leaked to the press the disclosure could violate an essential principle of confidentiality. If, moreover, the *Time* people got to know the entire contents, what use would the magazine make of this knowledge? Sharon simply did not trust *Time* to maintain the principle of confidentiality.

It was with immense relief, therefore, that he learned of the government's decision of Friday, November 30, to allow Justice Kahan to examine the documents and reply to Judge Sofaer's questions but not to allow the participation of the attorneys for the two litigants.

Judge Sofaer had nearly attained his goal. Time, Inc., however, was not yet willing to concede. They insisted that their Israeli attorney, Haim Zadok, also inspect the documents in the presence of Justice Kahan and that he be permitted to add reservations of his own, should he have any. Judge Sofaer, who was involved around the clock in the complexities of the trial, sent off a final appeal to the government of Israel. It was an eleventh-hour call for truth. Here is an extract from the judge's letter of December 12, 1984. It was addressed to Dennis Gouldman, who had become an essential part of the process.

The Government is no doubt concerned that our extraordinary application might create a precedent for such requests in the future. *Sharon* v. *Time Inc.* is, however, unique in several pertinent respects. First, it involves as plaintiff the former Minister of Defense of the State of Israel, and it involves very serious allegations about the performance of his official duties. As a practical matter, suits by high government officials are rare. Minister Sharon in particular has never sued anyone for libel before, despite the many harsh comments made about him.

Second, the Government of Israel itself has treated this alleged libel as extraordinarily serious. Prime Minister Begin publicly called for a retraction on February 14, 1983. Moreover, in the course of this litigation, *Time* has suggested that the Commission may have withheld from public view information arguably inconsistent with its most fundamental finding: that no element of Israel's political or military echelon was aware in advance that the Phalangists would intentionally harm noncombatants. Thus, the alleged libel in this case arguably reflects not only upon Sharon, but also upon the integrity of the Kahan Commission and upon the integrity of proceedings under Israel's Commission of Inquiry Law, which has served as a model of self-examination to all civilized nations.

Third, the nature of the libel alleged here is also unique. The story at issue was published in a magazine with the widest circulation of any publication in the free world. It concerns evidence allegedly in the possession of an official Commission of Inquiry with regard to a specific conversation between Minister Sharon and the Gemayels. *Time* based its story on reports from its Israeli correspondent, a lieutenant colonel in the IDF reserves, who claims to have received his information from unidentified IDF generals and

199

high intelligence officials. Disclosure of the evidence in the Government's possession in a manner that results in usable evidence could establish the accuracy or inaccuracy of these alleged sources. The Government possesses authoritative information about the allegations, and it possesses that information in a form ideally suited to conclusive proof. Releasing that information, particularly in the manner to which the parties in this case have already agreed, poses little danger of providing a precedent for disclosure of background evidence in future cases. . . .

. . . The beneficial effects of permitting access to the parties' attorneys would be especially profound in this case. The documents involved contain answers to central issues. If these answers can be obtained in the form of admissible evidence, then I am confident that constructive ends will be served. . . .

If the Government decides to allow access to the parties' representatives, we ask that the Government make it clear that the documents to which it grants access constitute all the sets of notes or minutes of the three meetings in question. We understand that access to Appendix B means access to any exhibits or attachments to that Appendix. We also repeat our request that any affirmative answer be explained, either by allowing us to see the material involved, or by quoting the relevant materials, or in some other manner; otherwise, the meaning of an affirmative answer may be too unclear to permit its use as evidence. . . .

SLOWLY BUT PERCEPTIBLY THE AMERICAN MEDIA
began to turn against *Time*.

The most devastating attack on the magazine came in mid-December in *The American Lawyer,* one of the most prestigious monthlies in the United States. In an open letter editor Steven Brill put the case boldly and incisively to Henry Grunwald, editor in chief of *Time*. The title, "Say It Ain't So, Henry!," was the only light note in the long article.

> ... I hope you can understand how dismaying this Sharon libel trial has become....
>
> ... It seems from the testimony of your own people that *Time* made up its story—that's right, simply made it up—when it reported in a February 1983 cover article that *"Time* has learned" that a secret appendix to a report by an Israeli governmental commission investigating the Phalangist massacre of Palestinian refugees in Lebanon concluded that then Israeli Defense Minister Ariel Sharon had visited the Phalangist leaders and "discussed ... the need" for them to take revenge....
>
> What's worse ... is that despite the now-compelling evidence that some combination of *Time* reporters, editors and rewrite people fabricated the story you recently declared [at a lecture at New York University] you are certain that *Time* "will be vindicated." ... Will you and your organization really have been vindicated just because General Sharon can't prove malice or damages?
>
> ... The pre-trial and trial record (such as it is so far) reveals an arrogant, bloated bureaucracy in which the reporter of the paragraph that Sharon is suing about is biased to the point of being a near-fanatic, your chief of correspondents isn't much of a chief and has a suspiciously selective memory when he's under oath, your managing editor ... doesn't know much of anything about what goes on in his shop, your much-vaunted research department is a sham, and your system for weeding out unreliable reporters is nil. Overall, the impression created by ... your people and inter-office communications is of a place where everybody strains to squeeze a "scoop" out of a series of forced assumptions, where stories go through a rat's maze of editing and rewriting ... and where nobody ever admits a mistake about anything....
>
> ... It's time to settle this thing with an outright apology. Not a

"clarification." Not a statement saying you were misled. But an apology. . . .

. . . The theme of your lecture was that libel actions have become "a serious menace" to a free press. Well, you're right. But even a First Amendment absolutist like me has to admit in looking at this suit, this is in large part a problem we've created and this is one suit that we deserve to lose—because of your magazine's arrogance. After all, with your policy on corrections, and your kneejerk process of standing behind your story, how else was General Sharon supposed to seek redress?

FROM GRUNWALD DOWN, THE *TIME* EDITORS
closed ranks, making a united stand for Halevy.

Richard L. Duncan, who as chief of correspondents was in
charge of more than eighty of them around the world, placed Halevy near the top of the correspondents of his magazine. "Of the
15 or 20 correspondents we have, whom we most normally rely
on, in an array of [highly placed confidential] sources," Duncan
told the court during his testimony, "I would say that Dudu [Ha-
levy] ranks among the top four or five."

Even Judge Sofaer couldn't conceal his amusement. His crack
at Duncan was barbed. "Is there a highly-placed-sources annual
award at *Time* magazine or anything like that, that led you to do
this at any point?"

Later Richard Goldstein came back to re-examine Duncan.
Under methodical prodding Duncan admitted that none of his
correspondents other than Halevy had ever been put on probation. Not one of them had received a "Dear Dudu" letter like the
letter he had written to Halevy after the "Begin health story."

"Is it still your position that Mr. Halevy was your fourth best?
Yes or no?" Goldstein asked flatly.

"Yes," Duncan answered, somewhat pale.

Halevy "is an excellent reporter and an excellent journalist"
was the award bestowed by the witness, managing editor Ray
Cave. Elegantly dressed, occasionally smoothing his beautifully
clipped beard, his eyes shifting to the ceiling or focusing on an in-
visible point in the courtroom, the editor was very precise in his
evaluation of Halevy. Cave had been managing editor of *Time*
since October 1977, and Halevy, he maintained, "has produced
stories, many of them from confidential sources, that have reflected what later turned out to be quite accurate assessments of
situations that were not publicly known at the time."

Under Gould's steady questioning Cave admitted he had not
known until recently that Halevy had been put on probation by
Duncan for his story on Begin's health. He also said he had
learned only in court of the story in *Time* in which Halevy put
Shimon Peres on a missile boat on a voyage to a secret conference
with the Lebanese, which was not true. Nevertheless, Cave continued, this did not affect his appraisal of Halevy.

Judge Sofaer wanted to be sure. "You have already taken it into account?"

Cave was emphatic. "Absolutely, Your Honor."

Stunned, Gould repeated the sequence. "You have taken that letter and the boat story into account, right?"

"Yes, sir," Cave repeated. "Everything that I know about what he has done, by definition, goes into my assessment of how valuable and able a correspondent Mr. Halevy is." The subjects of many, many questions put to Cave were unknown to him, so he could produce no answers. But about the bad apple there were few things he didn't know, and yet he had nothing but praise.

The bizarre chorus was joined by Henry Grunwald, editor in chief of *Time Inc.* since 1979. "I consider Halevy extremely reliable, extremely enterprising, and really one of the best reporters I have ever known, at *Time* or elsewhere." Grunwald's staunch support of Halevy evoked grins among the reporters in the courtroom. He had known Halevy some ten years, Grunwald said, and "My judgment is based mainly on his performance as a reporter."

"Even as a correspondent who has been put on probation for having reported inaccurately?" Gould asked.

Grunwald's voice became unctuous as he demonstrated forgiveness. "In the course of a long career, everybody makes a mistake once in a while. If indeed the Begin health story was a mistake. I have made mistakes too. . . ."

Judge Sofaer was puzzled. "But the logical alternatives in that story are such that it is not a conventional mistake. He may have trusted the wrong people—"

Grunwald hastened to agree. "That is correct, Your Honor, not a conventional mistake in the sense of getting a name wrong or something."

Before Grunwald had been summoned as a witness Sharon had asked Gould if he could discuss something with him privately. "Don't examine Grunwald," he said firmly.

From the outset Sharon had maintained that Judge Sofaer was drawing a clear distinction between the New York editors and *Time*'s Jerusalem staff—particularly Dudu Halevy. Sharon tried hard to put this across to Gould. There were only two lines of approach, he said. If Gould should examine Grunwald, it would have to be really tough. He would have to force the issue of an irresponsible attitude on the part of management. And even if the lawyers accepted this, there was another point: in view of the obvious line Sofaer had taken, differentiating between *Time* Jerusalem and *Time* New York, the judge might well disallow it.

The only other course, Sharon claimed, was to give up on Grunwald altogether—not call him to the witness stand. Because he would add nothing. On the contrary, he might well strengthen *Time*'s case. "We've got to remember that if Grunwald, a Jew, has managed to make it to the top, and to survive there for so long, he's a tough nut to crack."

Despite Sharon's reservations, Gould called *Time*'s editor in chief, Henry Anatole Grunwald, to the witness stand. White-haired, bespectacled, stocky, wearing the ubiquitous dark pin-striped suit, Grunwald told the court he had started work at *Time* as a part-time office boy in 1944 and eleven years later had become a department editor. In due course he'd become editor of the foreign affairs section. He had never worked as a correspondent.

Sharon, sitting in his usual place on the front bench, disappointedly whispered to a friend, "Look how they're treating Grunwald. Handling him with kid gloves. Not only our lawyer—the judge too. The judge isn't putting any pressure on Grunwald. He's creating a buffer zone between Halevy in Jerusalem and the editorial board in New York."

Grunwald had a glib explanation for everything. From Halevy's probation—"The word 'probation' is an artificial term"—to the absence of any requirement that stories obtained from confidential sources be double-checked—"If I trust my correspondent, if he has proved himself in the past, and if I am convinced that he has a reliable source of high standing."

Gould reminded Grunwald of Kelly's testimony that in Jerusalem he didn't have Sharon's home phone number. Hence Kelly hadn't called Sharon to get his reaction before sending his Take 9 Telex to New York. Kelly had said too that he had telephoned the Defense Ministry and left a message to tell Sharon that *Time* had called.

"Don't you think that under the circumstances he should have left a message about why *Time* was calling?" Gould asked.

Several journalists present in the courtroom smiled ironically at the arrogant reply nonchalantly tossed off by Grunwald: "I would have thought that the message that *Time* called—I believe it was left twice—surely suggests a desire for a return call."

Sharon was also smiling as he murmured, "Every top reporter in Israel knows my telephone number at home. They used to call me at night, even from Beirut."

"I am assuming Mr. Kelly was working against a deadline," Grunwald continued, and he "might not have been able to obtain the general's [Sharon's] telephone number." Grunwald gave an example: "If we were doing a story about Secretary [of Defense Caspar] Weinberger, I would be satisfied with two telephone calls placed to the Pentagon. I would not say you have to rouse Mr. Weinberger out of bed at his home."

Gould put another straight question to Grunwald. Why did *Time* magazine explicitly avoid apologizing to Begin when it learned Halevy's story was false? Why did the magazine insist on printing only "*Time* regrets the error." Was an apology different from a regret?

Grunwald was unfazed. He emphasized that to him apology and regret mean, "frankly, the same thing," but to the best of his knowledge, "as habit and tradition" *Time* has not used the word "apology" but simply expressed "regrets." This was an avenue that Gould wanted to investigate further.

Judge Sofaer intervened. "Someone might understand the words differently, in a certain situation, 'apology' and 'regret.' For example, if somebody punched Mr. Gould in the eye, and said, 'Mr. Gould, I apologize,' it might be understood one way. And if he said, 'Mr. Gould, I regret that I punched you in the eye,' you might understand it in a different way."

The newsmen in the court burst out laughing, along with the *Time* group.

"That is correct." Grunwald was affably grateful. He'd been saved.

Only Sharon was not smiling. His arms were folded across his chest; he was visibly angry. He looked straight at the judge, trying to catch his eye and give him the message he was saying to me in a low voice. "It's a shame, a disgrace. Look how the judge is making a fool of Gould only to flatter the editors of *Time*. It's disgusting."

Trying to take the sting out of the judge's joke, Gould rallied gallantly. "I think if I had the opportunity to remove my glasses before it happened, I might regard the use of one word as different from the other, Your Honor."

Had Sharon required further proof of this fine line the judge was drawing between *Time* in Jerusalem and *Time* in New York, it came the following day, when the trial was due to go into recess for the Christmas and Hanukkah holidays. Counsel for both sides had been arguing before the judge about the nature of evidence *Time* witnesses would be permitted to bring, since some of them, at least, had acknowledged themselves as politically biased against Sharon or against the Israeli government.

The judge's ruling put "paid" both to the immediate problem and to the more remote one. With regard to the witnesses, he said, "There is no one else who can testify to having spoken to these people, these sources, and to having heard them say the things Halevy says they did. It's all Halevy and so the issue is posed very starkly. Mr. Halevy is at risk in this litigation. Mr. Sharon is at risk in this litigation. I have said that to the parties from the outset.

"You are putting yourselves in the hands of the jury, not only yourselves as institutions or as law firms or as magazines, but as two people, Ariel Sharon and David Halevy."

Simultaneously the judge ruled on *Time*'s request to withhold Halevy's letter to Duncan. "I have ruled it's admissible. I have no doubt, having heard the testimony at trial, that the 1984 letter is admissible on actual malice. What it does is his statement about Sharon being the symbol of right-wing fanaticism, which is the way the jury can read that, and his statement of pain, personal anguish at Sharon's vindication, ties in altogether according to the plaintiffs.

"I am sure this is going to be argued. He is in effect revealing now [that] this is the motive he has had throughout in all the articles relating to the Likud government and to Mr. Sharon, that this has been his [Halevy's] purpose, to pull Sharon down. In fact, [this] would be what they would argue is his purpose, and this letter, in effect, states his political philosophy and his attitude in a highly confidential, highly reliable as a result, communication. . . . The jury has ample evidence in addition to Mr. Halevy's own testimony, upon which to make a finding of actual malice, intentional falsity."

Addressing *Time* attorney Stuart Gold directly, the judge warned, "This case, Mr. Gold, don't misunderstand me, if you people think that what is going to come out of this case is some kind of abstract truth, you are wiser than I."

When court resumed after the noon break on December 20, *Time*'s counsel made the unexpected announcement that they would rest their case.

Gould was taken by surprise. "I am astonished."

The judge's response was dry and also illuminating. "I am not astonished, just for the record."

By not producing a single witness of all those whose many depositions they had taken in Europe, Israel, and the United States, *Time*'s attorneys also legally closed the door for Sharon and his counsel to cross-examine, thereby preventing them from bringing out further testimony in the rebuttal phase of the trial.

The only additional evidence they were allowed to produce was that from the Israeli government.

THE VERDICTS

THE LAST DAY OF 1984, DECEMBER 31, WAS A CRITI-
cal one in the suit against *Time*. However, the scene of the grip-
ping events was Jerusalem, not New York. That New Year's Eve
Sharon faced a special committee of ministers, to whom he explained the decisive importance of Secret Appendix B in deter-
mining the outcome of the trial. Israel's new coalition prime
minister, Shimon Peres, headed the committee, assembled in the
prime minister's office. Alongside him sat the minister of defense,
Yitzhak Rabin, the vice premier, Yitzhak Shamir, and the minister of justice, Moshe Nissim. Attorney General Yitzhak Zamir,
several Mossad people, and various other security experts were in
the conference room as well. The atmosphere was tense.

Two days before the last proceedings were due to be renewed in
the libel suit in New York the Israeli government was finally prepared to decide if it would help ensure that justice was done.
Judge Sofaer's unstinting efforts for more than a year and a half
had paid off. Sharon too had made a monumental effort. Ever
since his return from New York eight days earlier he had been
trying to persuade the Israelis that it was time they did their part
to help vindicate him and, concomitantly, the State of Israel.
Moreover, when he returned home, after an absence of more than
seven weeks, he found a climate far different from the one he had
left. Not only was the weather warm and balmy, in sharp contrast
to the biting New York winter, but the Israeli media had been
forced to make an about-face and report that Dudu Halevy and
Harry Kelly had admitted that what they had written in *Time*
about Sharon had no basis in fact.

From an Israeli viewpoint there had been a drastic change since
the beginning of the suit. Sharon now seemed to have a good
chance of winning. The anti-Sharon circles and the bulk of the Israeli press were already discussing what would happen "if Sharon
wins the case." They were not loath to admit how much this
would distress them, claiming it could "very well pave his way to
the top."

Renowned U.S. attorney Floyd Abrams, an expert on libel and
the First Amendment, happened to be in Israel on a short visit at
the time. In New York he had been repeatedly asked for comment

on the trial. At a restaurant in Old Jaffa he asked me what I thought about this anxiety of the Israelis in reaction to what seemed to be Sharon's imminent victory.

I replied that a logical extension of their line of thought would require that Sharon should lose the case, even if *Time* had lied. All these staunch defenders of Israeli democracy, who protested their faith in a nation under law, seemed perfectly well prepared to abandon those same principles when it came to Arik Sharon. Their logic dictated that it was better that he lose, even if *Time* was wrong, just so long as it prevented him from becoming prime minister. "I cannot believe in a justice colored by politics," I told Abrams. "And I'm positive that in the States it wouldn't go over either. Here in Israel, though, political passions run so deep, they have managed to distort logic out of all proportion. It even portends deforming the legal system."

Immediately after his return to Israel, Sharon contacted Weissglas and told him, "We're going to lose if we don't get those documents. We've broken them down, but it's not enough. The judge has already said that what the jury must decide on is my word against Halevy's."

In that last week of December, Sharon knocked on every door possible. After a short rest at his farm on Saturday—lamenting what the winter drought had done to his land—he went to Jerusalem on Sunday to meet with the prime minister. Explaining to Peres that *Time* was counting on the secrecy of Appendix B, he contended that the very fact that it had been kept secret tended to prove the truth of what they had published. Sharon said that he felt *Time* already knew the truth, that they knew Appendix B would add nothing to their case. In fact, *Time* was quite happy that the Israeli government was prohibiting examination of the document; it served their purpose quite well. But, he stressed, it was not in Israel's interests, let alone his own, to maintain that secrecy.

Sharon knew Dudu Halevy was considered a friend of Peres. Permitting court examination of Appendix B, which would disclose the truth . . . Well, rumor had it that "Peres wouldn't do that to Halevy." Sharon was fully aware that despite his being a member of the same government as Peres, quite aside from having helped him become prime minister, Peres still regarded him as his major political opponent. So he wasn't suprised at Peres' dry, formal response. "I will do exactly what Professor Zamir [the attorney general] instructs me to do." Sharon hadn't expected more.

Thereafter Sharon took his case to Defense Minister Yitzhak Rabin. He emphasized that Halevy had testified before a New York court that he used IDF generals as sources whenever he felt like it. "If that's the case, we no longer have Israeli Defense Forces; we have Israeli Defense Sources," he said. It wasn't a pretty picture. It was also a picture that would remain on record, Sharon told Rabin, if he weren't allowed the minimum defense against all the lies about Israel already presented in court.

Nissim and Shamir were familiar with Sharon's arguments—they'd already heard them in the previous Shamir government. Shamir had refused to help Sharon then, but this time, Sharon insisted, they had to reconsider. Moreover, Sharon's political standing had changed since he had first filed suit. As minister for trade and industry he had become one of the stronger cabinet members. His opinion counted now, and he couldn't be ignored as he had been twenty months earlier.

Sharon next talked to the heads of the security organizations, explaining how the secrecy of the document in question would be safeguarded by following the method Judge Sofaer had suggested.

Exposing the substance of the Secret Appendix, Sharon knew, would be his gain and *Time*'s loss. His fellow ministers knew this as well, but did they want him to win the suit? Their arguments about state security clearly were only a disguise for their political jockeying. By the same token, Sharon surmised that there was one man who could not possibly be convinced that the Secret Appendix contained nothing significant—*Time*'s new Israeli counsel, Haim Zadok. The magazine had changed lawyers in midstream. Joshua Rotenstreich had initially been engaged to represent them, but owing to differences of opinion, they had later taken on Zadok, a prominent Labor party member and former minister of justice. Zadok was an avowed enemy of Sharon and had openly condemned him in the press and in public speeches. So Sharon saw it as self-evident that Zadok would hold fast to the theory that the appendix actually did contain relevant information.

But Sharon didn't much care what position Zadok took. All he wanted was that the document be examined, and he refused to be deterred. So when the committee, headed by Peres, finally met on December 31, he waited anxiously for its decision.

Meanwhile, on Friday evening, December 28, Sharon had consulted with five close friends and aides, including his Israeli lawyer Dov Weissglas. The upshot of the Friday-evening discussion was a consensus that Sharon should prepare himself for a negative response from the government. If his own friends in the Likud hadn't helped him when they were in office, how could he possibly expect a committee headed by his most determined political adversary, Shimon Peres, to help him now—Peres, Halevy's friend? It was clear that only Attorney General Zamir's legal decision, uncluttered by any political considerations, could possibly change the course of events.

Sharon decided that a draft letter to the prime minister should be prepared, explaining bluntly the fateful significance of his decision. The general tone of the letter should be direct. If Sharon lost the suit owing to the legal technicality insisted upon by the Israeli government, if he failed to prove that *Time* had published lies, then Sharon would lay the blame directly on the government of Israel. Furthermore, if the prime minister's response was negative, Sharon decided, he would publish the letter so the entire Israeli public would know the facts.*

The week ahead was critical.

Sunday, December 30, brought an agitated call from Milton Gould and Richard Goldstein in New York. They told Weissglas that if Sharon couldn't get the Secret Appendix examined, he might as well not bother returning to New York. The case would be lost. That same day, after long hours at the weekly Sunday cabinet meeting, Sharon arrived at his Tel Aviv office for a meeting with his aides, which began at 7:00 P.M. and ended at 10:30. Sharon read the draft letter to the prime minister, rewording here and there and correcting it. He read it with painstaking care; every word was vital.

At ten o'clock, Sharon called the head of the Mossad and in a fifteen-minute conversation stated his case clearly and precisely:

"I have nothing to hide. I want the Secret Appendix to be

*See Appendix for text of the letter.

214

checked. There is a reporter in the courtroom who claims he has a source in the Israeli Mossad who is none other than its deputy head. You and I have a common interest, both morally and for the good of the country, to prove that this is all unfounded. This can be done in one or more ways. Your man can appear before the judge in camera and tell him what he has already told you—that he never met Halevy in Bikfaya. Or else you can let them examine the Secret Appendix and the other necessary documents. If you do neither, I will have no choice but to make public debate of this, every way I know how. I'd like to make it clear: I won't let the matter stand."

At this point there was nothing left to do but wait for the New Year's Eve meeting.

On the afternoon of the thirty-first I had lunch with Sharon and his guests at a restaurant in Mishkanot Sha'ananim (the Artists' Quarter) in Jerusalem. He was playing host to Floyd Abrams and his wife, Efrat. It was their first meeting, but Sharon was well aware of the fact that Abrams strenuously opposed media-oriented libel suits in the United States and fought against any action impeding the freedom of the press. Sharon acted as if he had all the time in the world. He showed not the slightest sign of worrying about the imminent decision and amiably pointed out the details of the splendid view of the walls of the Old City of Jerusalem.

That day's issue of the *Jerusalem Post* had included its weekly *New York Times* weekend edition, which contained a letter from *Time*'s two top editors: "Even as the libel case of the former Israeli Defense Minister, Ariel Sharon, against Time, Inc., proceeds in a Manhattan courtroom, Mr. Sharon is conducting a propaganda campaign in the United States on his own behalf." They were indirectly admitting that Sharon's press campaign was giving them trouble. The editors also proclaimed that they were prepared to print a retraction if it was proved that the Secret Appendix contained no hint of the story *Time* had printed. However, they complained, they had not as yet been allowed to see this document. Their letter was a response to the article Sharon had published in the *Times*.

The editors also wrote that the reason Sharon had sued their magazine was that he was ambitious to become prime minister.

"We have tried for months to gain access to Appendix B, and we have declared that if it is demonstrated that the disputed material is not contained within the Appendix, we are prepared to publish a retraction of this point. But so far, we have not been given access to Appendix B."

"It's very unusual to have both *Time* editors—Henry Grunwald and Ray Cave—sign one letter," Floyd Abrams pointed out, adding, "In the last twenty years there hasn't been such a suit against *Time* in the United States." Abrams was curious to know how the outcome of the trial would affect Sharon's political future.

"In my opinion," Sharon said, "the way things go in Israel will not be affected by the trial outcome. Whether I win or lose won't make any difference to the political scene." The American guest said he had heard that the Israeli journalists were already wondering how to prepare public opinion in Israel for a possible Sharon victory. Sharon thought for a moment. "The main problem in Israel is not the economy, or the Arabs, or the Russians, or the state of the government. The main problem is the internal hatred among Jews. Self-hatred. That's what's so disquieting. And in my opinion, this is the country's greatest problem, in the short run as well as in the long run."

Abrams ventured the opinion that no matter what the outcome of the trial, Sharon had already scored many points. *Time* would never be the same. Articles such as the one by Steven Brill in *The American Lawyer,* in which he called *Time* to task, would have strong repercussions. Brill was known to be a strong opponent of libel suits.

Sharon finished his lunch and, taking his leave, left to appear at the prime minister's office, where his nine-page confidential letter lay on the table in front of the ministers—Peres, Rabin, Shamir, and Nissim.

And following that appearance the ministers finally approved Judge Sofaer's request.

Thus on Sunday, January 6, 1985, at precisely 10:00 A.M., Yitzhak Kahan, former president of the Israeli Supreme Court, arrived at the prime minister's office in Jerusalem for what was probably the last time he would deal with the report of the commission of inquiry bearing his name.

There was a lot of tension in the Sharon camp. The struggle to have the documents examined had created its own pressures. Now there were pressures of another kind. Only Sharon was calm. With his pragmatism and uncluttered intelligence, he calmed us down. There was no way, he said, that Kahan could find anything in the documents that hadn't been there when he headed the commission.

Ensconced in a tiny room not far from the prime minister's office, Justice Kahan and the two lawyers, Weissglas and Zadok, read the momentous documents. They read steadily for three hours. Security men hovered outside to ensure total secrecy.

First Kahan examined Appendix B. Then he checked the minutes of Sharon's meeting with the Gemayels at Bikfaya on September 15, 1982. Very methodically he followed this with the notes taken at the meeting between Sharon and the leaders of the Lebanese forces the same day. Then he read the testimony of the Israelis who had also participated in those meetings with Sharon, among them the chief of intelligence, the Mossad representative, and the head of the Shin Bet. There were also the testimony and documents from Sharon's last meeting with Bashir Gemayel on September 12.

It was, in every sense, a race against time. The trial had been due to reconvene in New York on January 2, but Judge Sofaer was so relieved that permission had been granted to check the documents that he had agreed to a postponement for another week. That, however, would be the last deadline. The jury couldn't be held indefinitely.

As we had expected, Zadok quibbled. But he hadn't reckoned with Justice Kahan. Calling in his secretary, Kahan dictated his answer to the New York court. There was no unnecessary verbiage. He took the questions unadorned.

Question A: Does the document contain any evidence or suggestion that Minister Sharon had a discussion with the Gemayel family or with any other Phalangist, at Bikfaya or elsewhere, in which Minister Sharon discussed the need to avenge the death of Bashir Gemayel?

Reply: In none of the documents or testimony is there any evidence or suggestion that Minister Sharon had a discussion with the Gemayel family or with any other Phalangist, at Bikfaya or elsewhere, in which Minister Sharon discussed the need to avenge the death of Bashir Gemayel.

Question B: Does the document contain any evidence or suggestion that Minister Sharon had any discussion with a Phalangist in which either person mentioned the need for revenge?

Reply: In none of the documents or testimony is there any evidence or suggestion that Minister Sharon had any discussion with a Phalangist in which either person mentioned the need for revenge.

Question C: Does the document contain any evidence or suggestion that Minister Sharon knew in advance that the Phalangists would massacre civilians if they went into the camps unaccompanied by IDF troops?

Reply: There is no mention in the said documents or testimony of the possibility of the massacre of civilians if the Phalangists were to enter the camps unaccompanied by IDF troops.

The conclusions to be drawn from the documents with regard to Minister Sharon's knowledge of the massacre—in the sense of foreseeing that such an occurrence was liable to happen—were considered in detail in the published report of the Commission. The above documents and testimony formed part of the evidence upon which the Commission based its conclusions. I have nothing to add and no comment to make regarding those conclusions.

Weissglas was elated. He went out to call Sharon. Zadok looked crushed.

Kahan left the moment his statement was ready. Attorney General Zamir arrived to see if he could help. It was sad that all this cooperation hadn't been forthcoming earlier.

Zadok saw an opportunity. He had several reservations, he said to Zamir. What else could one expect from a lawyer representing *Time*? Later that afternoon Zamir dutifully met with Zadok to discuss the wording of *Time*'s reservations. Clearly Kahan's letter had made *Time* nervous. That's what happens when you infer from or rely on body language.

When the trial resumed on Wednesday, January 9, 1985, the jury looked cheerful and refreshed. It was obvious that they had enjoyed the long break provided by the Christmas and New Year holidays after their seclusion in the courtoom for seven weeks. Sharon's meeting with the press after the holidays was like a reunion of old friends. He now had a close rapport with the media representatives, a rapport developed during the last four weeks of the trial. He would chat with them in the courtroom corridors, grant interviews on the courthouse steps—exclusive or for groups. They wanted it; Sharon was happy to oblige. The news that had reached New York even before Sharon's arrival was known to all the media. Sharon would be bringing with him the answers to the questions of the secret documents.

Judge Sofaer walked into the courtoom with the air of a conductor about to lead the last movement of Beethoven's *Eroica*. The plaintiff's legal team—Milton Gould, Richard Goldstein, Arnold Forster, and their assistants, Andrea Feller and Adam Gilbert—looked positively uplifted. Gould's face was transfigured: at long last he was beaming widely. The documents had been examined, and everything Sharon had claimed for almost two years had been corroborated down to the last detail.

But that day really belonged to Judge Sofaer; and he had every right to claim it as he described to the court his quite prodigious efforts to arrange for the examination of the documents. Presenting his unusual correspondence with Jerusalem, he sounded justifiably proud of his achievement. He instructed that copies of the correspondence be distributed to the press.

Once again the screen was put up before the jury, with Justice Kahan's replies projected into it. Bikfaya. Karantina. Gemayel. The Lebanese forces. The meeting of September 12. The meeting of September 15. By now the names, the places, the dates were old hat to these six ordinary Americans in Manhattan. At long last they could see and not only gauge the truth. The famous Appendix B contained nothing that *Time* magazine had published. *Time*'s report was completely false. After seven weeks of laborious contention, *Time* was now publicly exposed. The rock on which the magazine, and especially Halevy, had built its testimony was the secrecy of Appendix B. The fort had become a house of cards.

Judge Sofaer quietly reminded the jury that the Israeli litigator who had conducted the examination was none other than Justice

Kahan, the very man who had chaired the commission of inquiry.

For Sharon it was pure balm. For the American media, at last, it was significant. Their solid wall of support for a colleague in their closed world of communication had already begun to show a crack after Halevy's reluctant admission that he had lied. The crack had now widened into a gap, a credibility gap. But the respite was brief.

Time's Israeli counsel, attorney Haim Zadok, leaped into the breach. He announced that he had reservations about the formerly secret document, about its presentation. His reservations were presented to Judge Sofaer, and the judge ruled that they could be presented only to a closed court.

Time's legal team pounced. Zadok's reservations should be put before an open court.

Sharon did not forget that he was, above all, a member of the Israeli government. Anxious that no damage occur through misreading of Zadok's peculiar reservations, he called Minister of Justice Moshe Nissim in Jerusalem. Nissim consulted with Attorney General Yitzhak Zamir, who ruled that "court" included the jury but that disclosure of the reservations should still be in camera—a closed court.

After the reporters, vehemently objecting, were ushered out of the courtroom and while the reservations were being read, Sofaer suddenly heard that Floyd Abrams, legal watchdog for the freedom of the press, had made an appeal to the Second Circuit Court of Appeals against Sofaer's decision to have Zadok's reservations read in camera. Sofaer's ruling, in fact, did go against American legal and journalistic precedent, but he was determined to maintain faith with the Israeli government. He regarded himself as bound by his original undertaking, he announced, and he did not propose to deviate from it.

Meanwhile Floyd Abrams and other lawyers had hurried up to the top floor of the courthouse in order to submit an appeal to the appeals court on Sofaer's decision. They represented no fewer than twelve news organizations, including *Newsweek,* which opposed the court on First Amendment grounds. The judge was understandably distressed.

Abrams himself told Judge Sofaer in open court: "The law, as we understand it, is this—trials are presumptively open. All parts of trials are presumptively open."

The commotion in the courtroom grew. Sharon had finally succeeded in bringing the findings of the examination of the secret documents to New York, and now a new development was overshadowing that achievement. The media were going to blow it up out of all proportion—as if those secret documents really contained something terrible, as if this were the reason for the reservations being read in camera.

The judge's discomfort increased. A man of impeccable standing, he was suddenly being criticized by the media and by members of his own profession in New York. Another court was going to pass judgment on his action in making the agreement with the Israeli government. The judge had been heard to remark in private conversation that in view of the contents of Zadok's reservations, he did not understand why the Israeli government was insisting on in camera reading. The reservations did not contain any secrets.

Sharon saw the avalanche increasing in size and moving in the wrong direction. So he once more called Justice Minister Moshe Nissim, explaining what had happened and, most important, the unpleasantness now enveloping Judge Sofaer. This is the situation, Sharon said; you decide. The Israeli government had insisted on this extraordinary provision of secrecy for the reservations. Only the Israeli government could rescind it.

Nissim acted quickly. A rapid telephone roundup, and the message went to Judge Sofaer: the reservations could be read in open court.

CHAPTER
THIRTY-THREE

IT WAS A BATTLE EVERY INCH OF THE WAY, BUT Sharon was moving forward. Despite Zadok's "reservations," *Time*'s lawyers conceded the magazine was incorrect in claiming that Secret Appendix B contained an allegation against Sharon. Nevertheless *Time* maintained it would stand by its story that he had "discussed" the need for revenge with Christian Phalangists shortly before the massacre.

Richard Goldstein immediately asked Judge Sofaer to rule that there was not "a scintilla of evidence" to support *Time*'s claim that Appendix B included the charge. At that moment *Time*'s Tom Barr abruptly interjected, "I'm going to concede that point when I make my closing."

Robert Marshall, one of *Time*'s in-house lawyers, talking to the press added a corollary to Barr's comment. "While this discussion [of revenge] is not in Appendix B, it could be someplace else. There may be a detail that's incorrect, but that doesn't affect the substance of the story."

Sharon shrugged Mr. Marshall off. To him the concession was "an important achievement" and "a major step forward" in the battle with *Time*.

"*Time* based its lie and libel on something that was in Appendix B," said Sharon at a crowded press conference in the first-floor corridor in the Manhattan federal court building. "They wanted to give credibility to their lie. They have been found to be inaccurate." *Time* expected its story to hold up, Sharon said, because they never thought anyone would be permitted to examine the Secret Appendix.

Sharon was gratified to find that even *The New York Times* had joined the critics of *Time*'s journalism. Even before any verdict was handed down by the jury, Sharon observed that "the American media were honest and fair enough to attack *Time* magazine."

A news analysis by Alex S. Jones of the *Times* was critical.

> ... The journalistic issues have been sharpened by the announcement yesterday that, contrary to what had been reported in *Time,* a secret appendix to an Israeli commission report apparently did not contain some information damaging to Mr. Sharon, according to an Israeli jurist who headed the commission.

222

Unlike newspapers, newsmagazines ... routinely separate reporting from writing. Doubts are being expressed about this editorial process in which an article passes through so many hands that questionable reporting may not be seriously challenged because everyone assumes someone else is doing so. ...

The magazine's top editors have aggressively defended the article and Mr. Halevy's reporting. But questions continue to be raised regarding *Time*'s standard for accuracy and the degree of trust it places in its reporters. ...

For journalists, the Sharon trial highlights the balance that all editors must strike between trusting their reporters and yet remaining critical of the information that the reporters produce ...

ON FRIDAY, JANUARY 11, MILTON GOULD BEGAN HIS
summation to the jury. It was Gould's special day. For nearly ten
hours the attorney paced back and forth in front of the jury box
blasting *Time* magazine and the summation delivered by Tom
Barr the previous day. After more than two months of bitter conflict in the courtroom Gould had summoned all of his venerable
resources for the payoff. He was by turn sarcastic and ironic,
rasping and cajoling, as he called on the jury for a just verdict.

Courtroom 110 was packed. People had been lining up in hopes
someone might leave and vacate a seat.

Gould's opening went to the heart of the matter. ". . . Your verdict will go a long way to determine whether Ariel Sharon will go
down in history—not just in the history of Israel, the history of
the Western world, the history of all the countries that have
fought for decency and democracy, and I unhesitatingly include
this little country of Israel among them. Your verdict will determine whether he will go down in history as a great man, a great
soldier, regarded by countless people as the savior of his country,
or on the basis of the lies and the vicious speculation which I say
have been created, engendered by what *Time* has said about him
in this article, whether he will go down as a kind of monster, another Herod, a man who ordered a massacre of women and children. Your verdict is going to determine that, and that is a pretty
serious responsibility."

The jury listened intently. There was no question but that
Gould was presenting the historical dimensions of the case, far beyond the issue of libel.

"This really is a remarkably simple case," Gould continued. "It
centers on a single paragraph in an article in *Time* magazine, an
article which by this time you must be sick of hearing about, as I
am sick of hearing about it, 'The Verdict Is Guilty.'"

Gould mocked *Time*'s last-minute effort to discredit Judge
Kahan's examination by a legal maneuver: "If Zadok came from
Tombstone, Arizona, instead of from Tel Aviv, I'd call him Last-
Ditch Zadok!" he declared. "Zadok's reservations constitute an
affirmation of the resolution of *Time* magazine to die in the last
ditch of prevarication. I didn't make that one up, I borrowed it

from Edmund Burke. That is what they are doing. They are dying in the last ditch of prevarication, and Zadok provides them with the last ditch. . . .

"Three men sit in a room: one of them is our hired gun, Weissglas; the other guy is their hired gun, Zadok; but the real arbiter, the fellow in whom everybody has confidence, who is not hired, who is not the local counsel shoved in to louse it up, the one guy you can rely on is Kahan, and Kahan says it ain't so, there is no evidence. There is no suggestion. There is nothing. And for Mr. Zadok to come in at the last minute and throw some dirt in your eyes and call it reservations . . . Come on! It's an insult to your intelligence. I can hire a lawyer to give me a letter of opinion on anything I want, especially when I'm giving him money to give me a letter of opinion that is going to be used in a court 5000 miles away and he skips out of town before anyone can even call him a liar. . . .

"I am sorry for Mr. Zadok's family. I'm sure he is a fine, decent, honest fellow that goes to *shul* every Friday night and will take a fee for writing an opinion."

Gould was bitter about *Time*. "They wrote that Sharon had given them [the Gemayels] the feeling that he understood the need for revenge and assured them that they would be able to carry out their plan, their plan of slaughter, their plan of revenge without interference by the Israelis. I think that makes *Time*'s story all the more reprehensible in the face of these uniformly smooth statements from *Time*'s own people that, in fact, none of them had any reason to believe that General Sharon encouraged, intended or even knew that there would be a massacre. That people who were capable of sitting on the witness stand and in your presence in an American court could utter the words that they had no reason to believe that General Sharon encouraged, intended or even knew that there could be a massacre . . . that they could combine together to produce that little time bomb up there which conveys to the world that the Minister of Defense of Israel sat with the principals of the murderers and told them he understood their need for revenge.

"I think it offends decency to come in with an argument like that."

Gould had started his monologue at half past nine in the morning. By now the early twilight was dimming the courtroom. Respecting Jewish tradition and reluctant to offend the sensibilities of Orthodox Jews, Sharon avoids as much as possible carrying out his public activities on the Sabbath. Even Judge Sofaer himself would stop Friday court sessions long before the evening, before the onset of the Sabbath. This was heartening for the Orthodox members of the largest metropolitan Jewish community in the world.

When Sharon realized the evening would be prolonged he sent a message during recess to Judge Sofaer. He asked Bernie Fischman to tell the judge that the Israeli minister would remain in the courtroom although the Sabbath had already begun. It was inconceivable, explained Sharon, that he should leave during Gould's vital summation. Judge Sofaer confirmed Sharon's decision. "The duty of saving life overrides the Sabbath, and Minister Sharon is definitely struggling for his life."

It was a comment that characterized the entire battle in the courtroom.

Sharon, with Lily beside him, watched and listened as Gould passionately attacked the "filthy lie . . . flagrant, outrageous lie" published by *Time,* reminding the jury that Sharon had voted for the investigation of the events in Sabra and Shatilla, the investigation that resulted in the Kahan Report. "Well, I don't think anyone suggests Sharon is a maniac; but only a maniac knowing that he had sat there and had such a conversation, and that the conversation was taken down by somebody connected with the Israeli government, some Mossad fellow, stenographer, stenographic transcript, would say, 'I want an investigation.' You got to be nuts, and Sharon ain't nuts. He may be fat but he ain't crazy!"

Gould's earthy and direct words were followed by a burst of laughter from the entire courtroom, including not only the judge and the jury but Sharon himself, as well as Lily.

The previous night Gould's team had worked until dawn preparing all the necessary exhibits. While he spoke, they were ready with every document, projecting on the screen anything that was mentioned.

Gould bluntly called Halevy a liar, pointing out the discrepancies in his different versions of how he obtained the "secret information" from his "secret sources." "He didn't have any more of a source on this matter than he had on the Begin story. It's a cooked-up, made-up, fabricated story. He misled Kelly into thinking he had seen the notes but, in fact, he hadn't seen any notes because there aren't any notes. We know it now; there aren't any such notes dealing with Bikfaya."

Gould switched to travesty: " 'Halevy,' Kelly says, 'we have to find something out about Appendix B. What's in it?' Good question. About time. But you know, they didn't know about Appendix B until the Kahan Commission Report came out.

"Halevy doesn't hesitate one instant. This is the real war correspondent. When you hear his answer you understand this is the product of years of military experience. This is a heart-and-soul person. 'We have to find out what's in it,' says Kelly. Halevy says, 'I know one thing that's in it or I think is in it, or I think I know one thing that is in it and that's my December Memo item on the condolence call.' . . .

" 'So go and look,' Kelly says. 'Get the facts.' 'So,' says Mr. Halevy, describing the process of verification, 'I telephoned a source and I asked it what's in Appendix B, to which the source responded "I can't tell you that. It's a secret appendix." ' 'Well,' says Halevy, 'you know, you and I are buddies together. We were in Hebrew school together and you shouldn't put me off with that kind of stuff. You got to tell your old buddy about it. Well, tell me something about it.' So this same source says, 'Well, you see, Dudu baby, it's a code book, it's a reference book, and the names of intelligence officers identified in the public report are listed in Appendix B.'

"Well, he hasn't said anything about Bikfaya. . . . And we know it isn't there, and we know it from an impeccable source. We know it not from a Halevy, or a Kelly, or a Duncan or anybody else. We know from a Kahan that it isn't there, that it's a lie."

Halevy's political bias against Sharon was attacked too. "Why does Halevy want to conceal from anybody—from you in this case—what were his ties with the Labor party? With Mr. Peres, who's the head of the Labor party? He must have a reason.

There's nothing inherently disgraceful in being a member of the
Labor party. Some of the greatest people in Israel were members
of the Labor party. But you see, Peres and Sharon have for years
been arch rivals, and their respective parties, Labor and Likud,
are at odds with each other. Sharon isn't just a member of the
Likud. He's one of its founders. He's the guy who was largely responsible for the defeat that Labor suffered—you heard all about
that—a few years ago . . .

"So Halevy was well aware that if he admitted in your presence
that he had continued to support Peres after Duncan's warning, that might be seen, and properly seen, as a kind of conflict
of interest, especially when he is undertaking to write about
Sharon. And how do you write objectively and dispassionately
about him?

"So when he was asked here, he wasn't a member of the Labor
party. When he was asked earlier in a previous case, where was his
interest, his self-interest, his objective wasn't clear-cut, and he answered differently.

"Now, I don't think there's much doubt as to what happened.
Sharon is a member of the Likud party. Halevy's sympathies, at
the very least, were with the Labor party. Halevy had an affec-
tion, a great interest in Peres. Nothing wrong with that; but tell
the truth about it. Don't lie about it. Don't conceal it."

Gould suggested the jury "study Halevy's soul" by analyzing
his 1984 confidential letter to Dick Duncan. "He still shows in the
letter that in his mind Peres will be the savior of the country. At
the same time he worries over the political popularity of Sharon,
this fellow against whom he has no bias. . . . One of the things he
worries about is . . . 'the actual vindication of Arik Sharon.'

"Well, it indicates to you he has a very open mind on Arik
Sharon. Just the guy you want running around with his notebook
trying to get honest information and giving objective reporting on
Arik Sharon. This is the letter in which he compares the situation
in Israel with the situation in Europe—Europe and mainly Germany in the thirties and forties and so on.

"I think you ought to read that letter; but there's something
else in the letter. Do you remember the lengths to which this man
went to establish his devotion to the State of Israel, his deep patri-

otism, his identification in his own mind, in his own soul, with Israel?

"And what does he say to his boss? Get me out of here. Get me out of Israel. I want to spend some time in a place 'where the level of my personal involvement will be less acute. I can no longer become enthusiastic over here in Israel. I will not change my decision about leaving Israel when the weather improves, or when Peres will, if at all, become Prime Minister.'

"I don't think there is anything wrong with a man wanting to get out of a place and go live in another. I don't think there is anything wrong in a man wanting to improve himself; but I think that when a man comes into a courtroom here and puts on a parade of national devotion, puts on a show of the depth of his patriotism in the same year he's asking his boss to get him out of a place he compares with Nazi Germany, it is very, very important in one respect. It demonstrates to you the quality of the man, the nature of his sincerity and whether you can rely on him in what he says. . . .

". . . He is entitled to his political views, just as you and I are entitled to our political views, but we are not journalists reporting news about people against whom we are campaigning.

"Now, *Time* has conceded through its witnesses in the trial that political activity, political involvement not only affects the appearance of impartiality, it can affect the very credibility of a journalist. And I suggest to you that Mr. Halevy's letter, Mr. Halevy's political views, Mr. Halevy's secret feelings about the State of Israel and Sharon affect his credibility in this case."

Gould turned directly to the jury and summarized. "Ladies and gentlemen. You have become in this case virtual actors, virtual participants in an achievement. One man, a foreigner, comes these thousands of miles and he appeals to an American court, to a group of American citizens, to penetrate the wall these people have built around themselves: a wall which permits them to do what they please; a wall which permits them to defy any efforts to penetrate into their secret operation and find out how they work . . .

"It takes a lot of courage and a lot of effort; and Sharon has the courage and we have given him the effort, and we have penetrated their minds. And what's revealed in that penetration isn't a very pleasant sight. What's revealed is a vast organism working in its own way with a virtual license to destroy the reputations of other human beings. . . .

"What was done to Sharon was an infamy, and it falls to you six American citizens, who have never heard of these people and have no interest, to do your duty and eradicate that infamy.

"You know, about two hundred years ago there was a man named Voltaire. He was a great sage, a great philosopher, and he had dedicated the end of his life after all kinds of literary triumphs, he had dedicated the end of his life to stamping out infamy, as he called it; and he defined infamy for us.

"Infamy, he said, is bigotry. Infamy is discrimination. Infamy is superstition. Infamy is a disregard of the inhumanities visited on one group of men by another group of men. Infamy is doing it by recklessness, and Voltaire devoted himself with such passion to stamping out this kind of thing that every letter he wrote, every speech he made, every book that he put his name on, carried this little phrase in French, 'Ecrasez l'infâme'—'Stamp out infamy,' stamp it out, kill it.

"And I suggest to you that in this case you six American citizens can take advantage of Sharon's courage and the perseverance of the people who have associated themselves with him and his project, and you [can] help us strike out this infamy!"

Gould was pale. It had been a massive and effective indictment. The jury rose to leave the courtroom. Sharon got up and walked over to him. "Thank you, Milton, thank you," he said.

OVER THE WEEKEND, ON SATURDAY AND ESPE-
cially on Sunday, Judge Sofaer remained in touch with the lawyers for both sides and tried to convince them to reach a
settlement. After that it would be too late—he was about to
charge the jury.

Meanwhile everyone wondered what, if anything, was brewing
at *Time*. Appendix B had been examined and had revealed nothing to support their story. Gould and Barr had completed their
summation addresses to the jury. This was the moment for *Time*
to retreat with a semblance of grace. But anyone nursing this fond
hope had not reckoned with *Time*'s very special arrogance.

Even Judge Sofaer was taken by surprise when he saw *Time*'s
issue of January 21. Quite aside from extensive coverage of the
trial proceedings the previous week, there was a special statement,
prominently featured in a box.

> In its February 21, 1983 cover story, "The Verdict Is Guilty,"
> *Time* reported that Israel's official commission of inquiry found
> that Ariel Sharon, the defense minister, and several other military
> officials shared an "indirect" responsibility for the massacre by
> Lebanese Phalangist soldiers of hundreds of civilians in the Pales-
> tinian refugee camps of Sabra and Shatilla that began two days
> after the assassination of Lebanese president elect Bashir Gemayel.
> In one paragraph of its article, *Time* reported that a secret appen-
> dix to the commission's published report—known as Appendix
> B—contained further details about Sharon's visit to the Gemayel
> family on the day after Bashir Gemayel's assassination.
>
> Almost two years after Minister Sharon began litigation against
> *Time* over this paragraph, the Israeli government has permitted an
> Israeli attorney representing *Time* to examine the secret appendix.
> Based upon this examination last week, *Time* now issues a correc-
> tion: Appendix B does not contain further details about Sharon's
> visit to the Gemayal family. *Time* regrets that error.
>
> *Time* stands by the substance of the paragraph in question that
> "Sharon also reportedly discussed with the Gemayels the need for
> the Phalangists to take revenge for the assassination of Bashir, but
> the details of the conversation are not known." *Time* did not say,
> and has never said, that Sharon intended that the Phalangists
> commit a massacre, or encouraged such a massacre.

Blood Libel

> The Israeli government continues to deny *Time* the right to inspect other specific testimony relevant to this case that is known to exist as part of the record of the commission of inquiry.

In the same issue *Time* added another angle to that statement. It had an even more surreal quality: "*Time*'s sources for what was said at those meetings remain confidential, but as recently as two weeks ago they confirmed once again to *Time* that revenge had been discussed. *Time* pointed out that the question of whether the testimony is located in Appendix B or elsewhere is relatively immaterial and in no way undercuts the magazine's contention that revenge came up during the meetings and is irrelevant to the issue whether what *Time* reported was libelous."

Time was digging its heels in.

Not only had *Time* dismissed the findings of Justice Kahan but it had rechecked and reconfirmed with its sources—the anonymous and unreliable sources of two years earlier.

Judge Sofaer was not amused. Patently angry, he observed that he could not imagine that Barr had previous knowledge of this publication. It must have originated with the editors working with their in-house lawyers. "This special statement could constitute a repetition of libel," said the judge.

Worse, however, was yet to come. Not only had the editors reiterated their libel; they also had cloned the culprit. Herbert H. Denton, an enterprising writer for *The Washington Post*, asked managing editor Ray Cave who had done the rechecking. Said Cave: "Of course it was Halevy who checked the sources. They were his sources."

CHAPTER
THIRTY-SIX

WHILE LISTENING TO JUDGE SOFAER'S GENERALLY
monotonous tone as he read his charge to the jury, Sharon recognized that this was a highly complicated and involved case. He had watched the jurors' faces as they listened intently to the judge late that Monday afternoon of January 14, 1985. Even though Sofaer had chosen simple words in directing the jury, Sharon wondered whether the jurors were capable of grasping the complexities involved.

After eight weeks in court a certain sense of familiarity had developed among all those involved in the case—the judge, the litigants and their lawyers, the jurors, the media—all except Sharon and *Time* in respect to each other.

But now, while the judge was directing the jury, Sharon knew that all these relationships and other considerations were of no moment. Now was the time for the well guarded and secluded jurors to face what, for Sharon—and no less for themselves—was their biggest test. "You must decide who was telling the truth and who was not," the Judge said.

A time of decision for Richard Zug, forty-five, a computer programmer with IBM, who lived with his wife and children in northern Westchester County. A time of decision for Patricia Young, forty-five, of the Bronx, an executive secretary at a public relations firm; for Spencer James, Jr., sixty-four, a retired Con Edison employee, also from the Bronx; for Patricia DeLoatch, twenty-seven, from Westchester, a marketing specialist with AT&T; for Ingrid Tineo, twenty-four, a Manhattan secretary, originally from the Dominican Republic; and for Lydia Burdick, thirty-five, a New Yorker, management consultant, who on her jury questionnaire had written that her boyfriend was an Israeli.

Along with them, Sharon learned that afternoon that there was a huge difference between proving something "by a preponderance of the evidence" and "by clear and convincing evidence." The judge dealt with this in his sixty-six-page charge, in which he carefully defined the three essential elements for proving a libel—defamation, falsity, and malice.

With the patience of a schoolmaster he explained that, in coming to its verdict as to whether Sharon had proved the elements of his claim, the jury would have to consider the burden of proof a plaintiff must meet in connection with each element.

To begin with, Sharon bore the burden of proving that *Time*'s statement was defamatory, the first element, by "a preponderance of the evidence." In order to prove something by a preponderance of the evidence, Sofaer explained, one has to show that it is more likely to be true than untrue. In this case, if the jury felt that Sharon had not convinced them that the statements in question were defamatory, that is, "if you feel the evidence is equally divided or that *Time* has a better case, then Sharon will have failed to meet his burden."

Sharon's burden with respect to falsity, the second element, and malice, the third element, Sofaer emphasized, "is even greater." The burden one has to discharge in proving falsity and malice is the ability to persuade the jury "by clear and convincing evidence," not merely by a "preponderance of the evidence," that the statements included in *Time*'s article were published either in the knowledge that they were false or with a reckless disregard as to whether they were true or false.

Judge Sofaer went on to elaborate on the evidence needed to prove falsity and actual malice: "Clear and convincing evidence is a more exacting standard than proof by a preponderance of the evidence. Clear and convincing proof leaves no substantial doubt in your mind. It is proof that establishes in your mind, not only that the proposition at issue is probable, but also that it is highly probable. The higher burden of proof is required by the Constitution to protect the rights enjoyed by the press and public to speak freely about public officials and their conduct. On the other hand, 'clear and convincing' proof is not as high a standard as the burden of proof applied in criminal cases, which is proof 'beyond a reasonable doubt.' It is enough if plaintiff establishes falsity or actual malice beyond any 'substantial' doubt; he does not have to dispel every 'reasonable' doubt. . . .

. . . "Not every unpleasant or uncomplimentary statement is defamatory," Sofaer warned. "In reading the paragraph at issue, you must give its language a plain, natural, unstrained meaning, putting yourself in the position of the average reader."

On the issue of "actual malice" Sofaer gave the jury twenty-one pages of instructions. It was a kind of road map. Sofaer probably realized how unusual his charge to the jury was because he repeated his warning to the jurors: "You should draw no inferences whatever from this effort to provide new guidance in rendering your verdict."

It was clear to Sharon, now more than ever before, that if he had failed to prove one of these elements he would lose the battle. "What interests me more than anything else," he told us when court had again adjourned, "is to win on falsity. If we arrive there, I'll consider it not only a moral victory but a *factual* victory too—that I proved that *Time* lied and that I told the truth!"

RAY CAVE, *TIME*'S MANAGING EDITOR, STOOD IN
the corridor facing outraged journalists. They weren't just asking
questions. Top media representatives were shouting at him, were
actually screaming. Just a few moments earlier, after seventeen
hours of deliberation spread over three days, the jury had decided
that *Time* had defamed Sharon.

But *Time* thought otherwise. In an obtuse display of arrogance
or idiocy, or both, Cave simply refused to accept the verdict, stating that "the jury completely misread what *Time* said." *Time*
wouldn't even accept that Sharon might have won a partial victory.

Cave emerged into the corridor. He had a bunch of PR people
handing out *Time*'s news release. Outwardly he looked the
same—the three-piece pinstripe, the elegantly trimmed beard—
but this time clothes didn't make the man. As he faced a barrage
of hostile questions he seemed disturbed and embarrassed, very
much unlike his usual debonair self.

"What do you mean by 'misread'?" one reporter asked. "You
don't believe the jury can understand English?" inquired another.
"Do you mean to say you reject a decision by an American jury?"
demanded a third.

The atmosphere was explosive. The hostility of the journalists,
at the beginning of the trial so firmly directed at Sharon, had now
turned directly against *Time*. It wasn't only that Halevy had hurt
their professional pride by having to admit he'd reported something about which he knew nothing. But now, after the jury had
given Sharon a victory in the first of three rounds, the great *Time*
itself, at editorial level, was rejecting the jury's verdict, rejecting it
with a special statement backed by the managing editor himself.
Despite their lingering suspicions of Sharon, the American journalists simply couldn't take this. They bombarded Cave with
their questions.

At the other end of the corridor Milton Gould was beaming.
"One down and two to go," he said to a phalanx of journalists.
"General Sharon and I are delighted. I'm glad we didn't lose on a
point of grammar. Now we can get down to the critical issues,
whether that paragraph was false or not."

Sharon had been waiting since the previous Monday in that small back room. It hadn't been easy. He knew perfectly well that if the jury didn't find for him on the charge of defamation, he might as well pack his bags and go home. And this would mean losing the case before the issue of falsity had even been raised.

Notwithstanding *Time*'s defeat, Michael Luftman, the young man who ran the press campaign for *Time* during the trial, handed around its rather doubtful statement:

> *Time* continues to believe that the article was substantially true and we could have proved that had we been given adequate access to secret Israeli documents and testimony.
>
> To prove defamatory meaning, as the Judge instructed the jury, what *Time* printed must be construed to say that Sharon either "consciously intended" or "actively encouraged" the Phalangists to kill civilians in the camps. On this charge, the jury completely misread what *Time* said.
>
> This is only the first of the three issues which the jury must decide in this part of the trial and we remain confident that we will prevail.

Time's special statement, one of two prepared for both contingencies, infuriated the American journalists. It was hard to hear Cave across their angry voices while he admitted the magazine editors were "disappointed" with the verdict. Barr came to his aid. Both of them energetically defended *Time*'s position. "Sharon came here knowing we could not discover the substance in this case," Barr declared.

Then Barr came through with a remarkable piece of sophistry. Cave nodded in agreement as the lawyer spoke. "I don't see," Barr said, "why Libyan leader Muammar Qaddafi can't sue here too and then say every piece of evidence is a state secret."

All the press corps heard this astonishing comparison. And many of them went into print later taking the line followed by Ray Kerrison of the *New York Post*.

> On the lips of a battle-scarred old soldier, nothing is as sweet as the taste of victory at the end of a long, bloody war.
> Ariel Sharon, a general who has fought so many wars and skir-

237

mishes he cannot count them, got that taste yesterday when a jury handed him a significant first triumph in a $50 million libel campaign against *Time* magazine. . . .

He came to New York a solitary figure in a business suit with no marching columns to back him, only a ferocious pride, to do battle against a publishing empire with inexhaustible funds and resources. . . .

A foreigner, Sharon was striking into the enemy's very own territory, which itself was fortified by the First Amendment, cornerstone of the Constitution and guaranteeing freedom of the press.

No matter. If an old soldier is stripped of his honor, he is stripped of everything. So Sharon sold his home in Tel Aviv to build his war chest, then took a jet to New York. . . .

Israelis called him the Lion of the Desert. Military historians credit him with one of the most brilliant strategic victories in modern history when he crossed the Suez Canal with his tanks to split the Egyptian armies and encircle one of them. . . .

Sharon could not conceal the pleasure of his first victory against *Time*. "I came to New York for three reasons," he said. "I came to make it very clear that *Time* lied, to make the fact known to the whole world, and to make sure they do not do it again. . . ."

Sharon gives the lie to the canard that old soldiers fade away. Some keep fighting. . . .

TWO DAYS AFTER THE JURY RETURNED ITS VER-
dict on the question of defamation it returned its verdict on the
question of falsity. For Sharon this verdict was the essence of the
trial, the essence of his bitter campaign. Would the jury also decide what Sharon had been shouting from the rooftops for
twenty-three months—that *Time* had published lies about him?

Arik and Lily came to the court to await the verdict. They left
the Regency in the morning and, accompanied by their security
patrol, drove through heavy traffic along the snowbound East
River Drive. The dark-gray sky was the color of the river. In the
first-floor back room of the courthouse a coffee urn, bagels, and
orange juice were waiting for them.

The numerous security men stayed in the corridor outside the
room. They patrolled the length and breadth of the first floor of
the courthouse. The greater the publicity and attention generated
around Sharon's trial, the more anxious they became that someone would try something.

Hardworking Brenda Cameron, who was in charge of the
courthouse branch of Gould's law office, saw to refreshments. Not
only did she have to ask Lily and Arik whether they wanted Big
Macs again or pastrami or Chinese fast food; she also had to consult with the American security men as to where to order the
meals and who would deliver them. They would not even allow
her to inform the delicatessen for whom the meals were intended,
because they wanted to rule out the possibility of poisoning.

Sharon listened carefully to the conversations going on around
him—the guesses regarding the second verdict. But he himself
never uttered a word. I told him what I had heard over lunch
from two important American journalists—that they were afraid
the jury would determine that the paragraph published in *Time*
was the truth. They claimed that the judge's charge to the jury
had been too strict. Sharon reacted with indifference. He simply
didn't want to hear about it.

The jury was sitting in an adjacent room, opening on the same
corridor. All that the people concerned knew was that it had finished deliberating. Had they perhaps gone out to lunch?

The newsmen in the courthouse, who had been waiting there

for several days, engaged in guesswork. What was the significance of the jury's sitting for two days? How was it they had not reached a verdict sooner? Was that good for *Time* or for Sharon? They concluded that it was good for Sharon.

On Sharon's instructions, I had prepared a short announcement that would be suitable for both possible outcomes. It started with the words "I believe in the American judicial system. I have come to New York to prove that *Time* lied."

When, at last, on Friday, January 18, the jury found for Sharon on falsity, *Time* became the butt of a lot of newsmen's jokes in the courtroom and later in press reports around the world.

For most people there, and of course for Sharon and his friends in particular, the verdict on falsity was somehow sweetened by *Time*'s total confusion.

Managing editor Ray Cave had to carry the ball again. Looking relatively calm, he started reading from another prepared statement. Giving a declaratory "Hrm," he began, "*Time* is gratified that . . ." The TV cameras were already whirring when Cave fumbled to a stop. He rolled his eyes skyward for help. Momentarily it seemed as if he were going to pluck nervously at that well trimmed beard. He coughed. "Wrong statement," he admitted. His face turned a mottled red as the crowd of reporters laughed mercilessly. "Well . . . we had to be ready . . . ever hopeful . . ."

Cave's PR crew rushed forward to help him, hurriedly explaining things to the reporters. Amidst ribald comments, the least of which was "a communications breakdown in Time Inc.'s communications empire," they said they'd prepared two statements, one for victory and one for defeat. The hapless Cave had picked up the wrong statement.

Given the correct one, Cave settled his glasses on his nose and started again.

> Time Incorporated today issued the following statement about the partial verdict in the libel suit brought by Ariel Sharon, former Israeli Minister of Defense, against *Time* magazine: *Time* still believes that the article was substantially true. In our view, the only thing the evidence showed was that the disputed material was not contained in Appendix B—a relatively minor inaccuracy. We be-

lieve we could have proven that the paragraph was substantially true had we been given adequate access to secret Israeli documents and testimony. We have the utmost confidence in our editorial staff and in our editorial procedures, which have been tested for more than sixty years.

We continue to expect that the jury will find that *Time* did not libel Mr. Sharon.

Meanwhile the jury was already beginning its deliberations on the third verdict.

CHAPTER

THIRTY-NINE

THE LONGER THE JURY DELIBERATED ON THE

third verdict, the more demand there was for background stories on Sharon. Everyone in the media needed "color."

A New York *Daily News* reporter was told to get a shot of Sharon eating a hot dog. Sharon liked the reporter but, despite his exposure to the media, he has always fought shy of posed pictures. If photographers get a shot of him while covering an event, fine, but he has a phobia about posing.

But the reporter pleaded, "My editors told me to get it."

In the end Sharon relented. He would do it provided, he said with a cheerful smile, "you can find me a kosher hot dog!"

The *Daily News* editor had heard that Sharon was crazy about American hot dogs, and he was right. In spite of all the luxury banquets Sharon has to attend as part of his duties, he's happiest when he can find a hot dog. According to Sharon, only a hamburger can beat a hot dog. Whether waiting at an airport, or stopping at a roadhouse on the way from New York to Washington, or on Broadway, Sharon first looks for "a fresh hot dog."

Even in Israel he likes taking a break from a cabinet meeting and going to the Mahane Yehuda open-air market in Jerusalem to eat a felafel (fried chickpeas in a pita—a flat Arab bread) or a "mixed grill" in a pita. Once, after a long talk with Philip Habib in Jerusalem, Sharon invited him to continue the discussion over a felafel in the Mahane Yehuda. Habib preferred a flat-silver lunch, so Sharon drove over to the felafel stand and returned enthusiastically biting into the pita and felafel, impressively full of hot peppers. In Manhattan he never missed a chance for a hot dog.

On Sunday, January 20, the *Daily News* carried a picture of Sharon eating a hot dog on Forty-second Street and Fifth Avenue, with a story under Patrick Clark's by-line.

If Ariel Sharon seems larger than life these days there are two reasons—his big libel suit against *Time* magazine and his legendary appetite.

The 5-foot-6, 235-pound former Israeli defense minister doesn't deny that eating is one of his favorite pastimes, or that he loves American food—mostly hot dogs, hamburgers and southern fried chicken.

"My favorite American food since I first came to the United States in 1952 is a hot dog," Sharon said during a break in his $50 million suit against *Time*. "I like them best with sauerkraut, but I also like them with relish." Sharon's wife, Lily, who supervises her husband's diet and tries vainly to get him to eat sensibly, said he likes other things on his hot dog too.

"Look at him," she said jokingly. "Do you think he stops with only two? No. After sauerkraut and relish I know he has one with just mustard."

Six days later, immediately after the trial, a Bay Rigby cartoon ran in the *New York Post*. It showed a seedy individual near an outdoor stand yelling, "Dogs!" The caption read, "The author of *Time*'s Ariel Sharon story tackles his new assignment."

Whether or not Sharon's passion for hot dogs inspired the cartoon, no one can tell. But one thing is sure: despite everything that happened, Halevy wasn't sent by *Time* to sell hot dogs. Halevy exiled himself from Israel to Washington, on *Time*'s payroll. And all the *Time* actors in the drama stayed on in their jobs in a Mafia type of camaraderie.

HENRY GRUNWALD WAS ALMOST CERTAINLY
aware of the enormous damage done to *Time*'s reputation, not
only by what came out about the magazine in court but also by
Sharon's open media assaults on the news organization. He did
not sit idly by waiting for the next verdict. No other interpreta-
tion can explain how Grunwald came to send an extraordinary,
confidential, personal letter to the top people in such major
papers as *The New York Times,* the *Los Angeles Times,* and *The
Washington Post.* In the letter Grunwald sought to reassure his colleagues in the exclusive top media club that *Time* was still a credible newsmagazine despite the fallout from the Sharon libel suit.

Lally Weymouth, who brought Grunwald's PR campaign to
light in an article in the *Los Angeles Times,* insisted later that the
letter was sent out "in the trial's closing days"—after the earlier
verdicts, when Sharon first began claiming a "moral victory."
Michael Luftman, the ubiquitous *Time* PR man in the courtroom,
stated after the trial that the letter had, in fact, been sent to "a
very few people personally selected by Grunwald." He added that
it had been sent out before the jury began its deliberations. Luftman refused to disclose the full text of the letter or to reveal to
whom exactly it had been sent. But news reports claimed to identify some of the recipients as top op-ed page editors and writers
such as Max Frankel and Anthony Lewis at *The New York Times*
and two others at the *Los Angeles Times.*

Lally Weymouth explained that Henry Grunwald was taking
no chances and that his letter to leading newspaper editors was
"designed to forestall the negative commentary that might have
followed a total Sharon victory." In the letter, so Weymouth reported, Grunwald attacked the "great many misconceptions" regarding *Time*'s performance on the Sharon story.

Grunwald explained that reporter David Halevy "had several
very . . . confidential sources of the sort . . . any news organization
would not have hesitated to use." Grunwald glossed over *Time*'s
admission during the trial that it had incorrectly attributed the
damaging charge against Sharon to Secret Appendix B. "A lot of
people seem to have great difficulty in accepting the fact that the
truth of the information does not depend upon its actually being
in Appendix B," Grunwald wrote.

Ms. Weymouth was correct, while *Time*'s Luftman had gotten it wrong. Grunwald's letter is dated January 17, 1985, a time when the jury was in the midst of its deliberations on the second verdict. This is indicated by Grunwald himself in the first paragraph of his long and detailed letter:

> At this writing the jury in the Sharon case—I think mistakenly—has found against us on the issue of defamation. Whatever the final outcome, there is bound to be a lot of discussion now, not merely whether the verdict was right, but how *Time* performed journalistically. . . . I hope you won't mind if I offer a few comments for your background.
>
> Our reporter had several very solid, confidential sources of the sort I think any news organization would not have hesitated to use. Not incidentally, as recently as two weeks ago David Halevy's principal source reaffirmed the original information. . . .

Grunwald took special care to deal in his letter with the question of Secret Appendix B:

> . . . There is the matter of the Kahan letter to Judge Sofaer reporting that nothing in the Kahan Commission documents suggested any talk of revenge. We cannot accept them as conclusive. Kahan based his findings only on "some" of the documents, not including a large body of sworn testimony that was given to the Commission's examiners, but not passed on to the full Commission. . . .
>
> . . . Incidentally, the whole arrangement for Kahan to examine only some relevant documents, with our lawyers present under severe restrictions, plainly deprived us of due process. The Plaintiff in this case is a member of a government which controls the documentary evidence and has given us only limited access to this evidence and denied us virtually all witnesses who could have thrown light on the disputed story. Can you imagine what would have happened if an American public official were to sue a publication for libel and similarly tried to withhold evidence and witnesses.
>
> Finally, there is the matter of Appendix B. We were clearly wrong in reporting that it contained the information about the meeting. A lot of people seem to have great difficulty accepting the fact that the truth of the information does not depend on its location in Appendix B and indeed Judge Sofaer held that it might be

245

considered an aggravation, not the substance, of the alleged libel. Still, it was a very unfortunate error. The Jerusalem bureau based itself on what it considered circumstantial evidence. Besides, Halevy had a phone conversation with a source who did not want to talk about Appendix B, but gave hints and partial information. One is somewhat reminded of Woodward and Bernstein on the telephone to a source who didn't want to talk. They used the device of assuming a positive answer if the source didn't hang up by the count of ten. I don't want to push this analogy too far or to defend methods like this too strongly. I only want to suggest what investigative reporters are sometimes driven to when they are up against classified information—and, in this case, with leaks treated as treason. This does not excuse the error, but it seems to me that it mitigates it. Moreover, the printed passage in *Time* did use some qualifying phrases to indicate that we did not actually see Appendix B.

Mr. *Time* ended his letter with something of a personal appeal:

> At this writing the jury has yet to make a finding on actual malice. But I think you will agree, if you look at the judge's charge, that he has defined malice in an extremely broad sense that could be quite alarming to the press as a whole. What I am talking about here is not only the trial verdict, whatever it turns out to be, but the judgment of our peers. On that I only hope for a full understanding of the circumstances and the facts. On the larger issue, I still believe that libel suits of this sort by public officials are a threat to the press.

Thus, although from the date of the letter and its opening paragraph it purports to be written after the first verdict—which in any event was long after the time Luftman sought to suggest it was sent—the contents of the last portion show that it was, in fact, written after the verdict on falsity.

The situation seemed to *Time* to be so crucial that on Saturday, January 19, Duncan telexed Grunwald's letter to "All [*Time*'s] Bureau Chiefs worldwide"—thirty-two in all. Duncan prefaced his Telex carefully:

> As I am sure you all know by now, the jury in the Sharon case has found that the relevant paragraph in our story was false. This

is a finding which we, of course, dispute, but the jury is now meeting on the question of "actual malice."

Because this case is of such continuing interest and because many of the elements don't seem well understood, I am sending you, with Henry Grunwald's permission, the text of the letter which he wrote to a distinguished journalistic colleague, on another American press organization, this Thursday. You may find it useful in better understanding and explaining the case.

When Sharon heard about Grunwald's SOS letter, he told me it reminded him of an anecdote. The setting for this was Alexandria, Egypt, in 1979, when Sharon, in company with another Israeli cabinet minister, Dr. Josef Burg, were negotiating the Palestinian autonomy plan with their Egyptian counterparts. At one point Sharon became incensed by the fact that the Egyptians were not being truthful about their clandestine contacts with the PLO.

His cabinet colleague, Burg, who possesses a typical Jewish wisdom, tried to calm him down. "So what if the Egyptians aren't telling the truth? This, after all, is the Middle East, and some of the Arab leaders behave in accordance with their special credo of 'First let's cross the bridge—then we can double-cross it.' "

Time still had the bridge of "actual malice" to cross. Sadly for Sharon this was one bridge too many.

SHARON AWAITED THE JURY'S THIRD VERDICT IN
the little back room where he had spent days—adding up all the
hours—over the last couple of months. While he waited, his wife,
Lily, and Arie Genger went out to make telephone calls. Sharon
was left alone in the room, brightened by the wintry before-noon
sun of January 24, 1985. The door opened and in walked Richard
Goldstein; the jury had informed the judge that they had reached
a decision. After days of expectation this was pleasant news in itself. But Sharon did not move from his chair. He remained sitting, with his head resting on the palm of his left hand.

A messenger arrived carrying a parcel—lunch. Brenda Cameron, faithful as ever, was hot on his footsteps. Through the secretary of the court, the jury had passed on one question to the
judge: Were they entitled to read a special statement immediately
after having given their verdict?

Adam Gilbert and Andrea Feller also came into the room, their
faces showing the strain and the tension of the past months.

"Is this normal routine, for the jury to make a special announcement?" Sharon asked, breaking the silence.

"No, it's not routine at all," Goldstein replied.

Goldstein moved to leave the room, his face very pensive. I ran
after him into the corridor, passing the security man. "Is this a
good or a bad sign?" I asked him.

"I don't know," he responded with his usual caution.

By the time I got back to the room where Sharon was sitting,
Andrea Feller had managed to come back from the judge's chambers and report, "The judge has asked to see the statement the
jury wants to make before he decides whether to permit it."

Sharon, as is his custom in situations like this, when he knows
he has done all he can and things must now take their course, was
wrapped in his thoughts. He did not change his position at the
head of the table.

Brenda came in with the latest news: "The judge's secretary has
said that Judge Sofaer has decided to allow the jury to read its
special announcement."

Sharon got up from his place at the table and straightened his
waistcoat. For the last time in *Sharon* v. *Time* he moved in the di-

rection of the courtroom, with the security men struggling to take their places behind him among the enormous crowd that had gathered in the corridor.

In the courtroom there was no room to squeeze in another soul. Behind us sat the *Time* people. On the other side of the room the press corps sat crushed together, some with notebooks in their hands, others with their electronic typewriters all ready to go. Arik asked one of the security men to call Lily and Arie Genger into the courtroom.

Out of the corner of his eye Sharon could see the members of the jury taking their places. He sat with his arms folded across his chest. I was next to him. He didn't say a word. Genger sat on my left, and behind him was Ofer Nimrodi, a young Israeli lawyer who had done so much to help Sharon over the previous weeks.

The judge entered the courtroom with something of a spring in his step, went up to his bench, and sat down. It seemed to me that his face reflected satisfaction. He rubbed his hands together as if to suggest that this involved and complicated case had come to a fair resolution. His face seemed a trifle pale with excitement. Not a sound could be heard in the courtroom, which had waited for this verdict for seven days—and actually from the moment the trial against *Time* had begun.

The foreman of the jury stood up and read the verdict. The jury had not found actual malice, but he immediately added that the jury wanted to read a special announcement. "We find that certain *Time* employees, particularly correspondent David Halevy, acted negligently and carelessly in reporting and verifying the information which ultimately found its way into the published paragraph of interest in this case."

David Halevy was not present to hear this new indictment with his own ears, just as he had not been at Bikfaya at the time of the conversation about which he wrote his false story.

A ripple went through the courtroom. All eyes were fixed on Sharon. Everyone was trying to gauge his reaction. This time, even more than on the previous occasions, Sharon sat as firm as the Rock of Gibraltar—from the standpoint of dimensions and in that he didn't move a muscle. He kept looking straight at the judge and perhaps in the direction of the great seal of the United States above the judge.

For the first time since the trial had started broad grins appeared on the faces of most of *Time*'s lawyers. Barr sat back with a tired smile on his face. Gold and Saunders exchanged glances of satisfaction.

Sharon believed Judge Sofaer had gotten what he had set out to achieve—exactly what Sharon had estimated he would go for from the beginning. Sharon had proved that the *Time* story was false and defamatory, but he had not succeeded in proving actual malice. Thus justice was meted out to the Jewish Israeli general, but the Jewish American judge would still be able to live peaceably with himself in his own part of the world, with *Time* magazine, with the First Amendment, and with a great legal career ahead of him.

In other words, the judge had succeeded in bringing the jury around to decisions that—as Sharon had estimated even before the start of the trial—he could have been expected to hand down if there had been no jury at all.

In Solomon's famous judgment 2,800 years ago in Jerusalem, he suggested to the two women who claimed the same infant that they cut the infant in half and each take one half. The infant was saved because the true mother stood ready to give up the child and that was why the king awarded it to her in the end.

Some observers described the conduct of the *Time* trial as a latter-day judgment of Solomon, because of the wisdom of Judge Abraham Sofaer, a son of King Solomon's nation.

From the point of view of the results this was no Solomonic judgment. The infant, here the whole truth, was, after all, cut in half. The judge, on the other hand, remained undivided.

THE FIRST SIGNS THAT SHARON HAD LEFT THE
trial in New York behind him began to show the following Saturday, January 26. Sharon lunched with Bill Safire of *The New York
Times* at the Regency's pleasant restaurant. Safire had come in
from Washington to talk to Sharon "about everything except the
trial." They were at odds in their opinions about the case. Arie
Genger and I sat with them at lunch and listened to their conversation.

But it wasn't possible to avoid the subject of the trial completely. Sharon asked to say just one thing about part of an article
Safire had published in November 1984. He had written that
Time had apparently published the story about Sharon "in good
faith." At lunch Sharon said to him, "I think you were wrong
about that. There was no innocence there, right from the beginning. It began as malice—and it remains malice. Even though we
didn't succeed in proving it in court." Then Sharon went on to
other subjects. As if there had never been a trial; as if the past two
years had never taken place. Sharon turned his face to confront
the new Israeli vital front line: his country's inflation ridden
economy.

Two days later Safire wrote in his column in *The New York
Times* entitled "The Sharon Plan for the Israeli Economy":

> After battling *Time* magazine to an expensive standoff of the
> stiffnecked, Ariel Sharon returns to Israel with a plan in mind to
> help lift his country out of its economic morass.
>
> It's about time: while Industry Minister Sharon has been spend-
> ing months in New York removing a blot on his personal reputa-
> tion, the coalition government of which he is a member has been
> frittering away the same months doing the wrong thing: flinching
> from the austerity that would bring unemployment, preferring to
> deal with the symptom rather than the cause of inflation by im-
> posing wage and price controls.
>
> That's my view, not his: the burly general (who grouses that a
> piece of mine about *Time*'s absence of malice in its mistake about
> him might have influenced the jurors) is careful to note that the
> Peres-Shamir "package deal" freezing prices and wages provided a
> psychological blow to inflation expectations, and has moved to-

251

ward getting rid of what he terms "the mother of all economic sins, indexation. . . ."

Ending his essay, Safire noted: "Arik Sharon, the only foreign leader certified by an American jury to be a non-murderer, does not run Israel; Shimon Peres does. But Alternating Prime Minister Peres must appeal to Mr. Sharon's sizable constituency, as well as to free-market allies in the U.S., and would do well to consider the Sharon plan or lucidly explain his own."

APPENDIX

LETTER TO PRIME MINISTER SHIMON PERES FROM MINISTER ARIEL SHARON, JERUSALEM, DATED DECEMBER 31, 1984

Prime Minister,

The libel suit which I have instituted against *Time* magazine is set to recommence on January 2, 1985, and is due to end in a verdict a few days thereafter. In the few days which remain, the Israeli government ought to decide on three matters which may be of decisive importance to my efforts to reveal the truth and to expunge the lie which *Time* published about me in a matter relating to me in my capacity as Minister of Defense of the State of Israel.

My request deals with three subjects regarding the bringing of essential evidence which will prove that on the facts *Time*'s libel is completely unfounded, has no basis, and that there is not a shred of evidence in the Commission of Inquiry documents or in the appendix to its report. Such means of evidence will ensure that justice is done and will refute the libel, while at the same time remaining within strict observance of the rules of secrecy and security regulations.

A: The request by Honorable Judge A. Sofaer of New York court of December 25.

1. The libel published about me in *Time* magazine states that Appendix B, which is the secret appendix to the Commission of Inquiry Report, refers to the fact that in my condolence call to the Gemayel family I discussed the need for revenge with members of the family. Right from the start the question arose as to how it would be proved to the court in New York that there was absolutely no basis for *Time*'s allegation and that there is no mention of anything which would found this lie in Appendix B or in the minutes of the discussion which I held on that day. Judge A. Sofaer, who has displayed a great deal of sensitivity in regard to everything concerning the safeguarding of secret information of the State of Israel, a few months ago initiated a request to the Government of Israel in which he put forward various ideas as to how the secret appendix and the notes of the discussions could be examined in order to confirm or deny *Time*'s allegation without in any way prejudicing the security of the State of Israel.

2. As has been explained by my attorneys in the United States, this is a most exceptional procedure, which a judge does not have the power to apply on his own initiative but [which] requires the agreement of both

parties to the suit. The judge, who is fully aware of the crucial importance attaching to the examination of Appendix B and the notes of the conversations, in order to establish where the truth lies, virtually forced [an] agreement which allows the examination of the documents without *Time* or its lawyers and executives having to actually peruse or see such documents but which is nonetheless based on the clear understanding that the outcome of such examination would be binding on the parties to the suit for all intents and purposes.

3. After protracted negotiations between the judge and the Government of Israel by way of the exchange of considerable correspondence over a lengthy period, the judge's suggestion was summed up in a proposal whereby the documents mentioned below will be examined by a team of three people: the Honorable Chief Justice Y. Kahan, Chairman of the Commission of Inquiry, my lawyer in Israel, Advocate D. Weissglas, and *Time*'s attorney in Israel, Advocate Ch. J. Zadok. The team of examiners will be obliged to answer three well-defined questions in "yes" or "no" answers. In the event of any dispute arising among the members of the team as to the significance of any findings whatever in the documents, such disputes will be determined by Justice Kahan, and his answer—and his answer alone—will serve as evidence in the trial.

4. The lawyers and Justice Kahan will be prohibited from publishing the nature of any dispute between them—if there should be any—but they will be entitled to bring the fact of the dispute to the notice of the judge in the United States and to divulge the fact of its existence to their respective clients, without in any way revealing the details of the dispute, and such details may be disclosed only upon the approval of the Attorney General of the State of Israel.

5. The Honorable Judge Sofaer's proposal contains all the elements required to maintain the absolute secrecy of the information contained in the documents and will bar the use of this information in the legal proceedings.

This proposal does not reveal the contents of Appendix B to the people from *Time* but comes to the knowledge of only their Israeli attorney, who himself was for many years involved in the affairs of state and, inter alia, in matters of foreign relations and security, and to the knowledge of my own attorney, who in any case saw all the above-mentioned material in the course of his work at the Commission of Inquiry.

6. In light of the strict limitations which the New York court has taken upon itself in order to prevent the unauthorized use of any of the information contained in the appendix and the documents, I can find no sensible reason for not responding to the judge's proposal in the affirma-

tive. I would like to stress: the judge—after conducting lengthy negotiations with the Israeli government—has made it abundantly clear to the lawyers for the parties that the proposal he initiated is final and only the acceptance of the proposal in its entirety will give effect to the arrangement, which will enable a speedy and authoritative examination of Appendix B and the notes of the conversation. Such an examination will quickly and decisively rebut *Time*'s libel and the lies of its Israeli correspondent. I should point out that in terms of the decisions made by the Commission of Inquiry, Appendix B is available and will for many years be open to inspection by hundreds of people, and I do not believe that the team of examiners, of all people, should be prevented from examining the appendix and the documents when an examination of this nature could instantly refute the libel in question.

7. You, Mr. Prime Minister, and my fellow cabinet ministers, know full well—or you could know this at any time that you wish by simply referring to and reading these documents—that this story published by *Time* has absolutely no foundation, nor is there anything in the facts of the case on which it can rely and there is no semblance of a mention of anything of the sort either in Appendix B to the Commission's report or in any one of the notes of the conversation and that it is a total and complete falsification.

The repudiation of this lie could be effected by an inspection of the documents in a matter of hours, without the security of the State of Israel in any way being endangered or impaired, provided the judge's suggestion receives an affirmative response.

8. I must emphasize—any failure on the part of the government to cooperate in responding to this proposal might cause me to lose my case by reason of my inability to discharge the burden of proof on me, even though everybody knows that *Time*'s story is a barefaced lie and is libel. The judge made this perfectly plain on December 20, 1984, when he said:

"In all matters the onus is on the plaintiff and any failure of proof there through lack of cooperation on the part of the State of Israel will operate against the plaintiff's interests."

Thus, in his charge to the jury on how to arrive at a verdict, which he delivered only a few days ago, the judge instructed them that absence of proof due to lack of cooperation on the part of the Government of Israel would act against the plaintiff.

B: Requests for taking of a Deposition (Foreign Legal Assistance) from the deputy head of the Mossad.

Appendix

1. *Time*'s correspondent in Israel, David Halevy, the man who provided the "information" which was the basis for that story, testified under oath before the court in New York in testimony which lasted many days—all in the eyes and ears of the whole world—as to the existence of an unbelievable state of affairs in which the most closely guarded secrets of the State of Israel and other sensitive political information are available to him from a variety of sources, all of whom serve as personnel in the defense establishment. The reporter specified over 50 instances (!) in which, over the course of the years, he has published sensitive information in *Time* magazine in regard to secret peace negotiations, classified diplomatic missions, undercover military operations, and similar items and events, all of which are in the nature of being highly confidential state secrets.

2. From one of these "sources" in the defense establishment—as described in greater detail below—the *Time* reporter claims to know the contents of what was said in the meetings held on September 15 in Beirut, and he testified under oath that in that conversation I supposedly encouraged members of the Gemayel family to avenge the blood of the slain Bashir Gemayel.

3. This information was conveyed to the reporter—according to his sworn testimony—by four sources: two IDF generals, a member of the intelligence corps, and a high-ranking civil servant. That "source" who is a member of the intelligence agency, read to *Time*'s reporter the contents of the notes of the conversation which were taken by the Mossad representative who was present at my meeting in Beirut on September 15, 1982 (the very minutes the examination of which has been requested by the Honorable Judge Sofaer in his letter).

4. Contents of Mossad notes are divulged to the *Time* correspondent any time he likes: Thus, for example, after my deposition in New York, in September 1984, he sought to verify certain details in my testimony, and so, according to his version, he was given details by a Mossad person from the notes of the conversation regarding the identity of those who were present at that meeting. This is how the correspondent comes to allege that Mr. Uri Dan, my media adviser at that time, was not present at the meeting on account of the fact that his name does not appear in the document, whereas Mr. Fadi Frem supposedly did attend such a meeting. All these "corrections and modifications of the truth" serve only to support the reporter's version.

5. The details of 12 secret meetings which I held with Bashir Gemayel while serving as Minister of Defense and with the highest echelons of the Christian forces are known to the reporter mainly through the notes

taken at such talks—notes which were given to him "by the people who participated or took the minutes."

6. Other notes of the Mossad which also deal with my meetings with the heads of the Christian forces are, so he says, actually in his physical possession, and some of them were even brought by this reporter to New York (Appendix 8, page 1587).

7. *Time*'s reporter tried, in the course of his testimony, to conceal the identity of his sources, but a study of his testimony as a whole, and the many innuendos and inferences it contains, led the judge to conclude—on the strength of things the reporter had stated in his deposition—that the Mossad person in Lebanon who was present at any number of meetings and took notes at those meetings is, in fact, one of the *Time* reporter's "sources." These aspects are described by the judge on page 74 of his decision of November 12, 1984.

8. *Time*'s correspondent goes on to confirm that the Mossad person who took the notes of the conversation at Bikfaya—the same individual with whom he met and with whom he talked at Bikfaya—is none other than the Mossad person who presently serves as deputy head of the Mossad.

9. In the course of the *Time* correspondent's testimony the judge sought to clarify for himself whether the notetaker at Bikfaya was one of the "sources" to which the reporter had been referring. Thus, the judge put a very specific question to him, but the reporter declined to answer this, relying on the privilege accorded to a journalist in regard to the disclosing of his sources of information.

In other cases where he was asked whether some person or other was a "source" of his, he did not hesitate to answer in the negative. The reporter took pains to make it clear that such source is not "an intelligence officer" but "an intelligence person."

10. It is inconceivable that statements of this nature, which were made under the most stringent of circumstances—under oath, in a court of law, and being put on record in the presence of representatives from all branches of the media from all over the world—can be allowed to go unanswered, whether they are the truth or just a bunch of arrogant lies. This kind of testimony is defamatory and harmful to the defense establishment as a whole and to the intelligence community in particular and casts a giant shadow over the actions of two generals and of a well-known senior intelligence person of long standing as to their being guilty of grave criminal offenses—all of whom the reporter implicates, by way of inference, as being responsible for such deeds and casts suspicion on them.

257

Appendix

I would point out that *Time*'s attorneys sought to subpoena this senior Mossad person for a deposition in the United States, and they had no hesitation in identifying him by name or of describing the function he fulfilled at those meetings in a sworn affidavit which was filed with the court and which became public knowledge and available to one and all.

11. This testimony has put me in an untenable position from the legal point of view. The direct testimony of those who participated in the various meetings, which both I myself and *Time* magazine sought to adduce, was not permitted by the State of Israel. In consequence, the genuine content matter of those meetings has not been brought to the notice of the court. Instead of such direct testimony *Time* has been able, by way of the outrageous lies told by its reporter under cover of "journalist privilege," to bring so-called evidence into the courtroom the tenor of which is that I, as it were, am alleged to have encouraged avenging the blood of Bashir, and to ground such evidence, false quotes taken from Mossad notes are produced—all this when anyone who at any stage perused those notes at any time knows full well that there is absolutely no mention of such statements.

12. The judge himself was unable to ignore the gravity of the testimony given by the *Time* correspondent. In his application to the Government of Israel on December 12 the judge suggests to the Government of Israel that it allow the examination of Appendix B and of the notes of the meetings, among other things, for purposes of checking out and verifying the reporter's testimony: "*Time* bases its story on reports from its Israeli correspondent, who is a lieutentant colonel in the IDF reserve, who claims to have received his information from IDF generals and high-ranking intelligence officials. The revelation of evidence in the government's possession in a manner which allows for the use thereof in evidence could firmly establish the accuracy or otherwise of what has been stated pertaining to these alleged sources."

13. The rebutting evidence of the deputy chief of the Mossad is required in order to repudiate the lies related by the *Time* correspondent so as to clear the defense establishment, the intelligence agency official and myself of these grave accusations. The judge in the United States, when he was requested to allow this testimony, defined it as "very material evidence which would be important rebutting evidence and which would go to the very heart of the matter at issue."

14. From the beginning the various security agencies have taken the position of prohibiting the testimony of security personnel in the legal proceedings. Despite the fact that this posture has been extremely damaging to my own interests, I accepted it because this was the will of the State of Israel, which I respect. But in the wake of the testimony of the

Time correspondent, a new and dangerous state of affairs has arisen which demands a reply and a response. This reporter cynically and maliciously seeks to take advantage of the prohibition which the State of Israel has imposed on its personnel from testifying, and with a feeling of complete self-confidence that no one will come forward to challenge his statements—by virtue of such prohibition—he has defamed, lied and borne false witness against me and has contemptuously held the whole defense establishment up for ridicule.

This state of affairs constitutes a very weighty reason for allowing the testimony requested, so that, authoritatively and decisively, the statements and lies testified to by this reporter can be refuted.

C. Request for legal assistance: Mr. Uri Dan.

Mr. Uri Dan was present at the meeting which I had on September 15, 1982, and heard and listened to what was said and knows that *Time*'s story is an outrageous lie. I had wanted to call Mr. Dan as a witness in my lawsuit so that he could assist in revealing the real truth, but he was prohibited from testifying as to what took place at that meeting. In the light of the lies of the *Time* reporter as to what I supposedly said at that meeting about the need for revenge, Mr. Dan's testimony becomes of vital importance, and my request is that you reconsider the reasonableness of this prohibition of his testifying.

Mr. Dan will be requested to verify only that part of my own testimony which relates to the meetings I held on September 15, meetings the content matter of which was widely published in books and newspapers after having been approved by the censorship.

D. On the strength of the foregoing I would ask you to accede to the proposal of the United States court of December 25, 1984, to approve proceedings of foreign judicial assistance in Israel relating to the taking of deposition of the deputy chief of the Mossad and of Mr. Uri Dan. It is self-evident that at such proceedings involving the examination of the deputy chief of the Mossad all the necessary security precautions as prescribed by the competent authorities will be observed, and, among other things, the examination will be held in camera in the presence only of Israeli attorneys and without the identification of the witness by name and in respect only of the aspects approved of by the security agencies or their representatives.

Mr. Prime Minister and my fellow ministers, to the best of my knowledge and belief a clear-cut rebuttal of that libel can be effected in only one way—by acceding to my request. In your hands, therefore, lies the key to the outcome of this case.

INDEX

Abrams, Floyd, 175
  appeal filed by, 220–21
  on media-oriented libel suits,
    215–16
  Sharon's imminent victory and,
    211–12
Al Hamishmar, 32, 143–44
Allon, Yigal, 48
Alsberg, Paul, 92
American Lawyer, 175, 201–2, 216
Anti-Defamation League, 42
Arab terrorism in Israel, 12, 147
Arafat, Yasser, 12, 13
Arens, Moshe, 30, 175
Associated Press, 139
Auletta, Ken, on libel, 173–74

Barak, Justice, 163
Barr, Thomas, 72, 137
  Dan's deposition and, 122
  defamation judgment and, 237
  Gould's opening address and,
    137–38
  Gould's summation and, 224
  Halevy's testimony and, 183,
    189–90
  health of, 104, 132–33, 139, 144,
    177
  opening address of, 139–45
  points conceded by, 222
  proposed settlements and, 117–18,
    177–79, 180–82
  Secret Appendix B and, 143
  Sharon's deposition and, 89–90,
    91–92, 97–98, 104, 110
  Sharon's files and, 95–96
  Sharon's testimony and, 146, 151,
    152–59, 163–64
  summation of, 222, 224, 231
  Time's special statement and, 232
Beethoven, Ludwig van, 219
Begin, Menachem, 12, 13, 19, 33,
    41, 48, 86, 91, 93

anti-terrorism and, 84, 115
Grunwald's testimony and, 204,
    206
Halevy's story on health of,
    53–58, 60, 203–4, 206, 227
Israeli elections and, 50–51, 54,
    90, 99
Israeli-held documents and, 74–75
on Kahan Commission Report,
    35–36, 39–40
Secret Appendix B and, 37, 39,
    56–57, 120, 143
Sharon's meetings with, 14, 15,
    17, 39–40
Sofaer's personal appeal to Israel
    and, 199
on *Time*'s Sharon report, 35–36,
    37
Ben-Gal, Avigdor (Yanosh), 52–53,
    185–87
Ben-Gurion, David, 33, 91, 151–52
Bernstein, Carl, 246
Bikfaya meeting:
  Dan at, 19–20, 43, 121–23
  Gould's summation and, 226–27
  Halevy's testimony and, 166–68,
    183–84, 187–89, 190–91
  Kelly's testimony and, 192–95
  minutes of, 43, 45, 46, 72–73, 76,
    90–91, 92–94, 104, 157–58, 167
  Secret Appendix B and, 37–38,
    45, 104, 166–68, 175, 190, 201,
    215, 217, 219, 227
  Sharon and Gemayels at, 17,
    19–20, 22–25, 29, 35, 36, 37–38,
    43, 75, 79–80, 157–58
  Sharon's recap of, 44–46
  Sharon's testimony and, 157–58
  Sofaer's personal appeal to Israel
    and, 199–200
  Time on, 17, 19–20, 25, 29, 45–47
Brill, Steven, 175, 201–2, 216
Burdick, Lydia, 233

Burg, Josef, 247
Burke, Edmund, 224–25

Cameron, Brenda, 239, 248
Carter, Jimmy, 50
Cave, Ray:
  appearance of, 236, 240
  Begin health story and, 55, 57
  defamation judgment and, 236–37
  falsity judgment and, 240–41
  media criticism of, 236, 237
  Secret Appendix B and, 57,
    215–16, 232
  testimony of, 203–4
  Time's special statement and,
    232
Central Intelligence Agency (CIA),
  45, 50, 125
Chamoun, Camille, 51, 63
Chicago Tribune, 139
Christian Phalanges, Lebanese, 13,
  24
  Barr's opening address and,
    144–45
  Brill's criticism of *Time* and, 201
  Halevy's testimony and, 189, 192
  Israeli assistance to, 51–52, 64,
    137
  Sabra and Shatilla massacres and,
    14–15, 16–17, 37–38, 154
  Secret Appendix B and, 37–38,
    57, 106, 201, 217–19, 222,
    231–32
  Time's special statement and, 231
Clark, Marsh, 49
Clark, Patricia, 242–43
Commission of Inquiry Law, Israeli,
  199
Constitution, U.S., 234, 238
Cravath, Swaine and Moore, 89, 95,
  122, 133, 137
  Bikfaya minutes and, 72–73
  Duncan/Halevy correspondence
    and, 207–8
  Dutch journalists' report and,
    72–73
  Halevy's testimony and, 189–90
  Secret Appendix B and, 190, 198
  Sofaer's appeal to Israel and,
    197–99

Dan, Oron, 33
Dan, Uri:
  at Bikfaya, 19–20, 43, 121–23
  deposition of, 43, 121–23
Darrow, Clarence, 136
Davar, 32, 130–31
Dayan, Moshe, 49–50, 91, 111, 143
  Sharon/Ben-Gurion conflict and,
    151–52
defamation:
  jury's decision on, 236–38
  Sofaer's definition of, 134–35,
    233–34
Defense Department, U.S. (DOD),
  11
Defense Ministry, Israeli, 11, 17,
  31–32, 33, 41, 46
DeLoatch, Patricia, 233
Denton, Herbert H., 232
Dorban, 48
Draper, Morris, 64, 116–17
Duncan, Richard L., 36
  on Begin health story, 55–56, 58
  Gould's summation and, 227–29
  Halevy's correspondence with,
    58–60, 84–88, 114–15, 123, 203,
    207–8, 228–29
  testimony of, 203
  Time's public relations campaign
    and, 246–47

Eban, Abba, 133
Egypt, PLO contacts of, 247
Eichmann, Adolf, 34
Eitan, Rafael, 14, 31, 137, 185
etzlenu, meaning of, 163–64
evidence:
  "beyond reasonable doubt," 234
  "clear and convincing," 233, 234
  "preponderance of," 233–34

falsity:
  jury's decision on, 239–41
  Sharon's desire to win on, 235, 239
  Sofaer's discussion of, 135, 233,
    234–35
Fein, Jack, 54, 56, 57
Feller, Andrea, 104, 106, 137, 248
Financial Times (London), 141–42
Fischer, Dean, 55–57, 59

Index

Fischman, Bernie, 104
  background and character of,
    96–97
  Gould's summation and, 226
  proposed settlements and, 106–7
  Sharon's files and, 96–97
Forster, Arnold, 42, 46, 96, 104
  Gould's opening address and, 138
  at Gould's reception, 180
  Israeli-held documents and,
    75–77, 94
  Sharon's confidence in, 71, 77
Frankel, Max, 244
Freedom of Information Act (1974),
  94
Frem, Fadi, 62, 145
Fund for Financing Legal Expenses,
  Israeli, 162

Gart, Murray, 49
Gemayel, Amin, 13, 61–62
  Barr's opening address and, 145
  at Bikfaya, 17, 19, 23–24, 29, 35,
    36, 37–38, 43, 79–80, 157–58
  Gould's summation and, 225
  Kelly's testimony and, 193–95
  Secret Appendix B and, 37–38,
    105–6, 111, 217–19
  Sofaer's appeal to Israel and,
    199–200
  Time's special statement and,
    231–32
Gemayel, Bashir, 13, 62, 63
  assassination of, 14, 17, 19, 20, 23,
    29, 35, 37–38, 64, 79–80, 137,
    144–45
  Barr's opening address and,
    144–45
  funeral of, 188–89
  Halevy's testimony and, 183,
    188–89
  Kelly's testimony and, 193–95
  Secret Appendix B and, 37–38,
    105, 217–19
  Sharon's meetings with, 14,
    21–22, 24, 105, 137–38
  Time's special statement and, 231
Gemayel, Pierre, 13, 51
  Barr's opening address and,
    144–45

at Bikfaya, 17, 19–20, 22–25, 29,
    35, 36, 37–38, 43, 45, 79–80,
    157–58
  Gould's summation and, 225
  Halevy's testimony and, 183–84
  at Karantina, 21–22
  Kelly's testimony and, 193–95
  Secret Appendix B and, 37–38,
    45, 105–6, 111, 217–19
  Sharon's meetings with, 61–64
  Sofaer's appeal to Israel and,
    199–200
  Time's special statement and,
    231–32
Genger, Arie, 251
  malice judgment and, 248–49
  proposed settlements and, 106–8,
    181
  Sharon's deposition and, 90, 91
  Sharon's testimony and, 156
Genger, Saguy, 112
Germanos, Assad, 15
Germany, Nazi, Israel compared to,
    84–88, 114, 189, 228–29
Gilbert, Adam, 106, 137
  Halevy's personal file and, 115
  malice judgment and, 248
  Sharon's deposition and, 89, 97,
    104
Gold, Stuart:
  Kelly's testimony and, 195
  malice judgment and, 250
  Sharon's deposition and, 110–12
  Sharon's testimony and, 152–53
  Sofaer's warning to, 208
Goldenberg, Amnon, 69
Goldstein, Richard, 42, 47, 137
  Draper's deposition and, 117
  Duncan's testimony and, 203
  Halevy's personal file and, 114–15
  Halevy's rewritten scoop and, 82
  Israeli-held documents and, 75,
    94
  Kelly's deposition and, 119
  malice judgment and, 248
  proposed settlements and, 98,
    106–7, 177–81
  on Secret Appendix B, 214
  Sharon's confidence in, 71
  Sharon's conversations with, 67

Sharon's deposition and, 89–90,
97, 104
Time's correspondence file and,
78, 82
Gotsman, Mervyn, 58
Gould, Milton, 67, 76
banquets in honor of, 180
Barr's opening address and, 141,
142, 145
Bikfaya meeting and, 44–47, 73,
104
Cave's testimony and, 203–4
Dan's deposition and, 121, 123
defamation judgment and, 236
Draper's deposition and, 116
Dutch journalists' report and,
72–73
as eager and alert, 42
Grunwald's testimony and, 204–7
Halevy's personal file and,
115–16, 118
Halevy's rewritten scoop and, 82
Halevy's testimony and, 165–69,
174–75, 183–89
Israeli-held documents and, 94
jury selection and, 130
jury trial preferred by, 129
Kelly's testimony and, 192–93,
195–96, 205–6
opening address of, 131, 136–38
press coverage of, 236
proposed settlements and, 106–8,
117–18, 177–78
rulings called for by, 222
Secret Appendix B and, 45, 104,
165–69, 174–75, 190, 214
Sharon's advice to, 204–5
Sharon's anger at, 97, 131, 137–38
Sharon's deposition and, 92, 97,
104
Sharon's meetings with, 42–43,
44–47, 74
Sharon's testimony and, 146–50,
158
Sharon's trial preparations and,
131–33
Sofaer's appeal to Israel and,
197–98
summation of, 224–30, 231
team of, 137, 192, 226

Time's correspondence file and, 78
Time's news sources and, 72
Time's New York vs. Jerusalem
staffs and, 204–5
see also Shea and Gould
Gouldman, Dennis, Sofaer's appeal
to Israel and, 197, 199–200
Grunwald, Henry A., 203
Begin health story and, 55, 57,
204
Brill's criticism of *Time* and,
201–2
cross-examination of, 204–7
Kelly's testimony and, 205–6
proposed settlements and, 178,
182
on Secret Appendix B, 215–16,
244, 245–46
testimony of, 57
text of letter by, 245–46
Time's reputation and, 244–47

Ha'aretz, 32
Habib, Philip, 13–14, 21, 116, 242
Haig, Alexander, Sharon's meetings
with, 11–12, 21
Halevy, David (Dudu), 39, 71, 129,
137, 139
arrogance of, 168
background of, 140, 148–50
Begin health story by, 53–58, 60,
203–4, 206, 227
Ben-Gal's collaboration with,
52–53, 185–87
Bikfaya meeting and, 19–20,
79–80, 166–68
Cave's testimony and, 203–4
confidential news sources of, 165,
166–68, 183–89, 213, 215, 227
credibility of, 229
cross-examination of, 165–69,
173–75, 183–91, 196, 220
Dan's deposition and, 121, 123
deposition of, 123
Duncan's correspondence with,
58–60, 84–88, 114–15, 123, 203,
207–8, 228–29
Duncan's testimony and, 203
ethics of, 51–52
Gould's summation and, 227–29

Index

Halevy, David (Dudu) *(cont.)*
  Grunwald's testimony and, 204–6
  Harnof's collaboration with,
    187–88
  image of, 48, 115
  Israel compared to Nazi Germany
    by, 84–88, 114, 228–29
  Israeli media and, 211
  jury's statement on, 249
  Kelly's collaboration with, 78,
    80–81, 192–96, 227
  Kelly's testimony and, 192–96
  Middle Eastern affairs briefings
    by, 189–90
  Mitzna's collaboration with,
    185–87
  patriotism of, 140, 228–29
  Peres supported by, 50–51, 86,
    203, 212–13, 214, 227–28
  personal file of, 114–16, 118
  political bias of, 48–50, 227–28
  self-exile of, 243
  scoops by, 51–52, 53–60, 78–82,
    85, 140, 164, 167, 189, 192–96
  Secret Appendix B and, 56–57,
    81, 165–69, 173–75, 190, 212,
    214–15
  Sharon's credibility and, 151, 159
  testimony of, 56–57, 81
  Time editors' support for, 203–7,
    223
  Time's public relations campaign
    and, 244–46
  Time's special statement and, 232
  U.S. press and, 173–76, 184, 189,
    220, 223
Hammer, Armand, 117, 161
Hannibal, 33, 143–44
Harnof, Elkana, as Halevy's confi-
    dential news source, 187–88
Harzion, Meir, 151–52
Harzion, Shoshana, 151
Heritage, 133
Herzog, Chaim, 114
Hobeika, Eli, 145
Hod, Motti, 111

Industry and Trade Ministry, Is-
    raeli, 160, 181, 251–52
infamy, Gould's definition of, 230

In Search of History (White), 78
International Red Cross, 155
Israel:
  Arab terrorism in, 12, 147
  economic crisis in, 160, 161–62,
    251–52
  elections in, 50–51, 54, 90, 99
  Halevy's disenchantment with,
    84–88, 114, 189, 228–29
  Jewish terrorism in, 84–86, 115
  Lebanese Christian community
    and, *see* Christian Phalanges,
    Lebanese
  Lebanese ties with, 61–64, 189
  postelection situation in, 100–103,
    114
  secrecy laws of, 122, 197–98
  secret documents held by, 46–47,
    73–77, 92–94, 98, 104, 111,
    119–20, 132, 158, 197–200
  Sharon's political enemies in,
    74–77, 98, 101, 151, 161
  Sofaer's personal appeal to,
    197–200, 211, 219
  Time's clashes with, 53–58, 60
Israel Bar Council, 69
Israel Bonds drive, 180
Israel Defense Force Journal, 12
Israel Defense Forces (IDF), 31
  Halevy's confidential news sources
    in, 165, 166–68, 183–88, 213

James, Spencer, Jr., 233
Jerusalem Post, 125, 215–16
Jones, Alex S., 222–23
Justice Ministry, Israeli, 220
  International Department of, 197

Kahan, Yitzhak, 16, 76
  Gould's summation and, 224–25,
    227
  Secret Appendix B checked by,
    216–20
  Sofaer's appeal to Israel and, 198
  Time's public relations campaign
    and, 245
  Time's special statement and, 232
Kahan commission, 15–17, 31
  Begin and, 35–36, 39–40
  Brill's criticism of *Time* and, 201

conclusions of, 16–17, 25, 35, 67–69, 78–79, 158–59
Dutch journalists' report to, 72–73, 76, 92
mandate of, 16
Sharon's opening address to, 163–64
Kahan Commission Report:
court examination of, 219–21
Gould's summation and, 226–27
Halevy's testimony and, 165–69, 174–75, 190
meaning of *etzlenu* in, 163–64
Secret Appendix B of, 37–39, 45, 56–57, 81, 104, 105–6, 111, 119–20, 143, 165–69, 173–75, 190, 198, 201, 211–21, 222, 227, 231–32, 244, 245–46
Sharon's appeals for release of, 211–17
Sharon's reaction to, 39–40
Sharon's studying of, 131–32
Sharon's testimony and, 153–54, 158–59, 163–64
Sofaer's appeal to Israel and, 198–200
Sofaer ruling on, 68–69
Time's public relations campaign and, 245–46
Karantina meeting, 21–22, 75
Halevy's testimony and, 166, 168
Secret Appendix B and, 166, 168, 219
Sharon's testimony and, 156–57
Kelly, Harry, 36, 85–86
credentials of, 139
cross-examination of, 192–96, 205–6
deposition of, 119–20
Gould's summation and, 227
Grunwald's testimony and, 205–6
Halevy's collaboration with, 78, 80–81, 192–96, 227
Halevy's scoops cleared by, 78, 80–81
Halevy's testimony and, 165–66, 169
Israeli media and, 211
Secret Appendix B and, 81, 119, 165–66, 169

U.S. press coverage of, 195
Kerrison, Ray, on defamation judgment, 237–38
Kibiye affair (1953):
Barr's opening address and, 140, 142, 144
Sharon's testimony and, 146–47, 148–50
Time's report on, 149–50
Knesset, 40, 41
Begin's address to, 35–36
elections of, 86, 90–91, 99

Lebanon:
Israeli ties with, *see* Christian Phalanges, Lebanese
PLO bases in, 11–12, 14
PLO expelled from, 13–14, 21–22, 61, 63
Sharon's importance in, 30, 61–64
Syria's relationship with, 12, 61–62, 63
U.S. ties with, 61–64
Leshem, Israel, 95–96, 122
Levy, David, 74
Levy, Moshe, 31
Lewis, Anthony, 244
libel:
Auletta on, 173–74
Sofaer's discussion of, 134–36, 233–34
Los Angeles Times, 174–76, 244
Luce, Henry, 78
Luftman, Michael:
defamation judgment and, 237
Sharon's deposition and, 110–11
Time's public relations campaign and, 244–45, 246
Luttwak, Edward, 175

Ma'ariv, 29, 32
McFarlane, Robert, 64
malice:
jury's decision on, 248–50
Sofaer's definition of, 135–36, 233, 234–35
Malkin, Peter, letter to Sharon by, 34
Marshall, Robert, 222
Meir, Golda, 86, 91
Meridor, Dan, 75

Index

Mitzna, Amiram, as Halevy's confidential news source, 185–87
Montreal, anti-Sharon protests in, 43–44
Moor, May, 33
Morgenthau, Robert, 180
Mossad (Israeli intelligence), 19, 23–24, 45, 49–50, 75
  Halevy's confidential news sources in, 188–89, 215
  Secret Appendix B appeals to, 211, 214–15
Mubarak, Hosni, 117

National Security Council, U.S., 125
Neff, Don, 49
Netanyahu, Benyamin, 180
Newsweek, 142
New York *Daily News*, 173–74, 242–43
New York Post, 237–38, 243
New York Times, 36, 70, 99–100, 101, 181, 215, 222–23, 244
Nimrodi, Ofer, 249
Nissim, Moshe, Secret Appendix B and, 211, 213, 216, 220–21

Official Secrets Act, Israeli, 122
Olmert, Ehud, 119–20
Oz, Amos, 85

Palestinian Liberation Organization (PLO), 44, 155
  civilian targets of, 12
  Egypt's clandestine contacts with, 247
  expulsion from Lebanon of, 13–14, 21–22, 61, 63
  Lebanese bases of, 11–12, 14
  as sponsor of international terrorism, 12, 14
Pattir, Dan, Begin health story and, 57–58
Peace for Galilee operation, 12, 53
Peres, Shimon, 13, 17–18, 48, 117
  Gould's summation and, 227–29
  Halevy as supporter of, 50–51, 86, 203, 212–13, 214, 227–28
  Israel's economic crisis and, 251–52

political campaigns of, 86, 99–100
  Secret Appendix B appeals and, 211–14, 216
  Sharon's Dec. 31, 1984 correspondence with, 214, 216, 253–59
  Sharon's negotiations with, 101–2, 114, 212–13
  Time's intimidation campaign and, 124
Poran, Ephraim, 51–52

Qaddafi, Muammar, 175, 237

Rabin, Yitzhak, 13, 30, 50, 103
  Secret Appendix B hearing and, 211, 213, 216
  secret Lebanese missions of, 51–52
Ramzor, 48
Reagan, Ronald, 13, 21, 124, 125
Rifkind, Bob, 107, 122–23
Rigby, Bay, 243
Riklis, Meshulam, 181
Rotenstreich, Joshua, 95–96, 213

Sabra and Shatilla massacres, 31
  as act of revenge, 17, 29, 32, 35, 37–38, 79–80, 83, 145, 163–64, 183
  Begin on, 35–36, 37
  casualties of, 155
  Gould's summation and, 225–26
  Israeli press on, 32
  official inquiry into, *see* Kahan Commission; Kahan Commission Report
  Phalangists and, 14–15, 16–17, 37–38, 154
  Secret Appendix B and, 218
  Sharon's denial of responsibility for, 29–30, 32
  Sharon's knowledge of, 14, 17, 68
  Sharon's testimony and, 152–54, 158
  Sofaer's appeal to Israel and, 198
  Time's press release on, 17, 29
  Time's special statement on, 231
Sadat, Anwar al-, 57
Safire, William, 99–101, 251–52
Saguy, Yehoshua, 23
Sarid, Yossi, 120

Shamir, Shulamit, 112
Shamir, Yitzhak, 14, 23, 39, 251
  Israeli-held document and, 74–75,
    77
  Secret Appendix B hearing and,
    211, 216
  Sharon's communications with,
    117
  Sharon's deposition and, 104,
    112
  Sharon's negotiations with, 99,
    102–3
  Time's intimidation campaign
    and, 124–25
Shapira, Avraham, 99
Sharon, Ariel, 42, 70
  ambitions of, 215
  anger of, 97, 131, 137–38, 206
  appetite of, 160, 242–43
  banquets attended by, 180, 242
  bravery of, 176, 229–30
  brazenness of, 158
  charisma of, 91
  childhood of, 156
  credibility of, 151, 152
  cross-examination of, 151, 152–55,
    156–59, 163–64
  curiosity of, 67, 129
  Dec. 31, 1984, letter to Peres by,
    214, 216, 253–59
  Defense Ministry message of,
    31–32, 33
  deposition of, 89–90, 91–92,
    97–98, 101, 104, 110–12, 114,
    117, 138
  favorite foods of, 242–43
  files of, 95–97
  government hearings attended by,
    163–64, 211, 216–17
  as Industry and Trade Minister,
    160, 181, 251–52
  innocence of, 47
  intelligence of, 160, 217
  international press on, 141–42,
    156, 215
  international support for, 30–31
  interviews given by, 99–101, 159,
    175–76, 219, 251–52
  on Israeli/Lebanese ties, 61–64
  Israeli press on, 32, 33, 89, 90,

91–92, 97–98, 101–2, 124–25,
    140, 143–44, 152, 161–62, 211
  law firms investigated by, 42
  legal expenses of, 162, 181
  libel suit initiated by, 17, 18, 29,
    32, 35, 36–39
  military career of, 146–53, 238
  in Montreal, 43–44
  national unity government nego-
    tiated by, 101–3, 114
  news background stories on,
    242–43
  nickname of, 238
  physical capabilities of, 160
  political analyses by, 100–101
  political campaigns of, 90–91, 99
  popularity of, 33, 90, 180, 228
  pragmatism of, 217
  press conferences of, 222
  press rapport of, 219
  pride of, 238
  prominence of, 30, 50
  propaganda campaign of, 215
  proposed settlements reviewed by,
    98–99, 105–9, 113, 117–18,
    177–82
  reputation of, 67–68, 141–44, 230,
    251
  speeches delivered by, 20–21,
    31–32, 33, 180
  on terrorist activities, 11–12,
    13–14, 21
  testimony of, 146–50
  trial preparations of, 131–33,
    160
  troops addressed by, 20–21
  turmoil of, 40–41
  U.S. investors courted by, 161,
    180
  Zahala house of, 111–12
Sharon, Gilad, 111, 133, 137, 154,
    155
Sharon, Gur, 111
Sharon, Lily, 32, 41, 111, 133, 136
  anxiety of, 155–56
  Barr's opening address and, 139
  falsity judgment and, 239
  Gould's summation and, 226
  husband's appetite and, 160, 243
  malice judgment and, 248–49

Index

Sharon, Lily (*cont.*)
  proposed settlements and, 105–9,
    179–80
Sharon, Margalit, 111
Sharon, Omri, 111, 155
Sharon v. *Time*:
  Barr's opening address in, 139–45
  Barr's summation in, 222, 224,
    231
  Cave's testimony in, 203–4
  closed court session of, 220–21
  damages sought in, 43, 45–46
  Dan's deposition in, 43, 121–23
  defamation decision in, 236–38
  Draper's deposition and, 116–17
  Duncan's testimony in, 203
  evidence acceptable in, 207–8
  falsity judgment in, 239–41
  Gould's opening address in, 131,
    136–38
  Gould's summation in, 224–30,
    231
  Grunwald's testimony in, 57,
    204–7
  Halevy's deposition in, 123
  Halevy's testimony in, 56–57, 81,
    165–69, 173–75, 183–91, 196,
    220
  historical dimensions of, 224
  initiation of, 17, 18, 29, 32, 35,
    36–39
  jury charge in, 231, 233–35
  jury members in, 130–31, 134–36,
    153, 164, 218–19
  jury's statement in, 248–49
  as jury trial, 129
  Kelly's deposition in, 119–20
  Kelly's testimony in, 192–96,
    205–6
  malice judgment in, 248–50
  meaning of *etzlenu* debated in,
    163–64
  press coverage of, 110, 130–31,
    136, 153, 168, 173–76, 195, 206,
    211, 222–23, 236–37, 239–40,
    249
  pretrial clashes in, 67–69, 72–74,
    78–83
  proposed settlements in, 98–99,
    105–9, 113, 117–18, 177–82, 231

  Sabbath observed during, 226
  Secret Appendix B important in,
    197–200, 211–21
  Sharon's deposition in, 89–90,
    91–92, 97–98, 101, 104, 110–12,
    114, 117, 138
  Sharon's imminent victory in,
    211–12
  Sharon's official denial and,
    29–30
  Sharon's testimony in, 146–50,
    151, 152–55, 156–59, 163–64
  Sofaer's appeal to Israel and,
    197–200, 211
Shea and Gould, 42, 43, 96
  Sharon's confidence in, 71, 73–74,
    77, 94
  see also specific lawyers
Shefi, Dov, 121
Shultz, George, 64
Six-Day War (1967), 111, 125, 140
Smith, William, 137
  credentials of, 139–40
  Halevy's scoop rewritten by,
    81–82, 140
  Kelly's testimony and, 195–96
Sofaer, Abraham D., 96, 208
  Abram's appeal and, 220–21
  on acceptability of witnesses, 207
  appearance of, 249
  background of, 69–70, 129
  Barr's opening address and, 143
  Bikfaya minutes and, 73, 76
  Cave's testimony and, 204
  cross-examinations conducted by,
    166–69, 174–75, 183–84, 191,
    192–96
  Dan's deposition and, 123
  defamation defined by, 134–35,
    233–34
  discomfort of, 221
  on Duncan/Halevy letter, 207–8
  Duncan's testimony and, 203
  Dutch journalists' report and, 73,
    76
  falsity discussed by, 135, 233,
    234–35
  Gold warned by, 208
  Gould's opening address and, 138
  Gould's summation and, 226

Grunwald's testimony and, 204–7
Halevy's personal file and, 115, 118
Halevy's testimony and, 166–69, 174–75, 183–84, 191, 196
Israeli appeal made by, 197–200, 211, 219
judicial focus of, 129
jury charged by, 231, 233–35
jury instructed by, 134–36
jury selection and, 130–31
jury's statement and, 248
Kelly's testimony and, 192–96
libel discussed by, 134–36, 233–35
malice defined by, 135–36, 233, 234–35
malice judgment and, 248–50
on nature of acceptable evidence, 207–8
press coverage of, 69–70, 221
proposed settlements and, 98, 105–8, 178, 182, 231
Secret Appendix B checked and, 217, 219–21
Sharon's deposition and, 89–90, 91, 101, 110, 112
Sharon's files and, 95–97
Sharon's objections to, 129, 250
Sharon's testimony and, 150, 153, 157, 159, 164
on *Time*'s New York vs. Jerusalem staffs, 204–5, 207
Time's postponement requests and, 133
Time's pretrial contentions and, 67–69
Time's public relations campaign and, 245–46
on *Time*'s special statement, 231–32
Solomon, King of Israel, 250
State Department, U.S., 11, 21, 116
Supreme Court, Israeli, 216
Syria, 12, 61–62, 63, 64

Talbott, Strobe, 56
Time:
as arrogant, 231
on Begin's health, 53–58, 60, 203–4, 206
concessions made by, 222
correspondence file of, 78–83
editorial policy of, 78, 82
Gould's summation and, 224–25
Halevy defended by, 203–7, 223
information sources of, 72–74
intimidation campaign of, 124–25
on Israeli aid to Lebanese Christians, 51–52
Israeli clashes with, 53–58, 60
Israeli press coverage of, 32
Jerusalem bureau of, 49, 54, 78, 129, 204–5, 207
legal team employed by, *see* Cravath, Swaine and Moore
mistakes made by, 37–38
New York staff of, 204–5, 207
postponement requests of, 132–33
press criticisms of, 173–76, 201–2, 216, 222–23, 237
press releases of, 17, 29, 82–83, 236, 237, 240–41
pretrial contentions of, 67–69, 73–74
professional standards of, 192–96
proposed settlements and, 98–99, 105–9, 113, 117–18, 177–80, 181–82
public relations campaign of, 244–47
Secret Appendix B appeals and, 212–16, 219
special code of, 57
special statements published by, 231–32
Worldwide Memos of, 79–81, 164, 167, 189
Time, Incorporated, 18, 36, 129, 198–99, 240–41
Time-Life News Service, 36
Tineo, Ingrid, 233

United Nations, 117, 180
United States, Lebanese ties with, 61–64
Uris, Leon, 95

Voice of Israel, 29
Voltaire, 230

Index

War of Attrition (1970), 140
Warren, Robert, 175
Washington Post, 142, 232, 244
Washington Star, 84, 139
Weinberger, Caspar, 11–12, 21, 206
Weinreich, Danny, 30
Weissglas, Dov (Dubi), 32, 35, 71, 93, 138
  Bikfaya minutes and, 46
  Dan's deposition and, 122
  Gould's summation and, 225
  Halevy's personal file and, 114–15
  proposed settlements and, 109, 113
  importance of Secret Appendix B and, 212, 214, 217–18
  Sharon's deposition and, 92, 98, 117
  Sharon's files and, 96–98
  Sharon's testimony and, 153–54
  Sharon's trial preparations and, 132
  on sources of *Time*'s information, 72–74
  suit brought by, 36

Weizman, Ezer, 53, 100
West Beirut, siege of (1982), 12–13, 154–55
Weymouth, Lally, 174–76
  on *Time*'s public relations campaign, 244–45
Woodward, Robert, 246
Worldwide Memos, 79–81, 164, 167, 189

Yediot Ahronot, 29, 32
Yom Kippur War (1973), 20–21, 49–50, 53, 125, 140, 160
Young, Patricia, 233

Zadok, Haim:
  Gould's summation and, 224–25
  Secret Appendix B and, 213–14, 217–18, 220–21
  Sofaer's appeal to Israel and, 199
Zamir, Yitzhak, 75, 93
  Secret Appendix B and, 211, 213–14, 218, 220
Zenger, John Peter, 174
Zug, Richard, 233